TECH JOB HUNT HANDBOOK

CAREER MANAGEMENT FOR TECHNICAL PROFESSIONALS

Kevin W. Grossman

Illustrations by Doug Ross

Apress®

Tech Job Hunt Handbook: Career Management for Technical Professionals

Copyright © 2012 by Kevin W. Grossman

ISBN-13 (pbk): 978-1-4302-4548-3
ISBN-13 (electronic): 978-1-4302-4549-0

President and Publisher: Paul Manning
Acquisitions Editor: Jeff Olson
Editorial Board: Steve Anglin, Mark Beckner, Ewan Buckingham, Gary Cornell, Louise Corrigan, Morgan Ertel, Jonathan Gennick, Jonathan Hassell, Robert Hutchinson, Michelle Lowman, James Markham, Matthew Moodie, Jeff Olson, Jeffrey Pepper, Douglas Pundick, Ben Renow-Clarke, Dominic Shakeshaft, Gwenan Spearing, Matt Wade, Tom Welsh
Coordinating Editor: Rita Fernando
Copy Editors: Carole Berglie, Teresa Horton
Compositor: Bytheway Publishing Services
Indexer: SPi Global
Cover Designer: Anna Ishchenko

Distributed to the book trade worldwide by Springer Science+Business Media New York, 233 Spring Street, 6th Floor, New York, NY 10013. Phone 1-800-SPRINGER, fax (201) 348-4505, e-mail orders-ny@springer-sbm.com, or visit www.springeronline.com. Apress Media, LLC is a California LLC and the sole member (owner) is Springer Science + Business Media Finance Inc (SSBM Finance Inc). SSBM Finance Inc is a Delaware corporation.

For information on translations, please e-mail rights@apress.com, or visit www.apress.com.

Apress and friends of ED books may be purchased in bulk for academic, corporate, or promotional use. eBook versions and licenses are also available for most titles. For more information, reference our Special Bulk Sales–eBook Licensing web page at www.apress.com/bulk-sales.

Any source code or other supplementary materials referenced by the author in this text is available to readers at www.apress.com. For detailed information about how to locate your book's source code, go to www.apress.com/source-code/.

This book is dedicated to my father and mother, my wife, and my daughters. It's a testament to their work ethic, love, and support, and a tribute to how my girls—the B-hive as they're affectionately known—keep my heart abuzz with hope for the future of work.

Contents

About the Author

Kevin W. Grossman is a human resources and recruiting B2B software-and-services marketing strategist, business development and sales professional, evangelist, entrepreneur, analyst, advisor, manager, and writer. His passion for writing extends over 25 years in the "world of work" including marketing, HR and recruiting, technology, and higher education. He's been a prolific business blogger since 2004, and his current website, Reach-West.com, encompasses all things HR, recruiting, and career management. It sometimes even includes a little bit of wit and wisdom. Kevin also speaks at HR and recruiting industry events and moderates HR/recruiting/marketing–related webinars and roundtables. He's currently the Director of Marketing at BraveNewTalent, the leading social platform where organizations build talent communities around relevant topics that attract, engage and develop their next-generation workforce. Most importantly, he's a proud father of two beautiful girls and a loving husband to his beautiful wife. He also enjoys reading and running, and he writes regularly about fatherhood, responsible parenting, and domestic violence awareness and prevention.

Acknowledgments

This book would never have been possible if it weren't for my amazing wife. Her help with research and reading, her tireless motivation and encouragement, and the way she constantly told me, lovingly, to "shut up and drive" made this all happen. I could never have completed the book without her. Thank you, Amy. I also want to thank my artist and illustrator friend, Doug Ross, whose fabulous technology-inspired artwork can be found throughout this book. A special thank you to all my brilliant HR, recruiting, career management, and technology industry friends for your insight over the years, especially my Twitter #TChat and world of work co-conspirator, Meghan M. Biro. And lastly, I want to especially thank my editor, Jeff Olson, who's initial e-mail pitching me this book I had considered spam. Thank goodness I called you back. The editorial process you've taken me through has been a journey unforgettable. Thank you.

Behind every decent writer is a damn good editor, a patient but motivating significant other, very smart friends, and the inspirational stories that make up the final one. To all of you IT professionals out there working hard to stay relevant and gainfully employed, I thank you. Keep reaching West, my friends.

Of Daddies, Downturns, and World of Work Dogma

It's a far cry from the world we'd thought we'd inherit; it's a far cry from the way we'd thought we share it.

—Neil Peart, Writer, and Rock Musician

Where your talent meets the needs of the world, there lies your calling.

—Aristotle

Four downturns in, this daddy takes a look back.

I was a teenager during the early 1980s recession, in my twenties during the early 1990s recession, in my thirties during the dot.com bust, and then, in my forties, when the global pool of investment money and financial algorithmic models melted down the world's economic engine, I became a father to two beautiful little girls.

During the first two recessions I lived in and through, I had steady jobs—working in the produce department at a grocery store in my hometown (and of course living at home since I was in high school), and then working in alumni relations and fundraising at San Jose State University, SJSU, my college alma mater. The third was a promising recruiting software company that became a dot.com demise. This latest downturn involved taking a shot at my own risky business endeavor that then led to various experiments, consulting and writing after leaving a long-time leadership position in a marketing software and services firm. Today I have a new career with an exciting (and always risky) funded software startup out of the UK and Silicon Valley. And I'm a writer. Always a writer.

Recently, I read that millennials (i.e., Gen Y, those born somewhere between the late1970s and the early 2000s) will have at least seven to eight careers in their lifetimes. I'm a Gen Xer and I've already had seven now myself. The top concern for many daddies (and mommies) of any generation today is to stay afloat financially in the Bermuda Triangle of jobs, homes, and keeping food on the table. Even in this latest (highly specialized) tech boom we're in, IT pros who haven't kept up with their skills to remain marketable and relevant, after being laid off and/or wanting to return to the workforce, will struggle with the rest of the world's perpetual recovery.

For example, men have struggled more so during the latest recession, experiencing over 70 percent of the overall job loss between December 2007 and June 2009. On the other hand, women have struggled more during the recovery, gaining back only 22.9 percent of the jobs added between June 2009 and September 2012. This means that during the recovery so far, "women have regained only 32.3 percent of the jobs they lost during the recession while men have regained 43.2 percent."[1]

Either way, it sucks.

Let's take an even further look back at the careers of my dad and my grandfather, because we all share generational contrasts in lifetime careers and the cobbling together of many others.

My dad grew up helping to work the family turkey farm, leading to a severe distaste for turkey, as you can imagine. (I'll talk more of him in Chapter 12). After high school, he joined the Air Force and became a mechanic, and then, after serving, he returned to his home town of Porterville, California, where he became mechanic foreman for the local Chevrolet dealer. This was back in the 1960s, when if you were a damn good mechanic, which he was, you could practically listen to a car, touch the hood like a Vulcan or a Jedi Knight, and diagnose its problem. After that, he went in a completely different direction and became a police officer, where he spent the rest of his career, complete with a short stint as a captain in the South Pacific. He eventually became a "special agent" (detective) in charge of the Forgery and Fraud division at the Visalia Police Department (my hometown), where he happily retired.

My grandfather (on my mom's side), according to his own incessant quoting, was a "Jack of all trades and master of none." A young family man during the Depression, he carried his pragmatic frugality with him in every career he embarked on. He worked on the railroads back in his home state of Missouri. He then moved the family West to California's Central Valley, where he worked odds jobs before working on the Friant-Kern Canal construction.

---

[1] http://www.nwlc.org/resource/modest-recovery-reaching-women

When he hurt his back, he went into life insurance sales until he retired. But even retirement didn't slow him down; he worked as a custodian in a middle school for many years after. And throughout his whole life, he was an avid tinkerer, watch and clock fixer, and home gardener. I remember watching with magnetic fascination my grandfather fixing the tiniest of watches and watch parts with the biggest of hands and fingers. I never imagined in a million years that I could tinker or fix like that, or to chase people across paper as my detective dad did. Then again, I never imagined the seven careers I've had to date, or the fact that I would write a book about technology career development and management.

Through thick and thin, including many recessions and even a depression, my dad and grandfather both took care of their families, just as many parents from all walks of life and every combination have done for generations, and continue to do so today.

For the most part, none of us—my father and grandfather's children and grandchildren—really knew of the periodic world of work struggles they went through, their economic ebbs and flows. That's because the greatest gifts a parent can give his children are love, security, and presence, all of which transcend change and risk when passed on in kind.

And of course behind every daddy is a "mommy" who knows where the hell everything is, who shows as well as tells, and who's truly the motivation behind the inspiration. At least for me and my family, that is. Growing up with strong, independent women as role models—my mom and sister in particular—was enough to sometimes to choke the Y out of my chromosome. God love 'em.

Then came my lovely wife, the mother of my two daughters, born in the belly of the economic beast. I affectionately call her "The Mama." The woman who approached me one day at the beach over 15 years ago. The woman who encouraged me to take the risks I've taken, to stretch myself in ways I never knew I could stretch (and I'm really not all that limber in the first place). The woman who told me to shut up and drive the time we had a rental car with a standard transmission while on vacation in Belize; I hadn't driven a stick for over a decade at that point. The woman who can't stand Macbooks but loves her PC and her iPad.

God, I love that woman.

All of them taught me about living the ultimate stretch assignment, doing something I hadn't done before, and learning something I hadn't learned before. Whether I failed or not the first time, or the third, wasn't the point. The growth, they would all tell me in their own unique and colorful ways, is in the stretch. I learned to develop my agile emotional intelligence in all things related to the world of work, career development, and management. They taught me to reach wisely, reach well, and "reach West" (which, appropriately, is the theme of my latest website and blog, Reach-West.com).

And now I'm passing all their wisdom on in kind to those who are reimagining, reengineering, reentering, or entering for the first time information technology careers, although much of what I write about in this book is applicable to any career. It's about you taking ownership and reaching West—taking chances and stretching yourself to be the best at what you do, or as close as you can get.

Somewhere to Turn

She took the microphone, paused, then asked, "So how do I get noticed when I apply to a company online, and my resume goes into an applicant tracking system with dozens of others competing for the same position with similar qualifications and skills?"

She feigned a smile, held the mic at half-mast, and then handed it back to me. Not just dozens of applicants, I thought, but hundreds, if not thousands. No matter how she served herself up, no matter the keywords used and embedded throughout her resume and online profile, she'll still most likely get lost in the proverbial black hole of the candidate experience.

My experience in volunteering to speak at Hirewire, a local organization to help job seekers in Santa Cruz County with career development and job search advice, verified this sentiment from the woman above as well as many others who attend the monthly event. Multiply that across similar gatherings in municipalities all over the U.S. Mercy, it's tough to get a job offer today.

The good news is that *Computerworld*'s 2013 Forecast[2] revealed that 33% of the 334 IT executives who responded to their survey say they plan to hire in the next 12 months. That's up for the third year in a row. Right on.

Ugh, but then there's this: According to an *HR Executive* article from earlier this year titled "Not Ready for Recruiting,"[3] companies are still not improving in finding and hiring the best people. In fact, in the 2012 Allied Workforce Mobility Survey from Allied Van Lines, a study highlighted in the article, two-thirds of the 500 HR professionals polled say they have "extensive" or "moderate" plans for hiring this year. And 80 percent of larger companies—with more than 10,000 employees—plan for "extensive" or "moderate"

---

[2] http://www.computerworld.com/s/article/9231486/10_hot_IT_skills_for_2013.

[3] http://www.hreonline.com/HRE/story.jsp?storyId=533348080.

recruiting. And yet, 52 percent of those respondents consider their recruiting programs to be only "somewhat successful."

Ho-hum, diddly dumb.

A big disconnect that relates to all this is the fact that although many companies have made progress in creating high-quality candidate-experience career sites, when it comes to actually applying for the jobs, it's like trying to traverse an M.C. Escher drawing where you end up where you never started from. Yep, read that one again. And then, imagine the painful application experiences you've had over the years.

Recruiting is getting more complicated than ever, and it's amazing to me that companies aren't making it easier for candidates to explore career opportunities—and this means new candidates as well as internal ones. Sourcing, recruiting, hiring, and retention should be highly collaborative activities, and yet we're truly still lost in that endless Escher maze, losing quality hires like you and me, and those seeking internal moves, along the way.

Which is why again I wrote this book as well as continue to volunteer for an organization like Hirewire and write about the world of work. I've experienced the same painful candidate experience more than once, as I'm sure many of you have as well. But thanks to my own trials and tribulations and some really insightful colleagues and peers over the years, I know a few career development tricks. I have some tried-and-true strategies that will enable you to find and get the job you want.

My goal is to give you all even a little bit of career development and management insight that you can take with you from job to job, project to project, promotion to promotion.

The Mama says shut up and drive. So let's do it.

> *Growth means change and change involves risk, stepping from the known to the unknown.*
>
> —Author Unknown

What You Know

Reconciliation

Career Management Means You

'Cause No One's Going to Do It for You

Against the run of the mill, static as it seems, we break the surface tension with our wild kinetic dreams.

—Neil Peart, writer and rock musician

"Nobody's going to do it for you." You're probably sick and frickin' tired of hearing that, especially if you were one of the millions who lost their jobs in the past five years. Or, if you're one of the many entering the technology job market that continues an accelerated rebound. Or, if you're one of the many currently in a dead-end programming job, banging away on code while management bangs away on you. And you're absolutely miserable.

Yep, sick and frickin' tired, but I'm going to tell you this a lot throughout this book, so sit tight: Nobody's going to do it for you. No one is going to take care of your career management, your livelihood, your family, or your future.

In fact, many of you mentioned above did what I did—you took a chance to start something of your own. Or in my case, it was to look to buy something to then make my own.

Early in 2010, at the very height of the recession, I had a great job running a marketing software and services company side by side with the founder, an East Coast transplant. The company had grown out of the fossilized remains

of Silicon Beach— what Santa Cruz, California, was referred to in the late 1990s—back in the dot-com days. Software sales were flat in 2010 and had been heading that way for a couple of years. This was unfortunately no surprise at the time, considering that most of the human resources (HR) technology companies that purchased our software had frozen their marketing budgets. Much of the world had ground to a halt. The saving grace? Our agency services business was growing, meaning that a smaller percentage of our market wanted to hire us to be their marketing and PR agency of record. One of those clients, a small leadership-development firm with what I thought was pretty cool intellectual property (IP) and a possible future software footprint in the HR B2B marketplace, was looking for a buyer.

And I was looking for a new opportunity—something to truly call my own. I had helped dozens of clients launch and grow their businesses, including my current employer, so why not me?

At the time I had an affinity for leadership development, emotional intelligence, and people development. (Still do, thankfully.) So after research and due diligence, and many, many sleepless nights (partly from a toddler in tow and a new baby on the way at the time), I parted with my partner, boss, and friend, and the only stability I had known for over seven years. I started down my new path.

A path that lasted about five months. Holy shit.

What happened? Fortunately, I think about that less and less these days. But when the realization came that the business just wasn't there; that I neglectfully didn't see the burning forest beyond the pretty green trees; that it would take at least twice as long to become a sustainable business, much less grow—it all came crashing down in a way that no career management coach or mentor could have ever prepared me for.

Throughout my career, including nearly two decades of Silicon Valley and HR marketplace product launches, marketing campaigns and business development, I had worked with hundreds of companies, C-folk, business owners, entrepreneurs, marketers, HR and recruiting professionals, and technology pros. I'd seen great ideas bounce from white boards to advisory boards to databases to Boomerang to (enter another platform and programming language of choice).

I'd seen 'em come and I'd seen 'em go. And the ones who keep coming are the ones who know no one's going to do it for them.

And like me, you've kept coming as well; otherwise you wouldn't be reading this book. In fact, earlier this year I attended a conference called "War for Talent," which I'll reference later, and I can't tell you how many times I heard the Silicon Valley investors and startup founders say they had failed, failed, failed, and then got right back up again.

And that's what they want in their teams—candidates who have an entrepreneurial mind.

And baggage. Thank goodness for that.

Mindful Moment   Think about the risks you've taken throughout your tech career. Were they fruitful? Why or why not? And if you never have taken a risk, why not?

WHO THE HELL AM I?

Great question, I know. Who am I to tell you how to manage your career? You be the judge, but I'll tell you this: I've sourced, recruited, hired, trained, managed, reviewed, and let go hundreds of staff during the various incarnations of my career—including technology professionals such as yourself. Over 25 years, I've learned a lot about myself and those I've managed and worked with, and I'll tell you, it's gotten more and more complicated with full-time, part-time, contract, and virtual work. And in the nearly 13 years I've been in the human resource and recruiting space, I've shared company with the likes of many diverse "world of work" thought leaders, practitioners, analysts, consultants, vendors, and employees of all flavors.

The good news is that I'm still learning (as it should be), and yet I do hope to pass on the knowledge I've gleaned over the years to you, the reader.

Who the hell am I? You tell me.

The Breakfast Club Career Panel

"I'm getting a really cool *Breakfast Club* vibe here. Are you? Do any of you know what *The Breakfast Club* is?"[1]

Most of the high school kids sitting with us in the circle nodded, some even smiled knowingly.

Right on, I thought.

Except that the cast in this real-life version included two classes of well-behaved hip and sociable ninth and tenth graders and a career panel made up of a very smart gay female DA wearing a man's suit and tie; a very passionate straight male martial arts school owner dressed in relaxed sports attire; and me, the marketing biz dev solopreneur social media product-launch guy dressed in a Silicon Valley sports coat and jeans.

And it became very real very fast—we all spilled personally about our worlds of work and life, and the DA even cried when she talked about the murder cases she prosecutes.

This career panel was put on by a local organization in Santa Cruz, called Your Future Is Our Business, a community-based 501(C) (3) nonprofit organization dedicated to fostering business/education partnerships that benefit students. Its mission is to support young people in Santa Cruz County in making informed educational and career decisions.

At first it was all pretty straightforward. We introduced ourselves and discussed what we do professionally.

I looked back in time and saw myself as the young, play-it-safe yet idealistic high school student, my world of work and life yawning before me in self-serving complacency. Christ, if I could tell myself then what I know now.

But, hey, I now had an opportunity to play it forward and give the high schoolers the benefit of my wisdom.

"When I was your age, many moons ago, I wanted to be an architect and a writer. Fast-forward through a lot of life—the obligatory crazy years, college, careers, marriages, and now young children—and here I am, an architect of sorts, helping companies launch new products, and a writer. Always a writer . . ."

The students then proceeded to ask us questions, such as:

---

[1] *The Breakfast Club* was one of many John Hughes's coming-of-age teenager movies in the 1980s and 1990s.

- What inspired you to do what you do now?

- What do you like most about your job? What least?

- When did you know what you really wanted to do when you grew up?

- Do you regret any of the choices you've made?

Each of us answered in kind, a diverse mixture of experience and inspiration and one interesting similarity—the fact that we didn't have any regrets, at least not the debilitating, need-for-meds kind that unfortunately too many people experience throughout their lives.

No, we were all quite honest and transparent answering the questions, including our ages, much to the chagrin of the class. Half of each class frowned when the DA and I said how old we were (while on the other hand, the martial arts school owner was only 26, having opened his business when he was 19—dang).

One student said, "Ahhh. I don't want to grow up."

I smiled, knowing that our lives were flashing before their eyes. "Try not to fast-forward. Enjoy the now, and every moment you're in it, going forward. Learn to be comfortable in your own skin."

Then I thought about an earlier question concerning regrets and choices, and I added, "But don't be afraid to fail. Ever. Assess and learn from it, and get your butts right back in the game."

Amen. I grew up in the belly of the Gen X beast, where there was only one winner per game and someone always had to lose. Always. None of this "everyone gets a trophy" crap and the fact that hard work doesn't always equate to success. Sometimes, but not every time. And the fact that it is through failure that we can learn to see the other side of what we could be, of what we're made of.

Each one of us on the career panel proceeded then to share our own aspirations and realities, our dreams and failures, and of course, our triumphs and what we're passionate about. As the students warmed to us, they felt more comfortable asking us more pointed questions, and they listened to every word we spoke—just as we listened to every word they spoke.

"Thanks for keeping it real," one student said to us when we finished. Others nodded in agreement.

Right on, I thought.

Queue the *Simple Minds* song from The Breakfast Club *soundtrack:* "Don't you forget about me . . ."

Or you.

Mindful Moment What did you want to be when you were in high school and why? Are you living your dream or someone else's? What would make the dream yours? In other words, do you want to build the next Facebook? Then build it, baby.

Why I Learned WordPress

I didn't forget about me, or my family, which was why I hung on after the short-lived business venture. Yes, I'd already experienced dead-end jobs and a dot-com demise, but nothing like this to date. That led to what I'll call a walkabout through the business wilderness that taught me to adapt and learn new skills quickly.

So I learned WordPress.

You laugh, but nobody was going to pick me up but me, and I had to rebrand and reposition—and quickly. I picked a new business entity name, bought a domain, and then launched a new website in the HR B2B technology space. But instead of using free blog services, I learned how to use WordPress, even how to code my own site a little, and I refined my social media marketing skills even further.

During this rebranding phase, a wise sage and mentor of mine reminded me of this:

"The magic doesn't happen just because you show up."

Holy crap, how true that was (and is), no matter how good you are— which is why I drank some of his Kool-Aid (instead of mine with extra sugar), and listened to his hearsay.

That's why I had named my new website Marcom HRsay, "Marcom" representing my marketing communications background and the "HR" in HRsay representing human resources, but it was to be read "hearsay."

Everybody kept saying, "Oh, Marcom H-R-say. Very cool."

They didn't really get it. Even when I started consulting and my clients, prospects, and other industry folk started reading what I wrote in my blog, they still said:

"Oh, Marcom H-R-say. Very cool."

Indeed, but it's served me well. However, I evolved Marcom HRsay and just launched my new site titled Reach-West. "Reach west" is a metaphor for the ultimate stretch assignment, doing something you haven't done before and learning something you haven't learned before. And if there's one thing I've learned in the last few years, it's that we're each our own best and worst individual contributors, managers, freelancers, solopreneurs, and business leaders—all wrapped up in one big, disruptive train wreck of an innovative person and personal brand.

It's a lot of hard work, though, and we have to own it, we have to lead ourselves first. We manage Me, Inc. We are the C-suite. We are the board of advisers. We are the architects. We are the shareholders. And we must have the fiscal fortitude and the physical and emotional endurance to survive. All of these people are one within us. Not that we don't need others' insights in the form of mentors and teachers (which I'll discuss later), but the messy magic is inside us all.

Let me digress sentimentally some more. (Hey, it's only the first chapter and I will get to the gold soon.)

As I wrote earlier, when I was growing up, I wanted to be an architect. And a poet/novelist. And a rock star drummer. I haven't mentioned that part yet—and I still want to be. Quite the triple threat, I know.

What started as drawing Snoopy and other Peanuts characters, then cars and hot rods, led to drafting classes in high school and a love for designing homes and buildings. And what started as writing sweet little rhymes led to the dark prose of teenage questioning angst, then to hopeful short stories of love and redemption into adulthood, with a few "novel" beginnings to boot (writing has always been my "coding"). And last, what started as air drumming and eventually practice pads has never gotten any further than the love of drumming.

Instead, I went into higher-education philanthropy, high-tech marketing communications, and business development, all with a college degree in psychology. Why didn't I major in architecture or English? First, because I had a touch of the early adult crazies that inspired me to want to learn more about the human mind and why we do the things we do, and maybe even help others along the way. (God knows I needed the help then.) Second, I actually did start a master's degree in English after finishing my psychology degree, but then another stage of life got in the way—a divorce and a move over the mountains to the ocean. That put an end to that.

Many of us can relate to the path of "I wanted to be this but I fell into that, and that, and that," and I had read a few years ago that millennials (i.e., Gen Y—those born somewhere between the mid-1970s and the early 2000s) will have at least seven or eight careers in their lifetimes. I'm a Gen Xer and I've already had seven.

From plan A to plan B to plans E, F, and G.

For those of you old enough, like me, you may remember the E-ticket rides at Disneyland. They were the most expensive ride tickets for the latest exciting and enchanting adventures Disney could dish up. E-tickets became a metaphor for an unusually interesting and thrilling experience.

And that's what I've been working on now—my plan E-ticket—and that includes this very book you're reading now (so thank you).

It's still not going to be easy for a lot of us, though. Even though the recent job numbers in Silicon Valley are positive and growing, at the same time unemployment has actually increased slightly. For those still out of work or just recently out of work, many have lost their homes, their savings, everything. What's the other side of that?

Many of us are still disappointed and angry, but we may still have a dream or three of what we want to be and what we want to do.

I'm also not going to sit here and write that you can do anything you put your mind to, because that's just B.S. There's not enough life and career-coaching herbal remedies out there to close this global economic wound that festers still, even if you're one of the lucky ones living in a tech center where dot-com part 2 is playing in 3-D.

I'm a cynical idealist: There just isn't an infinite number of possibilities out there for us. Only a finite number. Sadly, we spend so much time focusing on what we're not and how to get there that we fail to draw upon our strengths and develop them as fully as we can.

And instead we fail to get there.

You should always try to get there. Failure can and should always be an option when you're learning to be better and to dream bigger. Always dream bigger. That's what I'll tell my daughters when they're old enough to understand, because dreams are the catalysts for personal growth and change. Adaptability is huge these days in the world of work.

Hark, the HeaR-say.

So, to make a long story even longer, I put myself back out there on the street, going to networking events and conferences, sending out emails and making phone calls, and connecting and reconnecting with the industry folk I mentioned above—the C-folk, business owners, entrepreneurs, marketers, HR and recruiting professionals, and technology pros.

And, yes, I'm that architect and writer I've always wanted to be who now knows WordPress.

Taking ownership of my solopreneurial career path is what made all the difference in the world—and the fear of failure (and success) has subsided ever since.

That's what I hope to instill in you after reading my book: to take ownership of your path.

And to hell with misery and mediocrity.

Mindful Moment   What skills did you have to learn to remain relevant in the workplace? What are you doing today to prepare for tomorrow's career?

Did You Break Stuff at Business Band Camp?

All right, enough "Debbie Downer," "Me, Inc.," "Nobody's going to do it for me but me" crap. Silicon Valley has seen fairly consistent rate of job growth of late. Right on. Imagine the Muppet's Animal banging away on those drums. Once again it's an exciting time to be in tech. Opportunity abounds, at least more now than during the last six years. And that means aligning your career-ownership mindset with those employers who live and breathe it and who empower their teams.

In fact, it's fascinating to watch a new tech company team being built, to see it rise from emotive steam, sweat, and tears, then to take tangible shape into a business model, complete with product and/or service (that you hope rocks). I've been fortunate enough to be part of that process a few times and have witnessed it many times over. Maybe you have as well. Or maybe you will soon.

I've been out and about in Silicon Valley a lot lately, and there are startups sprouting up in multiple industries, including the HR/recruiting marketplace, from Santa Cruz to San Francisco.[2]

---

[2] Especially in San Francisco. As described in a recent San Jose Mercury News article, "In 2011, companies in San Francisco raised $2.87 billion in venture capital, according to PricewaterhouseCoopers' MoneyTree report. . . . According to PwC, San Francisco has led the world in venture capital since at least 2009." http://sanjosemercurynews.ca.newsmemory.com/publink.php?shareid=1e8eac555

Let's get you in front of those recruiters—now.

But wait—unfortunately many of these startups won't make it out of the Silicon Valley startup "club scene," as a recruiting technology friend recently told me.

Don't we wish that everyone was such a straight shooter in business today? There's no need for sugar coating when it comes to launching a new endeavor, even if there's a bevy of you and your fellow programmers ready to bang code until 3 A.M. and deploy, deploy, deploy.

The days of Pets.com and WebVan.com are long gone, right?

If you're being sought out by a new, preferably sound business model tech play, you may be one of the lucky ones lured and "hired" with stock options and sweat equity, or some overly competitive salary in a currently hyper-competitive market.

Or maybe you're a hungry systems administrator, or a hardware engineer, or a website developer, or a systems analyst, or a network administrator, or a QA pro, or one of myriad other IT positions, ready to move on to your next career adventure with an established company with a nice growth trajectory.

But whatever the position or situation, does your new gig seem like going to band camp? I'm not talking about the funny *American Pie* catch phrase; I'm talking about working in an environment where each new programmer is indoctrinated into the workplace culture with a series of fun activities, including free-form jams and breaking stuff.

Yep, breaking stuff—smashing metaphorical guitars on stage, shall we say. In other words, you are creating live code from day one, even if it crashes and burns (safely called agile development). For example, I've noticed that in the last few companies I've visited, the core development team sits at terminals in configurations that face one another, as if at any point in time of coding, fixing, and breaking they riff off one another, like jamming together on stage (and some with the same twisted rock-and-roll faces at times).

Can you dig that? Have you dug that? Would you like to dig that?

If you ever had the chance to see the Grateful Dead jam together back in the day, you'll remember how intense every concert was, how the play lists varied from show to show, and how musicianship and the music were the number one priority for the band mates.

Take Facebook, where according to an April 18, 2012, *San Jose Mercury News* article, every new programmer hire

begins the six-week journey of a new employee class in Facebook's "Bootcamp,"
an experience shared by every engineering hire, whether they are a grizzled
Silicon Valley veteran or a fresh-faced computer science grad. Since 2008,
hundreds of Facebook's engineers have passed through Bootcamp, which
may lack the physical tests of military basic training but does provide the
same kind of shared experience and cultural indoctrination into the world's
largest social network.[3]

So again, I'll call it "business band camp" since I'm partial to music and I want
to keep the metaphor going. If you're longing to be one of those talented
developer "musicians" (and I'm sure many of you are, as well as being Rush
fans, I hope), then the best way for you to *know* is to *do*, and that means
immediately working on whatever it is you're composing once you're on
board.

Of course, the band-camp metaphor is specific to software programming, but
if you take it figuratively as well, then we're talking about your going into your
new technical role empowered and managing your "personal enterprise," and
you immediately play in the greater rock opera known as your new employer.

That's what I want for you: to own your career management and to belong to
any and all band camp jam sessions that can and should occur spontaneously
every single, frickin' day (if the company you work for or are interested in
wants to stay in business). Because, besides helping you to gel with your new
colleagues and solidify you in the culture, you'll end up most likely broadcasting
how happy you are where you are. This is what makes the employment brand.

And if the company gets that, and they get you, then rock on with your bad
selves. That's the visceral epitome of career management and workforce
culture fit.

That's where I hope to take you in this book.

Mindful Moment   Have you worked for companies that embrace the business band-camp
concept? Were you able to break stuff to both fail and succeed?

The Tech Job Hunt Handbook Ahead

I'm sure you're ready to get moving along, right? Then let's.

I do hope the book ahead will give you a fresh perspective on the world of
tech work and career management.

---

[3] www.startribune.com/printarticle/?id=148024815

In Part I, "What You Know: Reconciliation," Chapters 1–7, I open with why career management is your responsibility. Next, I discuss why education still plays an important role, as well as learning other specialized tech skills; why contract work isn't always a bad thing; about staying cross-trained in other business skills; how volunteering can help enrich your skills; why understanding how employment assessments and background screens will affect your job search is critical; and why you must play well in video interviewing.

Then, in Part II, "Who You Know: Recognition," Chapters 8–12, I tackle how to manage your online profile across social and business networks, research the companies you want to work for, how and when to leverage your networks and your networks networks, why keeping yourself real in an ever-transparent world is so important, the power of finding and engaging mentors and mentor groups, and getting ready for the face time and final interviews.

And lastly, in Part III, "Where to Go and What to Do: Redemption," Chapters 13–20, I dig deeper into the various tools and services available today to help you get a job, how to make the business case of why you should be hired, how you will be tested on what you really know in today's final interviews, what you need to know after you're hired and the during first 90 days, applying everything you've learned to staying nimble for internal mobility, as well as the expanding careers in cloud computing; mobile, big data, and social analytics; and the traditional realms of IT, engineering, and manufacturing.

Let the hunting begin!

You're sharpening stones, walking on coals, to improve your business acumen.

—R.E.M.

2

Finish Your Education

'Cause a Little Book Learnin' Never Hurt Anyone

If I had never dropped in on that single calligraphy course in college, the Mac would have never had multiple typefaces or proportionally spaced fonts.

—Steve Jobs

So what if Steve Jobs didn't finish college. Neither did Bill Gates or Mark Zuckerberg, and look what that got them.

The rest of us aren't so fortunate. We still live in a global society that favors higher education and completion of college degrees. Enrollment in college is higher than it's ever been before. According to the Bureau of Labor Statistics (BLS), in October 2011, 68.3 percent of the 2011 high school graduates (over 3 million) were enrolled in colleges or universities.

However, we now owe more in student loans than we own on our credit cards, forcing more college students to find work prior to graduating. According to the "Pathways to Prosperity" study by the Harvard Graduate School of Education in 2011, only 56 percent of college students complete four-year degrees within six years. Only 29 percent of those who start two-year degrees finish them within three years.

So much for the frickin' college degree, right?

After my first year at San Jose State University (SJSU), back in the mid-1980s, I began working full time while taking a full load of classes. Not because I had to or because I had $50K+ in student loans (I did have student loans throughout college but paid them off in short order), but because I had an opportunity to make some real money working for the university, running a student fundraising program for academic programs. After having spent my first year in college working at McDonald's and washing motorcycles at a Honda dealer, this income helped me become more independent and pay for my own schooling.

Then something happened—I realized I just didn't like college. At all. I stopped going to classes, turned in projects late, if at all, and performed dismally on tests. That led to incompletes and failing grades. The crazies I mentioned in Chapter 1 caught up with me, and book learning just wasn't on the agenda. The irony (completely lost on me) was that I was a top student in high school, had great grades, was heavily involved in activities like student government and sports, and I had a scholarship to attend the local community college and start a civil engineering degree, which would then allow me to transfer to Cal Poly.

After the first few weeks of the semester, I dropped out of community college and I ended up working for a year prior to attending SJSU. But after two and a half years of nowheresville, I stopped registering for classes. I kept working at the university, of course, which is where I began developing my marketing communications skills via alumni relations and fundraising.

More irony, this time not lost on me, was that I worked for the very institution that was supposed to be furthering my education. And it was. With my working for it. Here I was learning the arts of philanthropy and marketing, along with hobnobbing with wealthy alumni, parents, and friends who gave to the university. Why the hell would I need a college degree? In psychology of all things?

But the painful reality was that I knew I would need to have one, if only to advance any further from where I was. Sure, I already managed nearly 100 student fundraising callers and 2.5 full-time staff, but I was going nowhere fast in the ranks of University Advancement, and in an institution of higher learning that issued bachelor's and master's degrees for those who completed them. [1]

And nothing kills an alum donation faster than, "Oh, no, I never finished my coursework at San Jose State, so I do not have a college degree. But I still love the school. Go Spartans!"

My boss and colleagues at the time constantly reminded me of this fact—that my time there had an untimely expiration date unless I finished my degree.

---

[1] University Advancement was the name of the alumni relations and fundraising department I worked for at SJSU.

Add that to the fact that getting a higher-paying, white-collar job in any industry, including IT, would have been very difficult even with the direct work experience I had been accumulating. It was (and still is) a rarity indeed for the entrepreneur to ditch school for the bright lights of big business. And back then my constitution couldn't deal. Plus, my irritable bowel syndrome rendered me virtually incapable of that kind of professional and financial risk, except for the "dropping out of college" part, of course.

I did finish my psychology degree after about a two-year break—with honors, all while taking a full load each semester and working full time at the university, thank you very much. I even immediately started a master's degree in English literature with a focus on creative writing. Didn't finish that one, but that's a story for another time.

You've read the articles in the past few years about how the unemployed "need not apply," even those of us with relevant tech skills. True, the employed always get preference in job searches; their experience is certainly more recent and their skills fresh and up to date. What's the solution, for both the unemployed and underemployed? Go back to school. It gives you some cover for not working full time. Always wanted to finish your two-year or four-year college degree? Get an MBA or a Ph.D.? Get technical certification? Then do it. Although education alone is no guarantee of job fit, companies do prefer educated applicants, preferably those with higher education, a college degree, and/or professional certification. And recency counts. This chapter is going to show you which credentials matter most and why, and how best to obtain them.

Mindful Moment   Did you finish college? If not, what's preventing you from going back? Means? Motivation? There's always a way, from community college to four-year state college.

Today's College Degree Reality

More than one-fourth (25.5 percent) of the class of 2012 that applied for a job already had one in hand, according to results of a National Association of Colleges and Employers (NACE) 2012 Student Survey.[2] That's up slightly from last year at this time, when only 24 percent of 2011 graduates who had applied for a job reported having accepted one. This is good news and a sign of economic healing.

---

[2] The National Association of Colleges and Employers (NACE) connects campus recruiting and career services professionals, and provides best practices, trends, research, professional development, and conferences. www.naceweb.org/s05092012/job-market-2012/.

The current class also outpaced last year's class in terms of job offers: 44.2 percent of those who applied for a job received an offer, compared to 41.4 percent of 2011 graduates.

Here's the kicker, though: those most likely to receive jobs offers (50 percent or more of those applying for jobs receiving at least one offer) have degrees in:

- Accounting
- Engineering
- Computer science
- Economics
- Business administration

Psychology and humanities majors—you're screwed. Unless, of course, you're going to grad school (and finishing), but then you wouldn't be reading this book and looking for tech job career-management advice.

Overall, the NACE student survey revealed that slightly more than half of 2012 seniors (52.1 percent) reported that they had actually applied for a job. That's well below the activity reported for the class of 2011—approximately 75 percent had applied for a job by the time of the survey—but it is consistent with results for the class of 2007 through the class of 2010, when the percentage of the class applying for jobs hovered between 42 and 50 percent.

According to the *Raba Review*, a moderate political, science, and technology blog, "[E]ducation in America produces more art majors than engineering majors, way more psychology majors than engineering majors, and four times more business majors than engineering majors. More disturbing is the fact that the trend is worsening with every passing year."[3]

Let's shine a light on the employment picture as it relates to majors and job categories. When you look at BLS data over the past few years, unemployment is high for the arts and media, while engineering, business, and financial operations are actually trending downward.

And according to a *Bloomberg Businessweek* article, and research by economists Nir Jaimovich of Duke University and Henry Siu of the University of British Columbia, about job recovery in the recession, "Ninety-five percent of the net job losses during the recession were in middle-skill occupations such as office workers, bank tellers, and machine operators. That's what we all assume happens in recessions: the middle class is hit hardest, then eventually climbs

---

[3] http://rabareview.com/2011/04/20/college-education-in-america-poor-choice-of-majors.

back. Only, that comeback isn't happening. Job growth since the end of the recession has been clustered in high-skill fields inaccessible to workers without advanced degrees or in low-paying industries." [4]

Without advanced degrees, indeed. Holy crap.

The U.S. Bureau of Labor Statistics can be a pain in the butt to pull data from, but when you do it and take the time to compare salaries across job fields, you again find engineering, business, and financial operations trumped only by management and legal positions.

Mindful Moment   Sure, that liberal arts degree sounded promising a decade ago when you thought you wanted to teach, but have you weighed the job market reality and what kinds of education make you employable? Time to do a cost/benefit analysis on going back to school.

The Other Side of College Degree Reality

Here are three economic facts:

1. Most firms are small.

2. Most workers are employed at large firms.

3. Startups create the longer-lasting sets of new jobs, but most startups fail.

According to economists' figures, from 2003 to 2007, startups contributed to more job creation than other types of businesses. When you compare the private-sector job growth at established companies to literal startup job growth, you see that the private sector created 2.5 million net new jobs, while startups created over 3 million. The point is that, in the period between the two busts of the early 21st century, startups have been the job engines, whether they grow into big companies or not—which many don't.

But here's the rub: some economists say that today's startups aren't creating the same level of new job growth as they did in the past; there's a downward trend, combined with the fact that many middle-skill occupations aren't coming back. That's not good news at all, because without startups there wouldn't be any net job creation. The downward trend is quite worrisome, especially since only 78 percent of college grads are working in full-time jobs

---

[4] www.businessweek.com/articles/2012-05-03/the-recovery-squeezes-the-middle-class.

compared to only 54 percent of high school dropouts. You'd think it would be higher on the college grad side and even lower for the dropouts.

In the middle somewhere are the high school graduates with either no college credits, or some with college credits but no completed degrees, and this is turning out to be a huge differentiator in hot-growth tech regions like Silicon Valley. Many startups that I've worked and spoken with are increasing their college recruiting activities, which includes internship programs. When it comes to IT positions, there's a "try before you buy" environment that gives the upper hand to the recruiters, hiring managers, and ultimately the employers.

When specific technical skills are scarce, recruiting students right out of college via an internship screening environment does not help the millions of other students who have been out of work for any length of time and who either don't have a completed college degree or who hold a degree in an unrelated field.

Like my friend Paul. That's not his real name, of course, but I want to share his story because some of you will be able to relate to his situation. Paul has been developing commercial database web applications for almost 15 years, gaining extensive experience developing in PHP and MySQL.

He works for a promising startup now, hired by an employer who wanted a local development team with the technical skills to build a quality B2B software product.

But the road was fraught with potholes and bumps along the way. He told me he preferred not to remember how many times he was told he wasn't qualified because he didn't have a college degree. He went to college and completed coursework here and there, but he never finished his degree. Maybe in the 1970s programmers without degrees could walk onto corporate campuses and get new jobs, but the reality in the decades since is that those days are long gone.

"Why can't my aggregate experience over time validate my credibility as a damn good web applications developer? Even if I completed real-world projects in classroom settings, that's still not enough to show how my skills shine and help a business take off, right?"

These are questions Paul and I chewed on, and ones I've debated internally and with others ever since my own college experience. Completing college, especially a four-year degree for either a B.A. or a B.S. (joke away if you want), has been a professional mainstream rite of passage, especially since the rise of the middle class following WW II. No longer was it only the upper classes that could pay for secondary education. College became accessible to the masses, even if today you want to argue that affordability.

Which you undoubtedly can, because private colleges now often cost anywhere from $40K to $60K per year (that's for full-time tuition, housing, and all related costs, of course). Even at public universities, of which I'm a product, tuition is subsidized by taxpayers, but state budgets continue to get hacked away and so students fees rise and rise and rise again.

Life gets in the way, and Paul started a family and learned his skills on the job, unable to take the time or devote the money to completing a degree. Yet his real-world experience eventually helped him land the job he has now.

However, when most IT job listings require a four-year degree, and senior-level positions prefer a master's degree, street cred goes only so far. And if you're one of the many lucky interns in college who gets plucked away to play in a new tech startup, like NFL rookie drafts in the first round, you'll get paid for it while you play with it.

In a recent college-cost protest, I witnessed a woman holding a sign that read:

Education should not be a "debt" sentence

Sadly, as I mentioned at the beginning of this chapter, it is that very thing. With the middle-class continuing to get hobbled financially, and the amount of financial aid and number of scholarships finite and only for those who qualify, the majority of college attendees have no choice but to incur student loan debt. However, there are alternatives, and I will touch on those at the end of the chapter.

▓ **Mindful Moment**   Are you in a position where you can leverage your skills and experience over an incomplete education? Do you think it's even possible? Find someone who has, like Paul, and listen to his or her story.

And for God's Sake, Don't Lie About It

We hear about them every year. The news stories of high-profile CEOs and other senior management folk who have lied on their resumes. Or they blame their recruiting firms about the lies on their resumes, as did the short-lived Yahoo CEO Thompson in 2012.

Basically, Thompson's undoing came as a result of incorrect biographical references that said he held a bachelor's degree in computer science from

Stonehill College, as well as one in accounting from the same college. A former eBay Inc. executive, Thompson had earned a degree in accounting from the Easton, Massachusetts–based school, and that information was correctly listed in eBay regulatory filings and on some Yahoo press releases. Yet the incorrect degree, the computer science one he never received, still showed up in Yahoo's April 27 10-K filing, as well as on the company's website.

Regardless of who screwed up where, and they're all at fault here—Thompson, the recruiting firm, and Yahoo—public indignation isn't something Yahoo's management and investors wanted dragged out to the center of the social information superhighway for the world to see, especially the Security and Exchange Commission (SEC). Thompson was out of a job faster than it took to type in the faux degree.

There are unfortunately too many egregious, high-profile examples to choose from, but a flip side of this problem involved Bausch & Lomb CEO Ronald Zarrella. In 2002, Zarrella lost a $1.1 million bonus after it was revealed that he did not have an MBA from New York University, as his official company biography had stated. While he had been a student at NYU, Zarrella never graduated (how many times have we heard this?).

Although Zarrella offered to resign over the incident, Bausch & Lomb officials declined to accept the resignation. He remained in his role for another six years before retiring in 2008.

There's definitely a Dilbert-like injustice to all of this, and it may motivate some of you to pull off an Office Space "shave a penny off the bottom line" computer program pyramid scheme to stick it to the man, but I wouldn't recommend that, either.[5]

No, you and I wouldn't get that kind of publicity; we just wouldn't get the job. Yet, we keep lying over and over again. According to my good friends at EmployeeScreenIQ, a background-screening firm, over 50 percent of resumes contain blatant lies and errors, purposely injected to boost the applicant's appeal and chances of making the selection short list. In fact, most of those blatant lies on resumes are related to education, direct experience, and accomplishments with previous employers.

Diploma mills and faux employment-verification factories are big business globally, but don't make the mistake of going down those paths. If you haven't heard of these institutions, and I'm glad if you haven't, know that, for a fee, a diploma mill can provide you with an illegitimate yet certified college diploma from a real or imaginary accredited university. And there are fake employment-

---

[5] Office Space is a 1999 American comedy film satirizing work life in a typical 1990s software company, written and directed by Mike Judge.

verification firms that, for a fee, will tell your potential future employer you worked for Acme Dy-no-mite, Inc. and that you helped develop an open-source desert-chase platform for Wile E. Coyote and Road Runner.

Does it matter if you're a programmer with a handful of classes under your belt and you lie about your software engineering degree? I guess if you get caught because you really can't handle the work, then, of course, that'll leave scars.

Mindful Moment Again, for God's sake—don't lie about it. Either go with the collected informal and format education you have or complete the formal degree.

Think Two-Year, Technical, and Online

The good news? Even with all the hubbub about our education system heading down the toilet, the United States has the best system of higher education in the world, according to a list released by university network, Universitas 21.[6]

Although this was the first time Universitas 21 created these rankings, their researchers looked at the most recent data from 48 countries across 20 different measures, including investment by governments and the private sector, research, and the production of an educated workforce, international networks, and diversity.

However, the rankings did not factor in the affordability of attending the colleges, which is, of course, something I discussed earlier in this chapter. This is still good news, though—the fact that higher education remains "higher knowledge." In fact, according to the Shanghai Jiao Tong University's Academic Ranking of World Universities, more than 30 of the 45 highest-ranked institutions are in the United States (as measured by awards and research output).[7]

---

[6] Universitas 21 is an international network of 23 leading research-intensive universities in fifteen countries. www.nytimes.com/2012/05/14/us/higher-education-ranking-judges-by-country.html.

[7] The Academic Ranking of World Universities (ARWU) was first published in June 2003 by the Center for World-Class Universities and the Institute of Higher Education of Shanghai Jiao Tong University, China, and is updated on an annual basis. ARWU uses six objective indicators to rank world universities, including the number of alumni and staff winning Nobel Prizes and Fields Medals, number of highly cited researchers selected by Thomson Scientific, number of articles published in journals of *Nature* and *Science,* number of articles indexed in *Science Citation Index - Expanded* and *Social Sciences Citation Index*, and per capita performance

Overall, the United States has a total of 4,495 Title IV-eligible (financial aid available), degree-granting institutions: 2,774 four-year institutions and 1,721 two-year institutions. In total, this is an average of more than 115 colleges per state. As of 2010, the United States had 20.3 million students enrolled in higher education, roughly 5.7 percent of the total population. About 14.6 million of these students were enrolled full time.

I'm going to skip the four-year colleges for now; there are lots of sources available today on going back to school and getting or finishing a bachelor's or a master's degree, as well as where to find the financial resources you'll need to go into deep debt—I mean, that you'll need to go back to school. For those who've started a four-year degree and are thinking about rolling the dice and hooking up with a progressive tech disruptor in the space, hang tight—we'll chat about that world a little later. (Plus, you'll find more resources in the appendix of this book.)

So let's start with the two-year institutions because this is where you can get a technical background and improve your skills, reasonably and in an even more compressed format than standard two years, which will make you more relevant and employable, especially those of you with only a high school diploma.

I'll bet you've got a community college near you. Here in Santa Cruz, California, where I live, we've got Cabrillo College, a great school with a Career Technical Education (CTE) program that includes compressed programs in:[8]

- Computer & information systems
- Computer networking and system administration
- Computer science
- Digital media
- Engineering technology

There are also traditional two-year programs in computer science and engineering. Whether you're just looking for the A.S. degree or maybe want to springboard into a four-year school, community colleges are where to start.

There are, additionally, myriad technical schools throughout the United States that offer flexible campus learning, as well as online learning and certification

---

with respect to the size of an institution. More than 1,000 universities are actually ranked by ARWU every year, and names of the 500 best are published on the web.

[8] www.cabrillo.edu/.

programs (in fact, many more colleges these days offer online learning; I'll discuss certification in the next chapter). Many offer online information technology degrees starting at the top, with a master's, and then moving down through a bachelor's to an associate's degree. These programs aren't as cost-efficient as community colleges can be, but they are convenient and highly targeted for your technology learning needs. But be vigilant—many of these "technical" institutes have been or are being investigated for predatory and deceptive recruiting practices.

It's as simple as doing a web search to find out the legit and not-so-legit. There are also plenty of online college and technical school directories available that you'll find once you've done your web search. (I'll also list education-related resources at the end of the book.)

Mindful Moment   Have you ever considered attending your local community college? An online technical college? Think about the alternatives that can help you integrate your current work and life situation.

Again, with the Book Learnin'

Whether you're like me, and you really want to go back to school and finish whatever degree it was you started, or if you're like Paul, who persevered and used his experience and timing to land a new startup gig, know that there's a broad spectrum when it comes to the world of tech work.

When we're in boom times, which in tech we are once again, regardless of the rest of the world's industries, there are those of you who take risks and jump to the job-creation engines—the startups—without a second thought about finishing your post-secondary education. And that may be a risky either way in the end, considering the likes of Facebook's IPO this year, as well as social networking and gaming companies tanking. Not quite dot-com bust number one, but still risky.

There are lots more jobs in tech fields these days. In 2011, Amazon hired 22,500 people, bringing its workforce up to 56,200, and Google hired 8,000 people—more than ever before in a single year.

While not all of these jobs require an engineering or software programming degree, getting a new gig today can be harder than getting into a top-tier four-year college—and paying for it. Competition among businesses for tech talent is crazy-tight for firms to hire those who are qualified, let along those who aren't qualified. In fact, demand for these positions is greater than the skills that exist in the marketplace.

Skills that you'll need to acquire to become competitive and remain relevant. Like I said, a little book learnin' never hurt anyone.

In Chapter 3, I'm going to carry the education theme further and talk about certification programs you can take to update your professional skills—everything from learning HTML5 to Ruby on Rails (or WordPress—don't make fun). This is yet another way to stay fresh and relevant in the marketplace that you're trying to get back into, or want to stay in, and then to use those new skills to promote yourself. As you'll see, this is the time for "solopreneurs" and technical artisans—professionals whose software and hardware development and programming skills are highly specialized and in demand for today's market and tomorrow's.

Mindful Moment   Competition for the best tech talent is crazy-tight these days. Firms have to ensure they differentiate more than ever those who are qualified and those who aren't qualified. Demand for specialized IT positions is greater than the skills that exist in the marketplace, so get yourself some education and shine a light on that specialization. A little ongoing book learnin' never hurt anyone.

3

Learn New Specialized Skills

To Upgrade and Market Yourself

Bill Gates is a very rich man today...and do you want to know why? The answer is one word: versions.

—Dave Barry, Pulitzer prize-winning American author and columnist

Maybe they didn't finish college, but I'll be damned if our famous (and infamous) tech captains of industry, and most of the minions who helped them get there, did one thing quite well—and that's this: they constantly strove to be bigger, better, and badder.

Badder to the bone, baby. Meaning that they acquired new skills and upgraded themselves, and they ensured that their teams did the same. These days are no exception, because those who do these things are the ones who will survive the greatest recession since the Depression. It's not going to be easy for them, though, as it's become more and more difficult for CIOs to find employees well-versed in ever-changing technologies like cloud computing, mobile, and big data and social analytics (which I'm going to cover at the latter chapters of the book).

According to a *Bloomberg Businessweek* article from 2012, "job growth since the end of the recession has been clustered in high-skill fields inaccessible to workers without advanced degrees or in low-paying industries."[1]

---

[1] www.businessweek.com/articles/2012-05-03/the-recovery-squeezes-the-middle-class.

If you're like me, you're probably fed up with hearing about the "war for talent." I mean, you just want a friggin' job, right? A job with other smart folk and smart chieftains who want to build and grow and stay in business. Which is why it's not really a war per se. It's a mobilization of innovation and motivated minds—the leaders, the builders, the doers, and you. It's all the combined latest and greatest skills that make up "rocket soup." (Rocket soup is what Rocket, one of the characters from my daughter's favorite Disney Junior shows, Little Einsteins, needs to run on.)

This is the way I felt early this year as I walked through Cruzioworks from my co-working space to the restroom and I passed the packed day-long classroom on covering HTML5.[2] Or maybe it was jQuery. Or C#. Or PHP. Or Ruby on Rails. The times I went past the classroom when they were all on break I heard the buzz of "open source" and "cool new idea" and "the next big thing." This is all happening in the heart of Santa Cruz, the laid-back little surfing community in the backyard of traditional Silicon Valley. Remember hearing "Silicon Beach" back in the dot-com day? That tide retreated and supposedly never came back in. Not true. It washes over me almost every day.

Skills, skills, and more skills—you may not have the means or the gumption to go back to school and complete a degree or certification, but you should consider taking special courses online, or via local community services, or paid programs to update your professional skills, or even learning on your own from others—everything from learning Flash to HTML5 to Ruby on Rails.

More than ever, it's critical to stay fresh and relevant in the marketplace you're trying to get back into, or want to stay in—to upgrade yourself—and then use those new skills to promote yourself in the marketplace. This is the time for "solopreneurs" and technical artisans—professionals whose software and hardware development and programming skills are highly specialized and in demand for today's market and tomorrow's. This chapter will show you that beyond credentials, you need new skills to keep you employable. It also shows which skills are in demand, why, and how best to get them.

▓ **Mindful Moment**   When's the last time you learned new IT skills? Have you investigated what employers are hiring for and why? Or are you sitting on your hands wondering where it all went wrong? Focus on getting off your hands and putting them to work.

---

[2] A co-working facility in downtown Santa Cruz, California, and a tech innovation hotspot.

Like Moore's Law on Meth

Although the following list of hot IT skills may change in priority and scope in the coming year, many of them will still be relevant to you and your career aspirations in the near future. Yes, the tech world moves pretty darn fast these days. Remember how intricately difficult it was to build an HTML website in the late 1990s? And now folks like me can learn WordPress and build them even better.

According to *Computerworld*'s latest forecast survey, there are bevy of new technologies being beta-tested or piloted that could be unveiled next year.[3] In fact, 77% of the 334 IT executives surveyed by Computerworld in June said so, which is up from 43% four years ago.

Here's a sample of what the IT execs said they were cooking up:

1. Virtualization including server, storage, network and mobile virtualization.

2. New mobile and wireless technologies for the medical industry, about a third of which are testing or piloting tablets.

3. Cloud computing projects involved in testing, training and development.

4. Security technologies that allow consumers to make payments in restaurants or stores without a credit card to help eliminate fraud.

These fields, in particular the cloud computing projects in training and development, include the most recent companies I've worked for and consulted with that are hiring. Remember, the world we live in is constantly changing—it's like Moore's Law on meth. As I mentioned earlier, back in the dot-com boom, the new Internet and Web 1.0 were all the rage, and new and old companies alike were scrambling to get online—to get anything online as fast as possible, without much thought to user interface and data extraction and other considerations we give to websites today.

Combine that with the fact that it took a lot of storage and processing power to run websites and data centers. Thus, IT expenditures were the highest ever through most of the 1990s, with the enterprise storing and managing more data and computing power than ever before that still needed a lot of hands-on, day-to-day project management. The IT labor shortage led to exorbitant

---

[3] www.computerworld.com/s/article/9231483/Forecast_2013_Giving_top_technologies_a_beta_test

salaries for those who got the training and the certification. And in many cases there were many more jobs than there were qualified IT pros to fill.

Post dot-com and the world changed, those huge IT budgets of yore slashed to near nothing while many IT folks lost their jobs. Then it changed again during this latest recession, with many IT positions consolidated, dissolved, and even outsourced to data centers inside and outside of the United States.

So while we're talking about the hot tech skills for 2012, let's also talk about how the future of IT is being consolidated into three kinds of jobs: consultants, project managers, and developers.

According to Jason Hiner, the editor-in-chief of *TechRepublic*:

> *More and more of traditional software has moved to the web. . . . Many technophobic Baby Boomers have left the workforce and been replaced by Millenials who not only don't need as much tech support, but often want to choose their own equipment and view the IT department as an obstacle to productivity. In other words, today's users don't need as much help as they used to.*[4]

Jason also divides the consolidated IT jobs future into consultants, project managers, and developers. Where do you fall today and where would you like to be?

The realities of these divisions are quite evident in the rise of the freelance worker, which I'll discuss in Chapter 4, and the fact that companies realize that writing project code in the Wild West of the new tech boom can be too uncontrolled if there isn't any hierarchical leadership and project management to, well, manage the results. You should consider learning skills from both camps.

So let's digress for bit onto the millennial/boomer divide and how it applies to your career management. Earlier this year I heard Malcom Gladwell speak at the SHRM Conference and Expo,[5] and the first words out of his mouth were, "Let's talk about millennials."[6] I immediately bristled and recalled how, in reality, there is no Gen X or millennial "type." My tendency is to think of all generations as *Generation Now*—anyone can learn anything at anytime.

---

[4] TechRepublic is a website that helps IT decision-makers identify technologies and strategies to empower workers and streamline business processes. www.techrepublic.com/blog/hiner/the-future-of-it-will-be-reduced-to-three-kinds-of-jobs/8717.

[5] Society for Human Resource Management's annual conference.

[6] Malcolm Gladwell is the author of these *New York Times* bestselling books, *The Tipping Point: How Little Things Make a Big Difference* (2000) , *Blink: The Power of Thinking Without Thinking* (2005), and *Outliers: The Story of Success* (2008).

This is a mindset that includes employers treating people nongenerationally and talking straight. It holds that being passionate about what a person does is a major tenet of the world of work, regardless of when that person was born. That today we're not only loyal and committed to the work that moves and schools us, but also to the people who are part of that committed work—because that's the work that moves us all to do greater things for the world.

That's the view of work that makes it easier for startups to start up and for established companies to grow—creating new jobs and replacing some of those that were lost during the past five years, including full-time, part-time, flex time, contract and project work, and any combination of those and more that you can imagine. That's the view of work that transforms technologies, processes, communities, and the very heart and soul of the world.

That's the work that you want *now*.

But that's not where Gladwell went during his keynote speech. What he talked about were two generational differences that *do* exist—and should co-exist.

These are:

- Hierarchy
- Open networks

What Gladwell explained so eloquently and intelligently is that we've gone from hierarchical, disciplined, and centralized social organizations (think boomers and Gen X) to collaborative, amorphous, organic, and open social networks (think Gen Y and Gen Z).

Which isn't really a good or bad thing, because they're two very different worldviews that have influenced dramatically the way we participate in the world of work. On the one hand, you've got the traditional top-down management structure that, according to Gladwell, began to break down in the 1970s when individuals started to demand more ownership of their career aspirations (and paychecks). And then those born in the 1980s and 1990s found knowledge and power in the collective world of work, those personal and professional social networks that have upended the traditional top-down structure.

But the amorphous nature of these open networks, versus the structured leadership of a strong few, tells a tale of two separate states of mind and heart. As an example, Gladwell highlighted the differences between the succinct success of the Civil Rights movement and the oblique success of the Occupy Wall Street movement.

However, when combined, these viewpoints are a force to be reckoned with. Think of Apple: open social networks internally, yet run by a brilliant business mind who's a formidable dictator. (And any of you who have worked at Apple would most certainly concur.)

You can apply this view as a strategy for your own career management. Keep an open-network mindset, but manage your career with smart and disciplined leadership. Embedding some hierarchy into open-learning networks brews a magic that unites hearts and minds, including those of peers and prospective employers. That magic is what truly transforms technologies, processes, communities, and the very heart and soul of the world of work.

WHERE TECH SKILLS FALL TODAY

1. Consultants. Since the big IT budgets of the 1980s and 1990s, large enterprises have been able to scale back on capital expenditures for equipment—and the staff that maintains that equipment. We're talking servers, network routers, hubs, and everything else technical the organization runs on. Hardware and software efficiencies have truly driven the need for more specialized IT pros, but fewer of them. Hell, IT pros can be expensive—you know that. Combine that with the scaled-back internal IT fiefdoms that have become even more hard-core gatekeepers. This is why you're going to see more traditional IT administrative work and related support functions outsourced to consultants, who range from global firms to one-man (or woman) IT shops for small businesses. This includes firms like HP, Amazon Web Services, Rackspace, and IBM, all of whom provide data-center space and IT pros to help implement, manage, and fix problems. Consultancies give organizations an opportunity to buy IT services on demand in order to lower costs, get higher expertise, and provide ongoing coverage.

2. Project managers. As the age of specialization has evolved over the past five years, many business units, departments, and divisions are pulling in remaining IT pros to be their tech business analysts, helping management make more informed technology decisions. They will be the ones who gather the sound and the "Dilbertian" business requirements, the inane and nonsensical ones, while ensuring there's only sound deployment, not a Dilbertian one. These individuals are the brave souls who have ventured away from the centralized IT fiefdom (or been exiled from) to help build and maintain better businesses from the business unit on up. These also the folks who help to vet outside tech vendors and consultants.

3. Developers. Because software runs the world—and if you don't think so, just look around—the greatest job opportunities for IT pros are in engineering, programming, and coding. Because hardware has been scaled to be more efficient, Internet broadband has increased in bandwidth, and cloud-based SaaS development is hotter than hot, the need for software applications to run and integrate smoothly with other software apps is critical. All things social and mobile development are the new layers of software integration across hardware and platforms, thus the need for these developers is exploding.

▓ **Mindful Moment** There's a lot of opportunity today in the tech field—if you have the right balance of developer and project-management skills in place. What opportunities would you like to work toward and make your own? What would it take to get there?

So It's All About the Coding, Eh?

There you have it. It's all about the coding: application development in the literal social media and mobile spaces, as well as pursuit of anything and everything via cloud computing, with a nod to big data analytics and a variety of other not as glamorous industries like manufacturing, medicine, biotech, housing, hospitality, and retail. The list goes on and on.

My point is that all of IT touches every industry, and that means that, with the right skills, you can find work most anywhere. Don't think only about social networking technologies, for example, because Instragram sold for $1 billion in less than two years. Just remind yourself where the valuations of Facebook, Zynga and others have slid to.

So where are you going to upgrade the skills that will keep you relevant and employable?

In Chapter 2, I discussed going back to school to finish your college degree or get some sort of technical certification. That's one place to start—by taking classes to acquire various new technical skills or to brush up on what you already know. Remember that this education can include night school or online courses, and you don't have to complete a degree or get certification to learn new skills.

Here are some other ways to learn new tech skills.

Read, and Then Read Some More

I've been avid reader since I was a little boy, when science fiction was very popular with me. The movie *Stars Wars* appeared on the big screen when I was 12, and that was all it took when it came to my romanticizing technology and the heroes who use and abuse tech. I read many of the early Star Wars universe stories and many other sci-fi books like those by Isaac Asimov and Robert Heinlein. Fantasy was also a favorite of mine, especially when it blended alchemy, technology, and science, as in the *Thomas Covenant The Unbeliever* series by Stephen R. Donaldson and the *Incarnation of Immortality* series by Piers Anthony. *Popular Mechanics,* and *Omni* were favorite magazines at the time.

For me, I relate coding to writing; it's built on a learning foundation and an open mind. A lot of reading goes into being a good writer—it's by reading the works of many others that writers find their unique voice. The same goes for programming and other forms of IT work; reading will expand your mind and give breadth to your understanding of what's possible. And this includes reading things outside your technical area of interest, as this broader exposure is what neuroscientists tell us helps us connects those problem-solving dots.

To begin, a quick search on Amazon.com for best-sellers in the field of computers and technology will give you the latest and greatest in tech books to choose from. Or use your online bookseller of choice to do the same and cross-reference. (There are some books in Apple's iBooks that may be cheaper, and vice-versa.)

There are also different technical publications and technical manuals, some still in print, although most are available online and user friendly these days. Besides *TechRepublic* and *Computerworld,* there are myriad others, including the IEEE Computer Society publications, *CNET News, Information Week, InfoWorld, Wired, Byte,* and *Technology Review.*

And by the way, along the lines of reading and learning new skills of all kinds, there are many free online courses and content offered today via what are called MOOCs[7]—Massive Open Online Courses—from major universities like Stanford and Harvard joining forces with private industry. (I reference great online resources in the Appendix.) Immerse yourself in topics inside and outside of technology and broaden your reach. Stretch that mind, baby.

Play with Others Online

And then there's playtime. No, I'm not talking about gambling or adult sites, either. I'm talking about collaborating with and learning from other like-minded IT folks in a variety of exercises, Q&A sessions, or just general shooting the tech-shit talk.

User groups and online forums have been around since before the Internet was public, and before all things "social"—groups like IBM's SHARE and UNIX networks, Compuserve, AOL, and Yahoo user groups. Also, when I worked at San Jose State University in the late 1980s and early 1990s, we were already online using e-mail, checking out other university websites, and collaborating with peers throughout the state university system.

Then came the rise of the social networks and now the talent networks, where prospective employers welcome you and your friends to talk among

---

[7] http://en.wikipedia.org/wiki/Massive_open_online_course

yourselves and with current employees and hiring managers to help figure out tech problems of all kinds—whether it's problem solving on virtual white boards, attending interactive webinars, or just hanging out in a virtual chat session.

With collaboration comes informal mentoring; current employees, recruiters, and hiring managers may mentor referrals they know (or non-referrals they don't); similarly, talent participants mentor each other on learning new skills, career development, and more.

Two technical sites in particular that are all about learning and sharing programming-related questions are Stack Overflow[8] and GitHub.[9] Stack Overflow is a language-independent, collaboratively edited question-and-answer site for programmers, and GitHub is a web-based hosting service for software development projects that use the Git revision control system.

Play with Yourself

Okay, maybe you're still making fun of me because I learned WordPress all by my lonesome, something maybe a monkey could do today, but it paid dividends in my career-development account and led to me learn more about building websites in the 21st century.

Maybe you've already done that—coded your own basic website by learning practical skills like HTML and CSS. And then later you learned PHP, MySQL, and RSS, so you could do some stuff cooler than simple HTML would allow. Or maybe you're in the process of doing that. Or maybe you're currently learning how to wirelessly network your home office and all the peripherals. Or maybe you're working on new algorithms that filter the overwhelming amount of online data to only what you want to know about.

That's right—you're playing with yourself. Ain't nothing wrong with that; it's only natural. The best way to know is to do, so get to doing, would you?

Mindful Moment   Make a list of your favorite tech pubs and online sites you frequent and write down the reasons why you like them and what you learn from each one. Same for where you go online to collaborate (if you do). And then make a list of projects you've tackled all by yourself, if nothing more than to learn. Do you see a pattern? What would you then change, if anything?

---

[8] http://stackoverflow.com/.

[9] https://github.com/.

Show Me, Don't Tell Me

So now I'm going to turn everything we've covered on its head and see what we have yet to cover.

It's important that I do this now, because of my friend Paul, whom I introduced in Chapter 2. Paul, who didn't have the college degree or even much in the way of formal secondary tech education. For any of you out in the same situation as Paul, you know how tough it is to stitch together your professional experience and your formal and informal learning to create a credible and desirable IT pro who should be hired.

So if you've got any of the following creds, highlight them in your resume and/ or your LinkedIn profile: professional accomplishments and awards, peer and previous employer recommendations, articles and posts written, speaking engagements, college degrees and certifications, and any classes you've taken in between. Maybe you even mix worlds in online social and business networking and you share your proudest dad-icated parenting moments (as I do). You share whatever you've got when you've got it, because that's what employers and recruiters are looking for.

Employ "Conspicuous Consummation"

Based on the economic term *conspicuous consumption* and the newer term *conspicuous conservation*, I call the above example "conspicuous consummation": the relatively recent phenomenon of engaging in online activities and sharing information that highlights your best professional (and personal) self in order to obtain or signal a high social status.

I'm certainly no economist by trade or training, but I do find the field fascinating, just as I find it fascinating how people show themselves in the best light online, whether they are doing a job search or just keeping themselves relevant and marketable.

I started thinking about this after reading about the economic term *conspicuous conservation*, naming a relatively recent phenomenon of engaging in activities that are environmentally friendly in order to obtain or signal a higher social status (for example, buying a Prius versus other hybrid gas/electric combo models). This concept was developed and analyzed by a brother-and-sister team of economists, Steve Sexton and Alision Sexton.[ ]

In my world-of-work concept, conspicuous consummation can be a valiant personal branding effort to get noticed, but is it enough to warrant a good evaluation when seeking a new job or consulting gig?

The obvious answer is no, which is why employers use myriad screening tools. Then they throw in the interviewing, maybe a scenario-based exercise or two, reference checking, and a few other housekeeping-to-hire activities, and they have themselves a new employee (or not).

But what if there were a way to show your current employer or prospective employer some actual, real-time examples of yourself shining in action? No scenario-based acting models; I mean actual footage of you kicking butt and taking names. There are surveillance cameras already in places of business for security reasons, like crime prevention (not to mention identification technologies that confirm our identities via fingerprints, retinas, breath, blood, DNA . . . whoa, Nellie!).

Agencies, vendors, and companies record external and internal meetings, with participants' consent (usually audio, but I'd bet more video today, too). So why not record your day-in-the-life highlights and accomplishments in video? I don't mean recording yourself alone at home, pantomiming a day in the life at work, but I do mean getting permission to record yourself in action—running a meeting, or collaborating with developers on a white board, or presenting a new product idea to your supervisors, or anything else that shows you and your skills in real time. Save those videos for your future employers or business partners, and share with them. Or, if you've got your own blog and/or website and/or YouTube page, be bold and post the highlights online.

Crazy, I know, but video interviewing and screening have become mainstream, in both live virtual and recorded formats (will be discussed in Chapter 7). But what I'm suggesting may get the EEOCs, the ACLU, and the blood of many other privacy advocates boiling—not to mention direct supervisors, executive management, IT, and legal counsel—unless you obtain blanket permission up front.

Maybe you have already realized that, on paper, you're only worth your weight in words; that alone isn't enough to display your past experience, education, and skill level, no matter what recent classes you've taken and skills you've upgraded.

This is the new millennium of tech specialization; smart generalists are going the way of the outsourced and offshored low-cost labor. It's already been happening, and it's leaving you behind.

Start storyboarding your "conspicuous consummation" movie. That's where I'm going with the rest of this book, figuratively and literally.

As my dad always told me, "Show me, don't tell me." Upgrade yourself to conspicuous consummation.

▓ **Mindful Moment**   Competition is fierce in tech fields today, especially for certain skills. Have you ever thought about recording yourself in IT action? Starting with a story is key, as is learning new skills, but then showing what you can do is the step that's going to help you rise above the noise. Plan your storyboard today.

Find and Take the Contract Work

Livin' on More Than a Prayer

You jump off a cliff and you assemble an airplane on the way down.

—Reid Hoffman, co-founder of LinkedIn

It's like that. Any chance we take with our careers is a leap of faith that includes a magic act of proving we've got the goods of 10 men (and women) while we free-fall to our potential professional and economical doom.

How's that for productivity and no sleep?

Oh, and while you're assembling that airplane on the way down, note that you may be working on only part of the plane because it's part-time project work you're doing with a group of other contractors. Now, that's accurate for many of us who've worked on project teams as full-time employees with other full-time employees as well as independent contractors—contract work isn't anything new to businesses today, especially for IT professionals.

But what *is* new is an interesting trend in the way we work: the rapid rise of freelance and contract work across traditional full-time roles and across industries. In fact, I've read multiple world-of-work pundits and economists who claim that, in the next decade or two, contract work may surpass full-time employment.

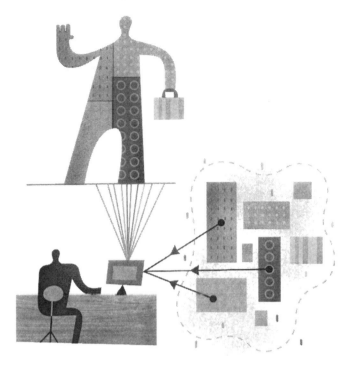

Makes sense, considering that many employers aren't offering competitive benefits packages and other perks—if they are offering jobs at all. In any case, the amount of freelance work being done has been increasing for some time, especially during the latest economic ice age.

It's feast or famine, but the flexibility of this feast is what can be so tasty, especially when you're hands-on in the creating. Sometimes that's out of necessity, sometimes it's out of want, and sometimes it's the very essence of survival so you keep food on the table.

Freelance workers, contract workers—"free agents," shall we say—are people who do not have any professional commitments that restrict their actions to whatever workplace role they fill, and that includes all nonsalaried jobs.

In 1997, author Dan Pink noted in an article in *Fast Company* magazine that there were approximately 25 million "free agents" in the United States.[1] Early in 2012, KellyOCG's latest research revealed that 44 percent of the active workforce in the United States is free agents.[2] That's nearly half for those of you keeping score at home, and that number is only expected to grow,

---

[1] www.fastcompany.com/magazine/12/freeagent.html

[2] www.kellyocg.com/.

potentially beyond the numbers for full-time employment, at some point in the future.

Companies have been operating leaner than ever in the past few years because of the economic apocalypse (that's still taking its toll), shedding millions of jobs of all shapes and sizes, many of which will never again see the light of day. For many different kinds of professionals, this situation has dire consequences: adapt or perish.

Sure, in this post-apocalyptic world, where pockets of economic prosperity glow warm and lush, there are people today who've made the leap and have found sound employment. Silicon Valley is one prime example where tech is (still) crazy-hot, job growth is strong, and salaries are increasing. A decade ago in the Valley, "the average wages of those in the lowest income categories were 66 percent below the average pay of the workers perched on the highest rungs of the income ladder. But 10 years later, the divide has reached 73 percent."[3] Meaning that tech positions continue to rise in salary as compared to non-tech positions that have decreased proportionally.

Damn. Good gigs for those who can get it, right? However, even for many IT professionals, there has been a struggle to stay relevant, to stay employable, to keep food on the table, especially if laid off. This has accelerated the freelance movement, where those who have the stomach for it (because they are hungry) have taken over their career management and have marketed themselves as lean businesses for hire. Indeed, freelancers are lean businesses incarnate.

More companies and freelancers alike want to dial up the professional services and tech work, then dial it down, then dial it up, then dial it down again. That's on-demand leanness, baby. That's how the world of work works today and how it will work tomorrow. But it also means those of us who've become lean businesses incarnate are also experiencing a renaissance of innovation. More freelancers and solopreneurs around means more ideas surfacing that can make a better business biscuit, some truly innovative and tasty.

For example, in the past 12 months I've come across dozens of new cloud-based startups in the HR and recruiting software space, from "freemium" applicant-tracking systems, to social-recruiting platforms, to employee-referral programs, to talent community systems, to new assessment products—and it's only the beginning. When it comes to software that may actually help you, the IT job seeker, find a good full-time, part-time, or freelance job, understand

---

[3] http://business-news.thestreet.com/mercury-news/story/wage-disparity-bay-areas-lower-paid-workers-fail-keep-inflation-while-top-earners-see-bigge/1.

that we're on the cusp of developing some of the most intelligent innovations yet. We'll talk more of these in future chapters.

That's really what it's all about: better business biscuits, hot from the oven and slathered with butter and honey.

We all gotta eat, you know.

■ **Mindful Moment** The amount of available freelance work is on the rise and has become a preferred choice by more and more companies, as well as professionals. Have you ever done any contract work? If so, how did the projects go? If not, have you ever considered it while looking for full-time work?

So Where the Heck Do I Go?

I'm sure many of you, at some point in your IT careers, have applied for jobs listed on job boards and employer career sites, so you're familiar with negotiating the M. C. Escher mazes and traversing the bleak candidate experience (more on that later).[4]

The good news is that there are five major freelance websites I profile here that you can use today. All are easy to get started on and to search for jobs. In no particular order, let's start with Elance.

Elance

At the time of this writing, Elance—"The Human Cloud," as their tagline states (and I like)—touted over 60,000 jobs posted in one month, with nearly a third of those IT and programming jobs. They were founded in 1999 in the Bay Area. See Figure 4-1.

---

[4] M. C. Escher was a Dutch graphic artist known for his often mathematically inspired woodcuts, lithographs, and mezzotints that featured impossible constructions, explorations of infinity, architecture, and tessellations.

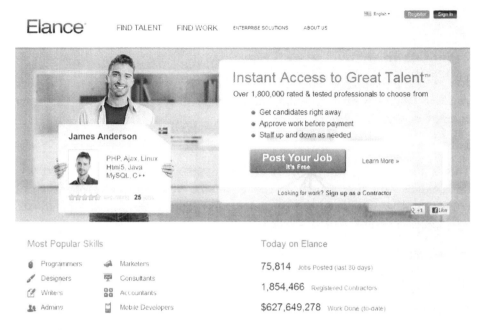

Figure 4-1. Elance home page. Courtesy Elance.com.

First, you need to set up an online profile and account. It's just basic name and contact info and your login credentials; you can also login in with your Facebook account. Read the terms carefully, because Elance requires all financial arrangements between you and the companies you work for to occur inside their payment system (not outside via checks or another service like PayPal).

Once you've logged in the first time, and have verified your e-mail address, then you pick the category of free-agent jobs you're interested in, which for most of you will be the IT and programming jobs. After that, you have a choice between a basic free account and a $10 individual account, the paid account giving you more visibility. But I'm just going with the free account—on a budget here, you know?

After that you get a nifty online prompt, as well as an email highlighting what you do next. This includes:

1. Building a Profile that Shines

In later chapters, I talk about the value of keeping your online professional profiles up to date, but it's important to mention here that your Elance profile is your online resume, so make it shine with your skills, experience, and volunteering efforts (see Chapter 5). The more complete your profile, the more likely you'll get noticed, which is the first step toward getting freelance work.

2. Familiarizing Yourself with Elance

Always make sure you understand the rules of the road for any online service you use. Elance is no exception. Follow their instructions before you start submitting work proposals.

3. Sending Great Proposals

This is true of any "work" you're trying to secure, but make sure that you understand what a prospective "client" needs, what the scope of the work entails, and what skills and experience are required. And always proofread your profiles and proposals! Always.

Elance also has what they call Elance University, which is filled with tutorials and resources for all Elance members. There's a great collaborative help section aptly called the "Water Cooler."

Now let's finish that profile (and move on to the next site).

Guru

Guru was also founded in 1999 in Pennsylvania, and at the time of this writing there were over 4,000 projects listed on their website, with over half of them IT related.

Setting up an account is easy, but I didn't find a "join with Facebook" link, which always makes joining new online sites much easier. If you're a programmer who's worked on these sites, please make them compatible with all social networks, without violating the terms of service. Thank you.

And remember, if you haven't filled out many online forms, though I bet you have, you can also sign up with minimal information and complete the profiles later; you don't have to sit for 30 to 60 minutes building your profile if you don't have the time right now. Save your work and come back to it. After that, you pick one primary skill category and up to five skill subcategories, and then you choose up to five industries you're interested in. Lastly, you can pick a basic free account or one of several tiered paid accounts (hey, these kids gotta make money, too).

After that you can continue to build your profile. There are lots of helpful profile completeness tips, and you get a nifty intro email as well. Another cool feature is that you can take a variety of skills tests—from .NET technology, to mobile technology, to Java, to you-name-it. But, if you're a free basic user, you'll have to pay for the tests, which run about $5 each. That's not a high price to pay when you're trying to show off your tech skills via credible skills tests.

Freelancer

Freelancer claims to connect with over 3.7 million employers and freelancers globally from over 230 countries and regions. That's a lot of reach. Founded in 2004 in Australia, it also claims to have over 1.7 million projects posted for free agents.

Again, signing up for an account is really easy, and you can register via your Facebook profile as well. Once you verify your email address, you're off to the profile races to add your skills and experience. (I actually received two email prompts to do just that—to add my skills and to complete my profile.) As with the other services so far, you can sign up for a basic free account and upgrade to supposedly better visibility via paid accounts. You can then select up to 20 skills that are relevant to you, but there is a limit to how often you can change your skills, so choose wisely the first time.

Freelancer also has a pretty robust internal accounting system called Milestone Payments to make it easier to manage your invoicing and your project payments for the work that you do..

Just as with Guru, there are lots of skills tests at $5 each that can help you stand out with potential employers, so make sure to score well! (You can take them as many times as you like, by the way.)

Freelance.com

Not to be confused with Freelancer, there's also Freelance.com. Founded in 1996 and headquartered in France, it's been around the longest, touting over 27,000 published jobs, which doesn't sound like much but note that they have a heavy French and European footprint. There are plenty of IT categories to choose from, but at this writing the current number of jobs open didn't seem like much compared to the other sites. Many of the postings I reviewed were jobs in Europe, which isn't necessarily a bad thing in this global "tech" economy—take the contract work wherever you can find it, right?

Registration is quick, and you can even sign up with your Viadeo and LinkedIn profiles.[5] Once you verify your account via email, and you're inside, you enter 255 characters' worth of your expertise (think a long headline of skills) and

---

[5] Viadeo, www.viadeo.com, is a Web 2.0 professional social network with over 45 million members worldwide. Members include business owners, entrepreneurs and managers from a diverse range of enterprises.

then you can begin to build your profile. The freelancer accounts are free, as are most related services for the job seeker once your profile is at least 60 percent complete.

oDesk

oDesk was founded in 2004 in the Bay Area and serves over 350,000 businesses. According to its website, they're ranked the number 1 free-agent marketplace by annual contractor earnings, posting nearly 400,000 jobs and serving nearly 300,000 job seekers in the first quarter of 2012. See Figure 4-2.

Figure 4-2. oDesk home page. Courtesy oDesk.com.

Just as with the others, creating an account an oDesk is as easy as filling out one short form, or connecting with your Facebook profile. Once you verify the registration email, then it's time to build the profile, as for all the other sites. oDesk is just as intuitive as the others from a usability perspective, and its help center and support services are the most comprehensive I've seen of all the sites.

Another cool part of the oDesk services is that there are more than 300 free skills tests; it's recommend that all contractors using their site check the list and take the tests that are relevant if they want potential employers to notice them. There is no penalty for failing any of the tests, and oDesk makes it free to retake the tests after 30 days. Freelancers can also hide any test scores they do not like, but don't forget to make your passing test scores public!

And Don't Forget About LinkedIn

Hey, you can also use LinkedIn to search for freelance work, for free, in your existing account. Most listed positions are for full-time work, but you will find a smattering of freelance jobs. It may not be the same selection as you'd get from the other freelance sites, but if you're like me, you'll invest the time in more than one site.

Again, finding contract work is a full-time job.

You can do it, though. Just know that investing the time on any of these sites, as well as others you'll read about in this book, is only part of the grind. You really need to complete your online profiles, keep them consistent, and steadily search for and apply for that contract work you find listed.

There is lots of technical project work being offered today, as validated by these free-agent marketplaces, so don't be shy about participating. Jump on the opportunities when they're offered. Of course, the more relevant any contract work is to your career path, the better—but not necessarily so, especially if you get an opportunity to "stretch" a bit on a tech assignment that adds new skills to your repertoire (remember Chapter 3 and learning new skills).

You are your own little business—full-time, part-time, project work—and so it's critical you take ownership of it and market yourself. No one needs to be shackled to professional bankruptcy today when they're trying to stay afloat, especially when they've got skills that are needed in the workplace. The competition is fierce for IT and programming jobs today, even contract jobs, so don't lose faith when cobbling together enough projects to eat.

Mindful Moment   Have you ever signed on with a freelance service site before? Review the freelance sites above and create a profile on at least one of them, and starting marketing your skills and experience.

And What the Heck Do I Do When I Get the Work?

C'mon, are you really asking me that? Some of the same principles of finding and retaining full-time and part-time work apply to the freelance world. One big exception, which I'm not going to cover in any detail here because I'm not a tax expert, is how to manage the tax implications of being self-employed (filing a Schedule C).

I can't help you there.

But I can help you with the following:

- How to manage the freelance work and your employer so you keep both.

- How you can use your successful completion of contract work to secure full-time employment.

- How to negotiate the fee for your contract work and what to do if the company changes the scope of the work but does not want to increase the pay.

How to Manage the Work and Employer

This is easy, at least in the relative contextual ease of what you've done in your previous full-time employment. If you're the consummate professional and you always do quality work on time, even finish early on, and you get along with most people you've ever worked with, then you're good. Not always, but usually.

This situation, of course, is different if you're attempting to secure contract work when your IT prowess may not be known to the potential company, they cannot see your past successes, and they may never meet you in person or virtually online (I'm talking face time).

If you find a project you're interested in, be sure to understand the scope of the technical work required (ask questions if you don't), agree to the payment terms (see below), acknowledge the deadline, and then . . .

Deliver. Deliver. Deliver.

Listen, I won't yank your chain (excuse me, ladies). The fact is, contract work can be a tough gig. You go from one project to the next, constantly negotiating the scope and payment for each. But I'm of the belief, based on experience, that when you deliver quality work for a company, you're more than likely to work for them again. Companies don't like to constantly search for trusted partners, vendors, and consultants, which is why the larger companies have a vetting process for "preferred vendors." This is especially true for partners in the tech fields, as well as those in marketing, sales, and business development.

How to Secure Full-Time Employment

If you follow the above recipe for delivering consistent quality work, then you're also taking steps toward securing more stable employment—but only if you're aware of those opportunities and/or you talk with your contract employers about them. As mentioned earlier, companies have been hesitant to hire full-time personnel in this latest downturn—with the exception of highly skilled, tough-to-find IT pros.

Like yourselves, of course.

Companies do screen their independent contractors for potential permanent gigs, but the incidence of this is much smaller compared to the growing number of freelance IT work assignments. Differentiating yourself among the global freelance resources just on the basis of your technical skills won't be enough to glean salaried opportunities. You'll need to really work on your soft skills as well—communications, collaboration, personal connections—in order to rise above the crowd.

I'm all about leading small and thinking big when it comes to those soft skills of career development, self-management, and personal leadership. The following "touchy-feely" activities will help you strengthen those skills.

Be aware of where you are in physical space in relation to those around you. In the world of contract work, you've got to be aware of everything around you, and be smaller in your immediate space while exerting control and energy over that space and influencing those around you. That's a mouthful, but more specifically it means you have to be crystal clear about the project requirements, the players, deadlines, "extra credit" opportunities, and the greater business context. Most important, you have to *ask* if there are further opportunities.

Be aware of where you are in your emotional space in relation to those around you. Being aware of your emotional state and of those around you is critical to managing both yourself and others (think emotional intelligence). That will pay back in kind with the right client or employer. How many times have you overreacted or underreacted to a situation? Knowing and living emotional an self-awareness facilitates better communications and team building in any organization, with and project, at home, and beyond. This doesn't mean being a nice guy or gal all the time, or being a tyrant all the time; but it does mean being nice when that's appropriate and being tough when that appropriate, too.

Keep the 360° focal strength. This is hard to do when you've got multiple projects going, maybe trying to launch a business at the same time, and/or trying to land the right full-time gig—all while sustaining your family. Having stamina is about being economical with your focal strength and decision making—that is, what to do, what to delegate, and what to dump. Having stamina is key to long-term physical and mental awareness, as well as effective leadership. We all get tired, and that sometimes takes a toll on our performance. So you must learn to manage yourself economically, to become aware of your endurance levels and longevity.

And again, do the frickin' work right and deliver it on time.

How to Negotiate Pay and Scope

So this is where it all comes together—the front end meets the back end. This is also where the world of freelance work gets the toughest.

I've done plenty of contract work in the past few years, and I've learned these two things (which are true for full-time employment as well):

- Most employers are looking to pay you the least amount possible.

- Most employers want to increase the scope of the work while continuing to pay you the least amount possible.

And I had a decent professional brand going into these contract gigs. You'll have the added baggage of not being known from Adam and of bidding on projects along with possibly hundreds of other IT pros. Maybe even thousands, depending on the project. This competitive bidding situation parallels the competitive side of full-time employment and mirrors the sheer volume of applications for work that employers are getting today.

Second only to receiving or giving performance feedback, negotiating fees is the most uncomfortable thing to do in the world of work. Most of us bend to the nickel and diming in order to get the contract.

But not everyone. I'm sure there are those of you who look a prospective employer right in the eye and say, "I want $XXX because of y and z, and not a penny less." And in response, there are employers who say, "Well, the project wasn't budgeted for $XXX, and even though you've got excellent y and z, I can't give you a penny more."

Queue the crickets chirping.

Then there are the rest of us, who shoot way too high or aim way too low. Been there, done that. And even when a percentage of bidders are able to score big in the hot-tech bidding wars, today's weak economy stymies things for everyone else. Plus, the variances in people's experience—starting a freelance project for the first time or not; having a solid brand and prior success or not—make a difference in what fees are paid.

My advice is simple: think and react proactively, like a seasoned marketing and sales professional. Marketing and sales pros understand how to do this:

Research, research, research. Sure, life moves pretty fast, and you usually don't have the luxury to fully understand the business you're bidding for, especially when it's project based and you're not given a lot of upfront information. But make the time to understand the scope and potential pay scale, as well as the future opportunities of your target "market"—which, in this case, is going from freelance gigs to a full-time position.

There are many sites today that show typical salary ranges by industry, position, and geography, including Glassdoor.com, Salary.com, and Payscale. They also show how to calculate your rates as an independent contractor. Don't go into your negotiations blind. Even a little knowledge can be a powerful tool when you attempt to ensure you're getting paid at fair market value. It may be a game of chicken: who will spill the salary numbers first?

Generate awareness to make the business case. Regardless of the size of the company you're working for, definitely document your own professional accomplishments after every gig you complete. And not just a random list— map as best as you can your accomplishments that helped the business grow, and show how you could bring even more value as a full-time employee. You must make the business case as to how your past experience and/or current project success has impacted the business—or will impact it—and why the company should invest in you further.

Build in a little wiggle room to close the deal. If you've ever had the opportunity to witness and/or read about how sales pros close consultative sales—ones that involve doing the homework, building the relationship, generating awareness and interest, making the business case, and then sealing the deal—you've got a pretty good idea that you don't just wing it.

But one thing you can do is to build in a little wiggle room regarding what you want to be paid, if you have the opportunity. This is an art more than a science because, as in sales, you're always trying to pad the margin as much as you can in order to make a profit if and when the deal closes. If you shoot too high, you'll insult and amuse the client and the negotiation may be short-lived. But if you aim too low, then you've wiped out your margin and any chance of going back up.

Think about it; it's much more difficult to negotiate up than it is to negotiate down. If you ask for $90 per hour and the employer says okay, and you go home and think about and realize you should've asked for more, and then you come back and ask for more, the odds are the offer won't change. However, the reality is that, until you've proven yourself with an employer, it will be difficult to negotiate very much on any projects. But just know that, as an individual contractor, you can beat out the bigger IT shops because you won't have the same margins on top of the base hourly rates. Plus, IT contracting rates vary greatly depending on factors such as location, skills required, and specialization.

Do your homework. Make the business case in your proposal. And good luck in sealing the best-paying deal.

▓ **Mindful Moment**   As with any job, it's important to understand the scope of the work, complete that work within budget and on time, and ensure you are communicating and collaborating effectively each step of the way. Having a professional brand and a previous track record help with securing freelance work. But if you don't have these, then start doing just that—creating the brand and the track record. Negotiating your pay and the scope of the work is an art more than a science, so do your homework and start pitching.

Cross-Training and Volunteering

The New Age of Enlightenment

Action is the foundational key to success.

—Pablo Picasso

Indeed, it is. Because you know that sitting on your hands and hoping the skills and knowledge assimilation will happen by osmosis is only imaginary action.

But I know you're up for the real action, though. I know that in your current world of work, or the one that you were just in before, you pushed yourself to learn other skills that may or may not have immediately impacted the core technical work you were doing. But it made you more valuable nonetheless. Maybe it was giving lunchtime presentations to your peers and supervisors to practice your public-speaking skills. Or maybe it was learning a database programming language like Cassandra because you're ready to move out of front-end work. Or maybe it was learning Photoshop and Illustrator because you want your flair for design to shine. Or maybe it was learning WordPress and basic HTML so you could launch a blog site that would help promote your personal brand.

Or maybe it was moving from using paper documentation, handwritten and typed on an IBM Selectric III typewriter, to inputting on your first Texas Instruments desktop computer with an MS-DOS operating system, Lotus 1-2-3, and WordPerfect.

That was me back in the SJSU college days. When I started working for the academic fundraising program, everything we tracked, from total calls made to donations pledged, was solely paper-based and stored in old-fashioned filing cabinets.

Then the magic box appeared on the desk that I didn't use—the TI desktop computer with the big ol' 5.25-inch floppy disc drives. The desk was a paperwork-processing station that no one person owned. And being the new student supervisor at the time, I wanted to own it; I wanted to learn how to use that new computer. All throughout high school I had used a manual and/ or electric typewriter (I had learned how to type on an IBM Selectric III during my freshmen year in high school), and although we did add a couple of early Apple II's to a side room in the administration building during my senior year—to later be called the "computer lab"—I never had the opportunity to use them.

Damn—did I want to learn how to use that computer! It wasn't in the cards, though. Nope. The program manager was going to be the only one to use it, and to manage all the inputting and reporting—no students allowed, even student supervisors.

But I was bold, and I pushed to be cross-trained on that amazing piece of alien technology (to me then, at any rate). This wasn't easy for me, as I despised directness and confrontation of any kind. Mercy, all I wanted was to be liked, but I'll be damned if the magical pull of that machine didn't curb my resistance to change and allow me to ask for what I wanted. Yes, I was young, naïve, and somewhat indecisive; and yet I knew exactly what could make it all better— being cross-trained on the computer and finally learning the new realm of electronic files, formulas, and fascinating DOS prompt commands.

I requested for weeks that I be the one to manage the fundraising program data. Granted, the data went from the lowly desktop to a larger mainframe system buried elsewhere on campus, but we had to start somewhere, right? And the program manager did his best to do it all himself. He hired and managed over 75 student callers, on average who worked six days a week across double shifts including Sundays (and sometimes Saturdays, which made it seven days a week), and then transferred all the calling data from paper pledges to that precious computer.

Until one day he asked me, "Kevin, do you want to learn how to use the computer?"

Abso-frickin-lutely, Brother. (I didn't really call him "Brother," but you get the gist of my enthusiasm.) And learning to use that computer exposed me to other forms of cross-training in the fundraising business at the university, opening the doors to promotion and eventually to managing the university annual fund progam; I did that for years while I was still a student and also after I graduated.

By the way, at one point while I was writing this book, I watched an interview with Geddy Lee and Alex Lifeson from Rush, my favorite band. Geddy explained how the band was criticized in certain circles because "their reach exceeded their grasp" of the musical ideas and ideals. Hogwash. That's the way they rolled, stretching themselves to grasp the next level of excellence, which they're still doing today.

Does your reach exceed your grasp? And are you stretching and grasping? I sure as hell am.

Back to the topic at hand. Were you ever cross-trained in any other facets of the business, other positions or skills? If not, then push your employer to cross-train you and your colleagues on the latest programming and platforms, as well as teaching you more about the business. Also, push for free time to explore and program some projects of your choosing (which is where some great technical innovation can come from).

Also, encourage your employer to sponsor volunteer projects and/or to focus on personal projects outside of work. This is a great way for you and your colleagues to learn other hard and soft skills, all of which will ultimately benefit the business as well.

If you're overworked and underappreciated, like many employed people are, sparks of collaborative caring and innovation will fly out the window along with your employer's customer service and revenues. This chapter explains that many learning opportunities exist within your current employ—or within the freelance work you may be doing—and it demonstrates how to uncover these opportunities and take advantage of them, as well as reaping the benefits of volunteering in the community and engaging in work outside of the workplace.

Mindful Moment   Remember when you wanted to learn that new task, to stretch yourself beyond your comfort level? Have you ever wondered how HR and recruiting personnel work with finance and executive management to locate and hire talent like yourself, as well as to run the company? Have you thought about how your role as an IT professional affects every facet of the business? Have you ever wanted to have a more well-rounded skills toolbox inside and outside to provide greater business value to your employer? Well, it's time to think about that and make it happen.

How Cross-Training Burns the Fat

If you're sitting there, chatting with your colleagues a good part of the day, are you one of the employed majority who are "actively disengaged"? That's fancy employee-engagement-survey results for, "I really friggin' hate my job."

Many American workers across positons and industries are "not engaged" or "actively disengaged" in their work, meaning they are emotionally disconnected from their workplaces and are therefore less likely to be productive.

"I really friggin' hate my job."

Particularly, those with at least some college (and possibly a degree or technical certification) often are more "unhappy" than those who have only a high school diploma. Why? So many jobs today are much more complex than ever before—they require more education and a diverse skill set, as well as soft communication skills and the ability to adapt quickly and efficiently to this ever-evolving world of work. It's the high school graduates (and nongraduates) who are especially struggling to find relevant and decent-paying work these days.

You, the consummate IT professional, may have been gainfully employed of late. But your feet most certainly have been held to the productivity fire, and you've been doing the work of three of your peers, so in a way, you've been pushed to stretch with little incentive (or only a few with big incentives) whether you like it or not. And unless, of course, you've been working for one of the progressive startups, with a bigger agenda of seeing their teams and products win big—and rewarding you for just that.

The more overworked, underappreciated, and underpaid you are, the less likely you will sing your employer's praises and evangelize the brand. You'll more than likely bitch and moan, or quietly uncouple your mind from the mothership and bide your time—bringing down your colleagues along the way—while you look for better opportunities elsewhere.

But what if you were given the opportunity to learn other parts of the businesses, to acquire related skill sets and experience that would complement your current domain and make you even more valuable to your employer (and to yourself as you become more marketable to others)?

It seems that this is possible. Maybe you've heard your supervisors or managers or HR, or all the bigwigs themselves, tout how the company's all one big, happy community working together across departments to build a better business and a better world, the epitome of evangelical elasticity.

You just gagged a little, didn't you?

Hold that gag just for a minute. Imagine if you were over 140 years old, had over 60K employees in over 36 countries, and were producing over $20 billion in annual sales by selling diapers and feminine hygiene products, among related items.

Yes, the "Glamorous Life" by Shelia E.[1] Indeed. What? Hey, I'm a happy daddy of two little girls and a contented husband of one lovely wife. I'm good with it all. My point is that even when you're 140 years old, and work for an old-time, bureaucratic institution, you can still change.

That was the message from Liz Gottung, the CHRO at Kimberly-Clark, whom I heard speak last year at an HR conference. That's right, CHRO—chief human resource officer, the most glamorous job of them all. Don't scoff. It's teams like Liz's that are going screen and hire IT folks like you when you apply for these conservative corporate jobs.

Again, imagine: you're over 140 years old and steeped in cultural tradition. Believe it or not, Kimberly-Clark is now in the midst of multiple change-management initiatives, including a complete overhaul of its compensation management, implementation of a new SaaS-deployed human capital management system, the institution of cross-functional career development and management paths for inside HR as well as for Finance, IT, Customer Service, and much more. The good news is that if big, old companies can provide their employees with cross-training opportunities, then so can most any other company. Many companies are in the midst of changing the way they hire, train, cross-train, and retain their workforce today—and that's a good thing for us all.

To cross-train and retain—truly an revolution. It's true that business and workforce management have evolved at a glacial pace compared to the speed of the technological advances that have made it easier to manage and share data across an enterprise. And the latest neuroscience research has revealed the true elasticity of the human brain—how we can *keep* learning and adapting throughout our lives. The next 5 to 10 years are going to be exciting!

Sometimes there are huge evolutionary spikes of change (relatively speaking, of course). I keep thinking that we're right there on the verge of massive change, right at the front edge of the mainstream. When you think about what motivates highly skilled IT professionals such as yourselves, you know it's the work you do, how you're compensated for that work, the flexibility and autonomy you have to complete that work, the people you work with, and the ability to see the fruits of your collective labor, whether they be

---

[1] Shelia E. is a musician, percussionist and singer whose career was launched in the 1980s with the popular song "Glamorous Life."

completed projects, new products, service offerings, security or systems integrity.

Although major change directives come from the top, all change has to get buy-in internally, meaning it has to catch fire with the majority for that cultural shift to happen and stick. This buy-in comes from the empowerment of ownership, not entitlement, and it lights the motivational fires.

Amen to evangelical elasticity.

The reality is that there are more motivated "communities" than other entities in any business organization. If you can more readily participate in the lateral, ladder, and lattice career-development moves described below, you and many others of the "actively disengaged" can burn the unhappy fat of inaction.

Mindful Moment   Have you worked for employers for whom it's always "business as usual" when it comes to career advancement— meaning little, if any? Or for employers that offered you different kinds of training and wanted you to understand the broader business? If the latter, what did those activities look like? Did you actually learn anything, or are you still sucking your thumb?

Laterals, Ladders, and Lattices—Oh, My

How many talent-development professionals does it take to screw in a lightbulb?

Well, it depends on what kind of lightbulb and what it's for. Meaning, it's contextual. For as long as I've been in the HR and the recruiting space, I've know many a great training-and-development strategy and talked with many a great training-and-development practitioner. I have applied some of their ideas to the companies I've worked for.

This isn't supposed to be a primer on talent management and development, but it's important for you to understand that there are different flavors of opportunistic career "blow pops" in any company you work for. There's a misconception that a smaller company provides more opportunities to learn all aspects of the business, but sometimes that's not the case. It's often the larger organizations that provide more career-development support, from onboarding to review time.

But then again, I've heard (and experienced) of new employees who have been parachuted right into the jungle and left there to fend for themselves. Keep these examples in mind as you examine your current employer's—or a prospective employer's—willingness to provide cross-training opportunities, career development, and mobility of any kind.

Lateral move *This is when you're unhappy with your current position and need a change of scene without leaving all together.*

Let's be real: IT is hot, but it also has an inordinate amount of pressure on top and from underneath—like a fat, sweaty man sitting sealed atop a pot of boiling water. It's not easy to move laterally if you don't have the skills to do so. If your employer won't help you get those skills, and you don't want to get them yourself, then maybe you should just get out. You'll know if you're in the IT hotness, and if you're not, then ask those who currently work there. It's kinda tough to pivot from systems administration to applying progressive enhancements.

As was mentioned in Chapter 4, IT has diversified into three camps: consultants, project managers, and developers. The latter two are the internal move potentials. Sometimes the grass isn't always greener elsewhere; the primary reason people leave their jobs is their immediate managers. You may have heard of other IT project management or developer-type opportunities in the company via your colleagues, internal job board, external job board, or your own horrible (or good-hearted) boss.

Of course, you'll have to weigh a lateral move against what you have now—compensation, bonus opps if available, the team you'd be working with, who your new boss would be, and any new skills you might learn that could increase your value long term. This can take time, but it's time you should take. (I'll talk in Chapters 9 and 10 about how to research jobs, people, and other organizations; some of the same principles can and should be applied to internal moves.)

The larger the enterprise, the more there might be opportunities to move. However, any kind of internal movement can be highly policitized, especially when you're unhappy with a current boss and/or co-workers. Keep your badmouthing to a minimum and focus on the professional growth that's possible when you want to move to the new business unit, department, or division.

Ladder move *This is he traditional career climb to the next best thing internally, if and when you qualify and/or are promoted.*

Again, with the reality. How often do IT pros get promoted to CTO? How often does *anyone* get promoted to anything beyond the front lines? Hey, there's always a chance to climb the ladder if you keep your nose clean, don't watch the clock, don't play Angry Birds of Warcraft or whatever the game *du jour* is (keep in mind that I had a first-generation Nintendo in college and played the original Legend of Zelda until four in the morning or until my cigarettes ran out), work your ass off, brown-nose your boss, never sleep—you get the idea.[2]

Traditional promotions do still ocurr in the world of work, so don't get me wrong. You may have steller performance reviews and recommendations from your immediate supervisors and peers, as well as amazing project-management prowess—enough that middle to upper IT management has taken notice and really wants to promote you. And maybe that happens. Some of you will get to CTO or IT management, in some shape or form.

But remember that seniority alone doesn't give you a free pass. You're battling it out with five generations in the workplace, for fewer and fewer full-time positions, so you better have the skills, experience, and specialized problem solving down to a science. Okay, throw in a little art, too.

Lattice move *This is the progressive move that takes you to new cross-trained realms within your organization.*

Now, we're talkin'. These are the rainbow, glitter, and unicorn mobility moves that all the HR industry thought leaders are proposing today. Here's what I recommend: start pushing your employer for empowered employment from the inside out. Tell your employer that you want more responsibility for managing your career development, as well as your learning of relevant and related new skills. Say that you want to be aware of other opportunities in the organization as well as the recommended paths for how to get there, not to mention the other colleagues and mentors who can help get you there. And it doesn't hurt to be able to control time and space, either.

Just like the lateral and ladder moves, lattice moves require you to not be afraid to find and ask for what you want and what you need. Controlling time and space is all relative. It doesn't mean you're going to get what you ask for; you may even get the proverbial squat. But you are the master of your career destiny (and yes, it helps when your employer plays along), and the development work you do in a career context while looking out for the next opportunity. This opportunity may mean specific responsibilities and projects in the role you love, or a promotion to the new role you'll love even more.

It's not a cliché, kids. You need to find a role that you love, with the kind of IT work that you love, with an employer that you at least get along with (you don't have to love the employer)—and you need to do it all well. Do it here, do it there, do it everywhere.

---

[2] The Legend of Zelda is a high fantasy, action-adventure video game series created by Japanese game designers and developed and published by Nintendo.

That is all. No, I am not Dr. Seuss.

The Value of Informal Learning

In a moment, we'll consider two different ways you can and should be cross-trained in your current position (or tomorrow's position) to potentially work yourself into the lattice. These suggestions are a blend of what I've experienced and the experiences of HR professionals I spoken with over the years. They focus more heavily on informal learning than formal.

It's been fairly well documented that handing employees a training manual and expecting them to understand the entire business accounting system they are supposed to maintain just ain't gonna happen. Yes, training manuals can be helpful reference guides, but since the majority of us don't easily absorb information this way, it's always best *to do* as the way to learn.

That's why informal learning rocks. That means hands-on application of the skills to the tasks, so as to become more proficient in those skills. Think about the "breaking stuff" I mentioned in Chapter 1—knowing through doing, adopting, and adapting.

Consider a study of time-to-performance that Sally Anne Moore did at Digital Equipment Corporation in the early 1990s.[3] The study showed the disparity between formal and informal learning and the fact that we do move from formal learning and knowing of new skills, to informal learning, to doing, to adopting, and to adapting those new skills. It's all in the practice and application of skills in real time, with real systems, software, and co-workers, that makes the magic work.

Two Ways to Gain Skills Informally

Think about these two learning paths:

1. Take a portion of time every month to "job-shadow" individuals from different desks, digs, departments, divisions—someone doing something that is of interest to you, relevant to what you do, and you can see how it impacts the bottom line. (Sorry, you can never get away from the bottom line, no matter how cool the CEO is.) Not only will this give you a better understanding of the business for which you work, you will meet others in the IT realm and beyond, some of whom could be mentors. But more important, you will learn new skills and brush up on those skills you thought you had nailed. You know—the soft skills, like

---

[3] Sally-Ann Moore, "Time-to-Learning" (Digital Equipment Corporation, 1998).

communicating empathically with your colleagues, subordinates, and bosses instead of shrieking like a banshee when you don't get your way (followed by breaking desk knickknacks and incessant crying).

2. There's the old-fashioned impromptu (or scheduled) meeting of mentoring minds that includes white-boarding, collaborating, and scenario-based problem solving, whether it's face to face or virtual. This is where sparks of innovation either ignite or are snuffed out like nasty-smelling scented candle. With regularity and practice, you just might learn a little something or two, teach a little something or two, get noticed by that boss and your snarky colleagues, and be celebrated in the annals of businessdom.

Being cross-trained is valuable to you and to the business. You're learning more, contributing more; you're getting the skills that will enable you to move around the company lattice work, either across the small company or across departments in are large enterprise. There's no guarantee of this, of course. There's no guarantee of anything in the world of work, unless you have a signed contract vetted by dozens of lawyers, Jesus, and Muhammad.

It Can Really Happen

So let me tell you more about me, since I've lived much of what I'm writing about. After the dot-com company I worked for went belly up, I worked as a marketing consultant and fiction/poetry writer. Don't laugh. I had a little success and notoriety online, and I was making progress toward landing print pieces, but I saw no monetary rewards. At all. I'm sure some of you also have some great stories of what you did between the real gigs. Am I right? Like my keep-it-real friends always joked with me back then, "So, how did that poetry thing work out for you, Kev?"

Dammit. Not well.

It was then that I met up with the firm I worked for most of the 2000s— HRmarketer.com, a marketing software and services firm. When I was hired, it was only as a half-time market researcher. I was to research and verify data that would then be entered into databases that were managed in the firm's software product on behalf of its customers (something they still do and I use in my latest incarnation).

But it was solid work and a good job, and the world was still coming out of the first downturn of the 2000s. And then the fabulous lattice appeared like a vision—the firm's founder was looking for leadership in the then-tiny ship, and I was looking for more. I began to take on more responsibility. I acquired new skills and experience as it related to developing, marketing, and selling B2B software—much more than the previous startup I had worked for. The more I aspired and proved myself, the more I became a trusted "partner" in a sense, eventually becoming and remaining president of the company until I left in 2010.

From part-time researcher to president in just less than seven years. The empowering lattice environment can help make that happen— to you, as well. It's not just at the smaller, supposedly more nimble firms, either. Don't forget the cross-training story about Kimberly-Clarke mentioned earlier in this chapter. That's a huge brand with over 60K employees.

It can happen. Really.

Mindful Moment Have you experienced job-shadowing or collaborative problem-solving sessions? Were they formal or informal in nature? What kinds of activities truly helped you learn new skills or adapt and grow in your career? Employers that offer lattice career-growth opportunities are the ones you want to work for.

So Much for the Job Have-Nots

They sat in the front rows listening to our advice. The air conditioning didn't work, so large fans swirled warm air back and forth between the open doors and open windows. They listened with guarded optimism, looking tired and a little lost.

We talked about resume best practices, and where to look for jobs, and how to optimize and leverage online professional profiles, and where to find freelance work. We talked about volunteer projects in your local community, not only to give back, but to exchange with one another via networking reciprocity; after all, we never know where our next opportunity could come from. At one point toward the end of my segment, I forced a smile, thinking of my own career path—the highs and lows, and the mediocre in-betweens. I wiped my sweaty brow and looked toward the windows, already somewhat regretting the cliché forming in my mind.

"Keep open all those windows of opportunity you find throughout your careers," I said. "You never know when you'll need them."

These were the job have-nots—working-class to middle-class folks who have lost their jobs, whose careers have ground to a halt, whose personal lives have gotten in the way of their professional ones. This was also an experience for me of volunteering with Hirewire, a local organization helping job seekers.

Consider one of the Hirewire attendees, an aerospace engineer in his late 50s. He had been out of work for nearly three years, struggling to fill the hole in his resume and remain relevant and become employable again.

Consider a service delivery professional in his early 40s, out of work for over a year and struggling to find value in the local employment-office workshops and counseling sessions.

Consider my best friend from college. In 1987, he wanted to be an airline pilot. He finished his college degree, flew hundreds of hours, finished all his flying certifications, and voilà! He became an airline pilot, first flying for a commuter airline and then for a global transport airline. But then just last month he was out of a job, laid off owing to the continued economic ice age.

Consider the thousands of men and women given highly skilled training to defend us near and abroad, who then find themselves as civillians drowning in a sea of the unemployed.

Consider the millions of high school graduates (and even more nongraduates) who fight for a finite number of low-wage jobs, shuffling from one social service agency to another, and then told to look ahead, figure it out, and find a job.

Figure what out, exactly? Sometimes the truth is contrary for the job have-nots, meaning that everything we knew before about hard work and career management need not apply. And then again, sometimes there's a breath of fresh air, like the note I recently received from another friend of mine:

> All is moving along for me. . . . I'm doing some interesting work with companies both inside and outside of the HR space, which is keeping things fresh. And still managing to find (some) balance in life by following your advice from the last time we spoke about "keeping all the windows open."

Ah, so much for clichés; so much effort is needed to warm the world of work again. So much has been lost during this darkest of modern economic winters. So much needs to be reinvented and reinvested.

So much for the job have-nots.

But we can all make a little difference. This is why I volunteer for an organization like Hirewire: to be able to give something of value back that I've learned over the course of my career, to give back to those who are looking for work, looking to reinvent, looking to learn new skills and ways in which to get noticed in this jobless recovery. Every month, the jobs report has been a mixed bag of piss and vinegar, as well as the tastiest IT Silicon Valley vino ever made. In fact, one journalist wrote, "It's like job growth is sideways."

Indeed. And that's putting it nicely.

I'm not saying that volunteering leads directly to employment, but it can open you up to new experiences, skills, people, organizations, and opportunities that you wouldn't have had otherwise. We ask Hirewire attendees to do just that—volunteer and thereby expose themselves to opportunities they may never discover via the Employment Development Department's manditory training classes. And it doesn't have to take a lot of time. Let's explore some more.

Volunteer

Volunteering for a cause you believe in can pay dividends for you and your career. I know that sounds so self-serving, but the reality is that giving in itself is reciprocal, whether there's an intrinsic or extrinsic return for the giver. And yes, your help will pay dividends for your cause of choice, as well as the company you work for, if you're employed.

Consider these facts, referenced on the VolunteerMatch site, a web-based volunteer engagement network of more than 86,000 nonprofits, making it easier for people and causes to connect:[4]

- More than 8 in 10 companies (84 percent) believe that volunteerism can help nonprofits accomplish long-term social goals, and are increasingly offering skills-based volunteer opportunities to their employees. In fact, corporate managers report that the top priorities when determining workplace volunteer activities include the potential to alleviate a social issue (36 percent), help the nonprofit function more effectively (31 percent), and serve more clients (31 percent).[5]

- Despite the tough economy in 2009, support for employee volunteering remained strong, with 83 percent of executives of large companies reaffirming their support. Treating Employees Well (81 percent) continues to be one of the top three areas of corporate citizenship most important to senior executives.[6]

- New research shows that companies that help employees volunteer with nonprofit organizations could have a leg up in

---

[4] Used with permission of VolunteerMatch.

[5] 2010 Deloitte volunteer impact survey.

[6] The State of Corporate Citizenship in the United States 2009: Weathering The Storm (Boston College Center for Corporate Citizenship, 2009).

recruiting Generation Y talent (18–26-year-olds). Nearly two-thirds of the respondents (62 percent) in a 2007 Volunteer IMPACT survey said they would prefer to work for companies that give them opportunities to contribute their talents to nonprofit organizations.[7]

Volunteering can also you improve both your hard and soft skills; encourage your job satisfaction and overall morale; upgrade your teamwork and leadership ability; enhance communication and collaboration with everyone you work with, supervise, and report to; and so much more.

Volunteering is a gut thing for me first, though. Volunteeing should be about something that moves you and that you feel passionately about—even more than what brings your paycheck every two weeks. When I had my first girl, I knew I wanted to ensure a loving, stable environment for her. Considering that I grew up with domestic violence and abuse, those memories became painfully real again and I decided that generating awareness of domestic violence, as well as volunteering at a local women's shelter and working with children of abusive homes, was exactly what I needed to do. A by-product of that effort was an increase in my empathic ability (not sympathetic, mind you), my listening skills, my patience, and my tolerance for those caught up in the messy confusion of physical and emotional abuse. I didn't go into it looking for those skills, but I honed them from the volunteering nonetheless.

The founder of Hirewire, Ken Winters, also went into volunteering because he felt passionately about helping job seekers. Being a recruiter for over 10 years, and running his own staffing firm called Staffback, Ken longed to help those he couldn't place in jobs by giving them pointers on everything from resume writing to job search to interviewing tips. He saw too many local viable employees in the Scotts Valley and Santa Cruz area—many of whom were and are IT pros (ironically)—go month after month without a bite. As I've already mentioned in this chapter, I've seen them (you) as well, which is why I wanted to volunteer and give job-search pointers. At the same time, I'm improving my public-speaking skills, something I've wanted to do anyway.

So whether you're looking for an opportunity to volunteer on your own or via your employer, be aware that many employers offer incentives for their employees to volunteer. You and your employer can find myriad volunteer opportunities listed at VolunteerMatch (see Figure 5-1) and Idealist.org.

---

[7] Deloitte & Touche USA, Volunteer Impact Survey (Deloitte & Touche USA, 2007).

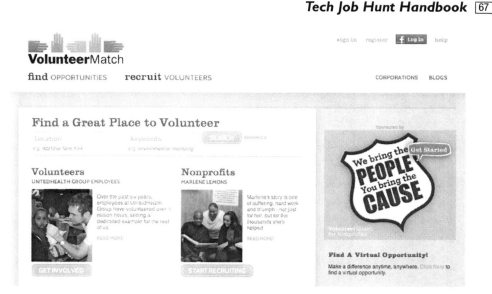

Figure 5-1. VolunteerMatch. Courtesy of VolunteerMatch.org.

The smaller firms I've worked for have given staff one or two days of paid time off per year in exchange for volunteer time with a cause of choice. At larger organizations, time off can amount to a large donation: Microsoft employees have supposedly logged over 1.5 million volunteer hours assisting their favorite nonprofit organizations.[8] And in 2009, the more than 1.5 million volunteer hours reported by Walmart associates translated to more than $11 million in grant contributions.[9]

I could make a list a mile long of these (thankfully), but you get the point. Consider volunteerism as yet another way to grow professionally. The personal returns are invaluble.

■ **Mindful Moment**   Giving your time can be hard when you're cobbling together enough work to make a living, but volunteerism has been proven to benefit employee, employer, and community. Volunteering can improve both your hard and soft skills, your teamwork and leadership ability, and the communication and collaboration skills.

---

[8] www.microsoft.com/about/corporatecitizenship/en-us/serving-communities/community-opportunities/employee-giving/.

[9] www.walmartstores.com/CommunityGiving/201.aspx.

CHAPTER 6

Background Screens and Assessments

Know Thyself (and Then Some)

It is discouraging how many people are shocked by honesty and how few by deceit.

—Noel Coward, English playwright

Maybe you heard about it. The fact (or lack thereof) that ex-Yahoo CEO Scott Thompson had published bios, including the one in Yahoo's annual report, that claimed that he had a bachelor's degree in both accounting and computer science from Stonehill College. Unfortunately, his degree was actually in accounting only, not computer science as well.

Now, anything the CEO publishes about himself in an annual report, a legal document that CEOs must personally swear is truthful, must be, well, truthful. Funny how that works, right? Who frickin' wants to be truthful when looking for work, particularly in the highly competitive IT world? We smirk about the high-profile idiots who lie about their experience, skills, and education—and there have been plenty of those. Then we shake our heads and curse them silently when we find out how much they'll still take home, even after being severed.

We don't get that. Not even close. If we lie on our resumes and our online profiles, and the lies are discovered after we're hired, then the only result is that we're fired. Bye-bye. Adios. Au revoir. Tschüs. Zài jiàn. Get out.

You Can't Hide

And forget about your future employers' not finding out about it, because in today's ever-connected networked world, word gets around. In the United States, federal and state guidelines may vary, but for the most part, past and current employers need only reveal your "name, rank, and serial number"— and your employment dates—during a reference check, but again, word gets around. Loose lips abound, whether they belong to the hiring managers, ex-colleagues, management, or the recruiters and HR people themselves.

Yeah, I know you fudged a little here and a little there. Everybody does, right? I have. Not blatant fabrications, but a little embellishment of the truth never hurt anyone.

But let's flip it for a minute. Imagine you're the one doing the hiring (you may, in fact, have hired your own IT teams in the past). I got the following examples from my friends at EmployeeScreenIQ, an employment screening company.

> *Your favorite candidate's resume is bursting with accomplishments, but a background check reveals a glaring discrepancy: he claims he attended a prestigious law college on a full academic scholarship and graduated in the top half of the class; however, he actually received a partial scholarship based on financial aid and finished 76th in a class of 85. Do you hire him?*

Please, think about it for a minute. Would you? Like most employers, probably not. Political affiliations aside, you probably wouldn't hire U.S. Vice President Joe Biden, who famously exaggerated his educational qualifications in this way when running for office.

Here's one more:

> *Your leading candidate is an unbelievable performer—a real superstar with a track record of making huge profits for his previous companies. However, he left his last job citing "creative differences," and a background check reveals several drug-related convictions. Do you hire him?*

Maybe you don't feel as strongly about this one, especially if you believe in giving people a second chance—but most moderate-to-conservative employers would not hire a troubled "star performer" (who might end up as a Charlie Sheen in the ranks, the primate example of this scenario[1]).

---

[1] When actor Charlie Sheen lost his job on the sitcom *Two and a Half Men,* he went a little crazy, touting that he was "winning" the dispute.

The Background on Background Checks

Most background-screening firms estimate that nearly 50 percent of all candidates distort or exaggerate information on their resumes. That's 50 percent, mind you. Half of you. One out of every two of us, thus, are full of crap—or somewhere around there, relatively speaking. The most egregious form of resume and/or online profile "crap" involves fabricating the educational qualifications. Reread Chapters 2 and 3, and rethink that fabrication.

Employers today face a lot of legislative and legal challenges connected with the hiring process. It's a minefield out there. The world's crazy-litigious, so background checks are critical to protect an employer's interests. Hey, I'm sure you're not who they're worried about, but there *are* many others who would sue at the drop of an "I'm with stupid" hat. Plus, background checks protect job applicants as well, especially if that employer screws up in a big way by screening you out for any unlawful reasons. Keep these points in mind:

- There are dozens of federal and state laws that affect hiring practices, employee rights, and labor relations—and new ones come into effect every year.

- There is increased enforcement by the Equal Employment Opportunity Commission (EEOC), challenging the use in hiring of credit and criminal histories (which is to your benefit, actually).

- Employers face a growing risk of being charged with discrimination (in 2011, the EEOC received 99,947 complaints charging discrimination—the highest number in its 46-year history).

- There are legislative attempts to expand "protected class" status to include the unemployed and ex-offenders (again, not such a bad thing).

- There's been an explosion of "failure to hire" suits, owing in large part to the tight job market and therefore a greater number of rejected applicants.

- There's been an increase in lawsuits charging violations of the Fair Credit Reporting Act (FCRA).

- There's been legal action taken related to the use of arrest records in hiring. (PepsiCo recently lost a $3.1 million settlement related to this.)

- There have been costly challenges to companies' not obtaining proper consent for conducting background checks that would ensure compliance with federal and state laws. (First Transit lost a $5.9 million settlement for failure to do so.)

- There have been "Ban the Box" initiatives at the state and local levels that call for the elimination on initial public employment applications of questions about past convictions.

- Social media and other new technologies are being used as screening tools, even though hiring decisions are not supposed to be made on this basis, according to the Equal Employment Opportunity Commission (EEOC) and the Fair Credit Reporting Act (FCRA); this is because information on social media isn't always verifiable, as is criminal or employment information.

The fact is that it's a pain for employers to recruit, hire, manage, and retain the messy human beings we all are. Because of our slobbery, we must have these pesky rules in place, making it really difficult to simply hire and fire.

BACKGROUND SCREENING—A HIRING MUST

By no means am I an expert on employment law—let's be clear about that. But what I do know is that background screening is a hiring must these days, for most positions and most industries. Background screening ensures that applicants are who they say they are in their resumes, online profiles, reference checks, and interviews. Background checks will expose or verify your criminal history, your employment history, your education history, your professional references, and sometimes your credit rating (depending on whether you'll be working with financial records and/or managing money). Again, employers really need to make sure they're hiring the right people—people who don't make mistakes that will come back and bite both the employer and the applicant in the ass. Really. We could spend hours just reviewing the lawsuits.

However, employers make mistakes as well, and they don't always make the right decisions when hiring is based on the background screening. You as the applicant have protections under the EEOC and FCRA.

For example, the Equal Employment Opportunity Commission "is responsible for enforcing federal laws that make it illegal to discriminate against a job applicant or an employee because of the person's race, color, religion, sex (including pregnancy), national origin, age (40 or older), disability, or genetic information.[2] It is also illegal to discriminate against a person because the person complained about discrimination, filed a charge of discrimination, or participated in an

---

[2] www.eeoc.gov/eeoc/index.cfm.

employment discrimination investigation or lawsuit. Most employers with at least 15 employees are covered by EEOC laws (20 employees in age discrimination cases). Most labor unions and employment agencies are also covered. The laws apply to all types of work situations, including hiring, firing, promotions, harassment, training, wages, and benefits.

And the Fair Credit Reporting Act "regulates the practices of consumer reporting agencies (CRAs) that collect and compile consumer information into consumer reports for use by credit grantors, insurance companies, employers, landlords, and other entities in making eligibility decisions affecting consumers. Information included in consumer reports generally may include consumers' credit history and payment patterns, as well as demographic and identifying information4 and public record information (e.g., arrests, judgments, and bankruptcies). Consumer report information may be used by entities to predict the risk of future nonpayment, default, or other adverse events. The FCRA was enacted to (1) prevent the misuse of sensitive consumer information by limiting recipients to those who have a legitimate need for it; (2) improve the accuracy and integrity of consumer reports; and (3) promote the efficiency of the nation's banking and consumer credit systems." [3]

The Social Media Window

But with regard to the social media, this is still a relatively new phenomenon, one that exposes us to broader networking and job opportunities but also to a helluva lot of risk. Thank God I didn't have social media in college—and I was a good kid.

Hey, if we all walked around naked all the time, with our curtains drawn and our shades down, which some of us do, then there would be a lot *more* reason for everyone else to stop and stare. Which is why background checkers and HR people are attracted to your Facebook page like a moth to the flame.

And then they judge and shake their heads, and sigh in disappointment, even in disgust (that's why I only post pictures of my kids, like a good social daddy). Thankfully, that's not the case for many of us, because otherwise we'd probably all see a lot more than just being naked. It's not just the silly eccentricities we exhibit from day to day. Maybe we'd also see violent activity, racism, or other intolerance, as well as illegal activities, sexually explicit material—you name it—things we'd have to call 911 about.

Maybe that hasn't happened literally, but figuratively? The Internet is a minute-by-minute, day-by-day online social playground. I'm talking about the vast amount of positive and negative information about us that's online via the social media and social networking sites. Go ahead—Google yourself. (We've

---

[3] www.ftc.gov/os/2011/07/110720fcrareport.pdf.

all done it at this point.) If you're disappointed that you don't find any dirt, then you and I should talk.

Sadly, more people than we'd probably like to admit are pulling up their online shades and opening their social media curtains to share sketchy, inappropriate, and negative behavior that can destroy their careers and their aspirations. As a result, recruiting professionals and hiring managers are scouring the Internet these days to find out what else they can about you and me when we apply for jobs—and then they're using that information to make hiring decisions, which is discriminatory and unfair, and could expose their companies to lawsuits.

Most hiring professionals I know are peering through your windows without hesitation and making those hiring calls based on what they see, regardless of what the Equal Employment Opportunity Commission or the Fair Credit Reporting Act says—or in spite of the sensationalized litigation we've seen of late.

So whether it's a legitimate background search your future employer is running on you, or if it's a review of your LinkedIn and Facebook profiles, Twitter streams, GitHub or Stack Overflow posts, BraveNewTalent talent community shares—whatever—keep in mind that the hiring personnel are looking for reasons *not* to hire you. So don't give them any, if you can help it.

Games to Avoid

Here's another list from my friends at EmployeeScreenIQ about what employers are looking for when they are screening applicants (and there are many background-screening firms out there today, all of which are going to help their clients with the following situations):

You provide a false date of birth with the intention of throwing off a criminal record search. That's because most criminal records are filed by name and date of birth. Remember, they might consider asking you for a legal form of identification, such as a driver's license or passport, that can be compared to the information you're providing on the background-check release form.

You provide a false Social Security number with the intention of hiding places where you've lived. Again, they're going to make sure you provide a valid form of identification that confirms your SSN.

You provide a false Social Security number to prove that you have the legal right to work in the United States. That's what I-9 forms and E-Verify are for.[4]

You intentionally omit a past employer from your job application. Listen, smart employers are going to compare your resume and/or your LinkedIn profile to the completed job application before they submit it for a background check. You may get away with a gap or two in the short term, but you should be the one to backfill the blanks in the best way possible.

You claim to work for an employer who doesn't exist. C'mon, really? Don't be an idiot and use an online employment mill that will charge you a fee to provide fake employment information and verification. You don't wear desperation well enough for that, and there is plenty of contract IT work available today that will give you immediate experience and funds (see Chapter 4).

You present a fake copy of your diploma when your degree couldn't be verified. Really? Again? Wasn't the employment mill experience enough? Yes, you could try to falsify your diploma for a degree you never finished. You can also buy a fake diploma outright from an online diploma mill, but do you really need the college diploma that badly? There are lots of better ways to get here, like finishing school or getting various tech certifications.

You wait several days to take a drug test. Hey, I'm not judging. Just be careful out there.

You claim to have worked for a company that went out of business, knowing that your new employer won't be able to verify the work history. Tricky bastard, aren't you? Well, savvier employers are even trickier, because they'll ask you to provide a copy of your previous W-2s. Damn, is right. Don't forget that your W-2s also show past salary, which employers know is the second-most falsely claimed information. And hey, you're an IT pro. Money is currently raining down on you.

You use multiple social media profiles to hide inappropriate behavior or offensive content. Remember the part about seeing you naked through the open window? Yeah, that part. Maybe you're smart and keep the nasties tucked away, but if you've ever hacked anything, you know there's a back door to be found.

---

[4] E-Verify is an Internet-based system that allows businesses to determine the eligibility of their potential employees to work in the United States.

You intentionally provide inaccurate information, knowing exactly what your past or current employer will or will not verify. Don't make me say it again—loose lips and W-2s.

It's harder to hide these days, so make it easier on yourself and don't.

And Another Thing...

I worked hard for my college degree at an accredited university. I'm sure many of you did as well. Although I was always a good student, there was a time in college when I thought I'd just scrap the whole plan. But I hung in there and finished it, with honors. That didn't mean I was guaranteed a job, but it did help pave the way, as I've mentioned already in this book.

Right on. Right?

And I'm all for allowing undocumented students to attend our universities, as well as undocumented residents to launch business ventures here that may create jobs. So when I read a report last year about a twist on the diploma-mill epidemic mentioned above—I'm talking now about "visa mills"[5]—it's frustrating and disheartening for those of us looking for work in this mixed-bag economy.

The deal is this: unaccredited schools are paid millions of dollars to help foreigners obtain student visas that authorize them to remain in the United States. Yep, you heard me right. This is a huge scheme fueled by a profit-sharing system that gave students who referred newcomers from abroad a 20 percent cut in the tuition. Damn. Screw the drug business, I'm gettin' into mills.

Entrepreneurism runs amuck in a black market, which is usually a big part of the legitimate business markets. Sadly the U.S. government currently condones these activities that allow such a black market in student visas. Think about this: over a decade after 9/11 occurred, when terrorists were in the U.S. on student visas, the Department of Homeland Security (DHS) allows universities to issue F1 student visas—some universities questionable enough that they should be ineligible to issue the necessary paperwork. In fact, the DHS lists these schools as institutions on the list that international students can consult before pursuing a degree in the United States.

The students who attend these institutions are attracted for another big, bad reason: the promise of jobs upon completion of the program. Unfortunately,

---

[5] Fraudulent universities operated for the sole purpose of helping foreign nationals obtain student visas to allow them to enter the United States., Canada, and other countries.

many students return home with little education gained, no accredited degree, and broke to boot. And for those who do get jobs, it's sometimes at the expense of those who have been unemployed for months, even years. Unfortunately, systems that recognize and accredit institutions of higher learning vary greatly around the globe, making it easy for diploma and visa mills to confuse and deceive. As of 2011, there had been nearly a 50 percent increase worldwide in the number of known diploma and accreditation mills, according to EmployeeScreenIQ and its partners.

As I said, screw the drug trade (but don't really go down this rabbit-hole scheme, either).

Lastly, if an employer requests your social media login credentials, and/or wants you to pay for your own background screen, then screw them.

Mindful Moment   Not every employer will run you through a background screen, but if one does, don't jerk them around with fabricated information. We're living in world of great transparency on both sides of the employment equation, and you'll screw yourself faster than you can buy a fake diploma online.

If Only We Could Send Everyone Back to Preschool

Ah, Toddlerville. The world of my two-year-old and four-year-old daughters is a world of playtime. As it should be. Full of experiencing life moment by moment, for the first time—playing with me and the Mama (as I affectionately call my wife), playing with other kids, exploring their new worlds freely, getting the world around them explained, learning to share, and learning empathy, or emotional intelligence.[6] Preschool starts again soon for my oldest, and my youngest will start next year.

Many of us think that this is Toddlerville normal, but for many disadvantaged children and children who grow up in violent, dysfunctional homes, it's not normal.

No playing. No learning. No empathy. No soft skills.

That's what these things are called—soft skills—the cluster of personality traits, social graces, communications, language, personal habits, friendliness, and optimism that characterize relationships with other people. These soft

---

[6] Emotional intelligence (EI) refers to the ability to perceive, control, and evaluate emotions.

skills can make us, and without them, they can break us later on in life. Without them, life can be full of jail time, less pay than your peers, dysfunctional socialization, and the like.

Those without the soft skills have a horrible time finding and keeping a job. Last year, I heard University of Chicago economist James Heckman on NPR's Planet Money[7] talk about the Perry Preschool Program study run back in the early 1960s, in which researchers took a bunch of three-year-olds from poor families and randomly divided them into two groups. They gave one group free access to preschool. Then they followed both groups for 40 years.[8]

According to Heckman, the results were astonishing. Kids from the preschool group were less likely to be arrested and more likely to have a job. Among those with jobs, those who went to preschool made more money than those who did not. Other studies show similar results. Heckman argued that using public funds to pay for poor kids to go to preschool actually saves the government money in the long run. Heckman stated:

> The cost to society of courts and crime is lowered. The cost of educating kids who are unruly and undisciplined in schools, that goes down. The benefits that the kid contributes to earnings and society, that goes up. And so on down the line.

In contrast, Heckman also reviewed government job-training programs that teach people new skills and help get them back into the workforce. He found that the success rate for these training programs was nil. Zero. Nada. And, in the case of men versus women, the men were worse off than if they hadn't done any training at all. The failure was the result of a lack of soft skills.

The fact is, if you don't acquire the soft skills by the time you're five or six, it is much harder to develop them; by the time you're a teenager or young adult, it's likely you will never acquire them.

Lastly, according to Heckman, for every $1 spent on high-quality preschool for disadvantaged kids, society gets from 7 to 10 percent per year in return based on those who develop soft skills, have better interpersonal skills, get better jobs and better salaries and have lower crime rates. Now, that's a sound economic investment. If only we could send everyone back to preschool.

No, I'm not trying to make you feel bad if you didn't go to preschool or if you've struggled with your soft skills and couldn't care less about your emotional intelligence. I'm starting here as a precursor to employment assessments, because many more employers these days are screening for

---

[7] www.npr.org/blogs/money/2011/08/12/139583385/preschool-the-best-job-training-program

[8] http://heckman.uchicago.edu

collaborative communication team-building skills; they see it as their way to build a culture of trust, higher productivity, and sound business growth for the organizational ecosystem, not just you and the engineering team you're seeking to join.

Laugh if you want, but these are the firms you're going to want to work for, startup, or established. These are the firms that are going to make it through the painful process of change management. I know what you're thinking: Larry Ellison and Steve Jobs couldn't give a shit about the unicorns and rainbows. But, hey, I never said you couldn't be a hard ass and also know how to orchestrate folks from all folds, did I?

Mindful Moment   Even if you've got the hard skills and experience employers want, and your background check was clean, more of them today are screening for the soft skills—the cluster of personality traits, social graces, communication skills, language, personal habits, friendliness, and optimism that characterize relationships with other people, and the ability to collaborate effectively. These are often the skills that can make us, and without them, break us at any point in our professional lives.

Assessing the Assessments

There are a gazillion different employment-type assessments on the market today, from upwards of a gazillion different kinds of companies throughout the recruiting and HR space. Of course, I'm being facetious, but I only want you to know that there are a lot out there. And these assessments are used more often by larger companies across industries than by smaller ones and startups (unless you're applying to an actual assessment startup). These applicant and employee assessment tools are provided by and/or included in talent-acquisition systems (also known as applicant-tracking systems and other sourcing platforms), and they align with talent management systems (once you're hired), training and development systems, performance review systems, workforce management systems, workforce planning systems, succession planning systems, leadership development systems, and even outplacement services systems. Beyond these software companies, there are assessment firms and/or professional services firms that offer all of these tools. That is, they use a variety of assessments on the market (including their own) to screen applicants and current employees of their client companies.

Some of their names you may have heard of: Taleo, Kenexa, SuccessFactors, Hogan Assessments, Development Dimension International, Profiles International, Halogen Software, ReviewSnap, Silkroad, TRACOM Group, Multi-Health Systems—and again, a gazillion others.

But this part of the chapter isn't about who and what these products are, or how to game these assessments. (Which I wouldn't tell you even if I knew how, which I don't.) You can't game most scientifically valid and reliable assessments, anyway. I'm just going to highlight the primary types of assessments you may encounter in your job search. You may have had experience with some of these in the past, but whatever the case, be aware of what employers are using to help them screen applicants for positions and current employees for promotions.

Emotional Intelligence Assessments

I list this type first because I'm a huge proponent of nurturing emotional intelligence, personally and professionally (it's all personal though, isn't it?) Emotional intelligence (EI) is your ability to be aware of your own emotional reactions to various situations and to be able to control those reactions in a productive and positive way, as well as your awareness of others' emotional reactions and be able to respond appropriately. This is a big part of the soft skills I've been pushing, and individuals (and organizations) with higher EI are more productive, provide more bottom-line growth, and are overall much better colleagues, peers, and bosses. The EI assessments may not be something you run across very much, but their prevalence in larger enterprises is growing. These assessments can include paper-based tests, online tests, and essay and/ or interview questions.

Personality Assessments

I'm sure at some point in your career you were forced to take a personality test and/or a career assessment and/or an aptitude assessment. Or maybe you took some of these on your own, just to figure out what the heck you're all about. There are many free assessments online these days. Personality, career, and aptitude tests help determine what your type of personality is, and what your values, interests, and skills are as they relate to your personality. These tests are used to assess your aptitude for specific occupations or careers. There's the Color Quiz and DiSC, and the Myers-Briggs Type Indicator, and IQ tests and myriad others.

Cultural Fit and Accountability Assessments

These are newer tools in the assessment market. Many people-development and leadership-development firms, some with their own proprietary tools and tests and others that license various tools and tests, are offering differing flavors for today's employers. These assessments evaluate whether or not you're a team player, if you're adaptable and can think on your feet, whether you're accountable and take personal responsibility for your actions, and other related characteristics. Like other assessments, these can include paper-based tests, online tests, and essay and/or interview questions.

Cognitive Ability Assessments

Although I'm a writer and a heavy reader, when I took the SAT way back in the day, I fell asleep during the reading comprehension part. Don't tell anybody. Anyway, these assessments measure a variety of mental capabilities, such as verbal and mathematical ability, reasoning ability, and reading comprehension. Historically, cognitive ability tests have been useful predictors of job performance, which is why they are used to select candidates for many different types of jobs. Cognitive ability tests typically consist of multiple-choice items that are administered via a paper-and-pencil instrument or computer. Get those number 2 pencils sharpened.

Job-Knowledge Assessments

Job-knowledge assessments are used to measure critical knowledge areas that are needed to perform a job effectively. Typically, the tested areas are technical knowledge. You'll probably run into versions of these where your IT domain expertise, whatever that entails, is put to the "test" to make sure you already possess the right body of knowledge. Like cognitive ability assessments, job-knowledge assessments usually include multiple-choice items via paper test or online test, although sometimes there are essay items included in these assessments.

Work-Sample Assessments

Work-sample assessments include tasks or work activities that will, it is hoped, mirror the tasks you'll be required to perform once you're hired. These tests can be constructed to measure almost any job task, but usually measure technical tasks, like operating hardware, repairing and troubleshooting hardware and software, organizing and planning your work, and other related activities.

Skills Inventories and Assessments

As with many of the other assessment categories mentioned, skills inventories and assessments literally capture information on your primary skills—what you excel at, what you're okay at, and what you need a helluva lot of help at.

You're asked to apply your technical knowledge, programming knowledge, systems knowledge—you name it. You can't fudge these babies, so brush up on what you know (and some of what you don't) and let your tech magic shine.

Employers are all about having adaptable and resilient workforces these days, and they are truly focused on three converging factors:

- Selecting employees with the right knowledge, skills, experiences, and backgrounds.

- Providing the right training and development once candidates are on the job.

- Establishing an organizational environment that facilitates innovation and creativity.

You have more control over that first bulleted item than you think. That's why I want you to consider all the things that make you *what* you are and *who* you are—your past, present, and future tech-scape. Remember, even once you're hired, you will be assessed periodically to ensure that you still have all the right stuff and that the right stuff is helping grow the business you work for.

Mindful Moment   Employers use a variety of assessments to help them make better hiring, internal mobility, and promotion decisions. Be aware of what kinds of assessments exist and sharpen your those hard and soft skills, much like the number 2 pencils of old. They are still used, aren't they?

Interviewing, Part 1

It's a Brave New Virtual World

In most cases, the best strategy for a job interview is to be fairly honest, because the worst thing that can happen is that you won't get the job and will spend the rest of your life foraging for food in the wilderness and seeking shelter underneath a tree or the awning of a bowling alley that has gone out of business.

—Lemony Snicket (a.k.a., Daniel Handler), from *Horseradish*

And nobody wants that. In fact, the even better news is that you may not have to drive to the place of business that wants to interview you. That means if you don't get the job, you don't have to slink away to the parking lot and drive home to that aforementioned bowling alley.

I'm talking about video interviewing, of which there are two types: recorded and live virtual interviewing. Each one is pretty new to the world of work and the job-search grind, and both are still finding their way, but they do work and more and more employers are utilizing the technologies.

However, let's first take a step back into maybe your own (perhaps painful) recent interviewing experience.

Job Interviews of Yore

Ah, the job interview. The all-important transaction between job candidate and potential employer. You've been phone-screened and assessed and included in the top tier of most qualified applicants. Maybe you're in the top

ten out of hundreds of applicants. Whatever the math, you're ready to be interviewed "face to face," for the first time.

You're invited to the office, and after a little small talk, one of the first things you ask is: "So, what are the benefits you offer? I've got a wife and three kids, you know."

Ugh, not the way you wanted to open, no matter how long you've been looking for work. Or maybe the interview starts off on the other foot, in his mouth: "Thanks for coming in today. We're very interested in you for this job. Very interested. Wow—did anyone ever tell you how gorgeous you are?"

Idiot. Or maybe you come prepared and ask questions like, "How do you see this position collaborating with product marketing to drive B2B channel growth?"

Damn, you're smart. Okay, maybe all of these are a bit contrived, but believe it or not they're not too far from the truth of what I've experienced, and I'm sure some of you have as well. (No, I wasn't the guy who told the candidate how gorgeous she was. I mean, she was, but that's not the point.)

And no matter how good employers try to get at interviewing, no matter the behavioral technique or casual and personable style (which we'll talk about more later in Chapter 15), no matter how prepared you are for any style of interview, we're only human. And as I've already written, really frickin' messy, but yet we do our best to answer the interview questions fully and honestly, as well as ask our own questions, and then read between the blurry lines . . .

. . . to trust our very gut. Very scientific, you know. For example, I remember back in the day when I was with Tapestry.net and I sourced and recruited software developers. Here's how it went after I did an initial phone screen and then presented the candidates—people like you—to the hiring managers:

RECRUITER (ME):   This candidate is great. You should interview him.

HIRING MANAGER: Try again.

RECRUITER: Why? What was he missing?

HIRING MANAGER: I don't know. The skills were there, but just try again.

RECRUITER: [Sigh]

You say *po-tay-to* and I say *po-tah-to*. Right? If he just would've given that applicant a shot, the guy could've shined in the interview. Right? Well, I spoke with an IT business systems analyst candidate earlier this year, and she said she couldn't count how many times she had heard, "Well, I was pulling for you, but others on the team wanted to go with an internal candidate."

Actually, she did count, because after 18 final-stage interviews in the course of one year looking for employment, she heard it 10 times.

You drove all the way from Palo Alto to Santa Cruz just to hear that crap? You would've been better off not being selected in the first place by that idiot hiring manager. You would've been better off driving to FedEx (what used to be Kinko's, then FedEx Kinko's) to do a live virtual interview. Alas, companies aren't paying for services like that anymore. Now, they have Cisco TelePresence high-definition video conferencing service and are using it for executive interviews, collaboration sessions, and other meetings, but not necessarily for the myriad other jobs they interview for.

But the fact is that companies are slowly warming to new options. For example, how about Skype, the free video and audio conferencing online service? It's easy to install and use. My family has been using Skype to see and talk with family and friends for the past two years now, and I've been using it on the job to see and talk with colleagues, peers, and management team members, whether they're across the globe or across town. Of course, the quality is highly dependent on your Internet connections on all ends of the conversation—I've been on some doozies where all you can hear is every third word and the rushing-air sounds of flying at 32,000 feet.

FaceTime—Apple's video calling software for MacBooks, iPad, iPods, and iPhones—is yet another program I use to talk with family and friends, but I've never used it in a business context (yet). Lastly, and believe it or not only in the past few months, I have been experimenting with Google+ Hangouts, and I'll tell you, it's pretty damn cool. Especially when you can add cute little animations to your face and head. Like a devil clown or a tiara on a Mohawk haircut. No, I don't recommend using those on an interview.

■ **Mindful Moment**   Think about your best and worst interview experience—what were the details that contributed to both results? Were they both in-person interviews, or did either involve video? Did video make it better, worse, or are you still on the fence? Think about these things as you read on.

Everybody's Doing It. Right?

"So how does this all help me?" you ask. Are companies really conducting more live and recorded interviews? Well, let's take a look at some recent research from my friends at GreenJobInterview, a live virtual interviewing platform.[1] They surveyed U.S.-based organizations about their current video interview usage and practices. Over 65 percent of respondents were in manager, director, vice president, or C-level positions—and not surprisingly, most respondents (85 percent) work in human resources and recruiting for their organizations. There were also more than 20 industries represented, so the survey represents a pretty good distribution of companies and hiring folk. What they found was that the incidence of video interviewing is growing rapidly in organizations big and small. For example:

- Just over half (52 percent) of respondents said they have used video interviewing.

- For companies with fewer than 100 employees, it's almost a 50/50 split (47 percent yes, 53 percent no). For companies with more than 1,000 employees, that figure goes from 58 percent (1,001–5,000 employees) video usage to 80 percent (more than 10,000).

- Almost 58 percent of the organizations that use live virtual interviews have done so for one to five years. In every time period, results show that large organizations are the early adopters.

- Most companies of fewer than 500 employees use FaceTime, Skype, or Google+ video chat to conduct their video interviews. Of those, nearly 50 percent report that their hiring and screening efforts have been good.

---

[1] http://greenjobinterview.com/video-interviewing-survey-2012-trends-and-insights/.

- Most companies of over 1,000 employees are using live virtual interviewing platforms. Out of those, 25 percent say that their hiring and screening efforts have been great and 25 percent say these efforts have been good.

Overall, larger employers have higher hiring volume and are looking for ways to shorten their hiring cycles, saving time and money; but they want more secure platforms that they can brand to do so. Because video interviewing has been perceived as expensive; at least until recently, smaller organizations have been less likely to pay for video interviewing, but that's changing for many reasons I'll highlight shortly.

Regardless, more and more companies are digging the fact that video killed the phone-screening star. For those who get that reference, do not scowl. I know you're pulling up the song on YouTube.[2] I know I am.

Recorded Video Interviewing

Let's review what each of the two video interviewing services entails. Let's start with recorded interviews. Maybe you've recorded your own "intro" or "experience" videos that you've posted on your tech blog and have shared with prospective employers. Maybe you've created a video resume or what's also known as a video CV (*curriculum vitae*—a fancy word for resume or online profile) using one of a few video resume services available today. (You'll see many more sprout up in the next few years.) If so, then you're familiar with recording yourself talking about yourself in a professional way that you hope gets you noticed. These can be useful methods to attract positive attention. However, what I'm talking about is something a little different, a little more structured, with a standard format.

For example, HireVue, Async Interview, InterviewStream, and Wowzer are among the recorded video platforms that hiring companies use to screen applicants. One primary way these work is that you apply for a job for company X. If company X is interested in you, then a recruiter, hiring manager, or whoever's doing the screening will invite you to the video interviewing platform. There, you log into the system, follow the instructions on setting up your profile, prepare yourself for the recorded interview process, and even do some test recordings to make sure you're comfortable with all the hip gadgetry and functionality.

Most of us have computers with built-in webcams these days, but for those who don't, the interview firms will send you a webcam, usually for free, to

---

[2] www.youtube.com/watch?v=lwuy4hHO3YQ.

use. Some hiring companies will require you not only to answer a series of questions via recorded video clips but also to answer other text-based screening questions, assessments, and other screening devices baked into the process.

Live Virtual Interviewing

The counterpart to recorded video interviewing is live virtual interviewing. I already mentioned the free services that smaller companies are using—FaceTime, Skype, and Google+ Hangouts. There are only a few true live virtual platforms out there built just for companies to conduct interviews, GreenJobInterview being one of the best to date (keep in mind that the free services listed above weren't built specifically for live virtual interviewing). With the live virtual interview platforms, once you apply for a job for company X and if company X is interested in you, then a recruiter, hiring manager, or whoever's doing the screening will invite you to the video interviewing platform. There, you log into the system, follow the instructions on setting up your profile, prepare yourself for the live virtual interview process, and even do some tech tests to make sure you're comfortable with all the hip gadgetry and functionality.

Sound familiar? The big difference between this and recorded interviewing is that during your scheduled interview, you'll be live with your interviewers, not recording yourself answering predetermined questions.

So when are employers utilizing video interviewing in their recruiting processes? Primarily they're using it to screen out-of-the-area candidates. Most are also using video interviews after the phone screen as an interim step before bringing in a candidate for the face-to-face interview. It allows both you and the employer to gather more information and determine fit and interest level. Based on what they experience in this fairly new level of screening, the hiring folk can decide whether it's warranted to bring you in again, even begin the reference-checking process if they so choose. Meaning they dig you.

Smaller companies use the free video services because, well, they're free and their hiring volume is smaller. There's no need for a software platform that can scale. Larger companies that have more investment in employment brand initiatives and Internet security—who can access information inside and out—need a scalable, more secure video interview platform (just as they need for most of the company-wide software purchases, many of which you're probably been involved in).

Think about it, though: it's a huge savings for organizations. We're talking upwards of thousands of dollars saved on candidate travel expenses, per many open reqs, when they bring in top applicants for in-person interviews only. Video interviewing has allowed organizations to maybe consider candidates than that they would otherwise have relegated to the black hole of "We're sorry, but we're going to pass on you this time due to other, more qualified applicants"—if you even get a response. (Sadly, even with all the assessments and background screening and interviewing and other filtering methods I discuss in this book, hiring is such a subjective human endeavor that many times we miss out on the A talent that we somehow mistook for B talent.) But new and inexpensive methods of reaching out to more candidates at least offers the hope that recruiters and hiring managers will make fewer such mistakes.

Also, video interviewing saves you and your prospective employer tons of time. You don't have to reorganize your schedule to meet the hiring manager, recruiter, HR, or whoever might be in the office when it's inconvenient. You know how stressful it can be just to make time to research the companies you're interested in, much less also take time to jump through their early screening hoops, and then to make time again for the sucky phone interview. (Unless you're applying for a customer-facing position, like a sales engineer or usability engineer, just how valuable is that brief phone screen anyway?)

With video interviewing, there will be no more days missed at your current job to go on interviews for a new job. You won't have to fake doctor's appointments, or being sick, or taking care of your parents or children. Listen, we've all been there, when we've "checked out." Even when you work for half-wits, they can pick up on the fact that you're sick a lot or not meeting your deadlines because of your rash of other appointments and responsibilities. With video interviewing technology, you can interview conveniently, even at a prescribed live interview time—from a mobile device, a laptop, or home desktop, or when you get to recording your answers to preset questions from the companies interested in you. It doesn't matter where the company is; as I've already stated, they could be across the street or around the globe.

The good news? Your stress level goes down when you don't have to worry about making up stories for your current employer so you can get to that interview. You're going to avoid all the many different travel-related inconveniences. If the interview is close to home, there's driving your car that's been overdue for an oil change since the first dot-com boom, or any worries that you may run into a co-worker—or God help you, your boss. And again, what if the interview is going well—and going long—and you still have to drive back to work? With video interviewing you'll be in the comfort of your own homestead. And if the interview is for a company in another state, or another continent, you can avoid airport crowds, security shakedowns, flight delays, jet lag, wrinkled interview clothes, and potential out-of-pocket expenses (which are never potential, right?).

■ **Mindful Moment**   More companies are offering video interviewing to potential candidates, which saves wear and tear, time, travel, and your nerves, leaving you better mindfully prepared for the interview (I can't help you with the other prep). Smaller companies leverage the free video interviewing services while larger companies prefer more scalable and secure video interviewing platforms. Either way, you can interview in the comfort of your home office.

Be Prepared; You're Not That Cool

All right—you don't just turn on the webcam and start babbling away about why you're so frickin' cool. Nope, sorry. That's not how it works (and none of us is that cool, anyway; there's somebody always cooler than you—queue the Ben Folds song[3]).

Here are some very important things to keep in mind prior to jumping into a video interview:

- I know you're a smarty pants IT pro, but make sure you have the right equipment to participate in video interviews: up-to-date computer, decent webcam (preferably built into the computer), decent headset (it doesn't have to be a mono one from 1975, and even though you can use your computer speakers and mic, a headset will reduce the white noise around you), and solid broadband Internet connection.

- Make sure you have a well-lighted, quiet place at home where you won't be interrupted (not a public place like a Starbuck's or Denny's, please). Ensure that there's either a blank wall behind you or something conservative and non-offensive, like pictures or a painting. Don't fight with me on this one; you do not want to distract, only to accent your surroundings. Take down the Mötley Crüe and Lady Gaga posters, please.

- As in in-person interviews, find out ahead of time what kind of attire is appropriate. No, I didn't say wear a suit and tie or a pantsuit; I said find out what is appropriate for that company and culture. When in doubt, default to between business

---

[3] www.youtube.com/watch?v=XxkM_cnjFfw.

casual and business formal. Remember, Davenport, Iowa, isn't the same as Palo Alto, California.

- If you're recording your video responses via a platform, you usually get the opportunity to redo questions if you aren't happy with your responses. Make sure you understand how the system works and use the practice sessions most of them allow.

- In a live virtual interview platform, you may be interviewed by multiple people at once, just as if you were in a panel in-person interview, so be prepared no matter what!

- Here's something that's difficult even for those of us who have communicated via video chats and interviews: that we look at ourselves looking back at us in the little square on the screen, and not at our webcam, or at the very least, the people on the screen. Look at the camera and the others as though you were right there in the room with them. Oh, vanity.

- Somebody from the hiring company will usually contact you to explain the video interview process, recorded or live virtual, so make sure to take the call!

- Most video interviewing platform companies offer tech support services that will ensure you can interact face to face, in real time, with the hiring companies (their clients), anywhere in the world, and usually 24/7 (or something close to that). They'll tell you what to wear, the best lighting to use, and so on. However, the free services do not offer any such support. So if you're being interviewed by somebody via Skype, keep that in mind and double-check that everything works fine before the scheduled time.

- The video interviewing platforms also offer choice of VOIP services (computer audio) or a dial-in number so you can use a landline or your cellphone. With free services, it's all computer audio (unless they're using a free conference-call service to augment).

- Last, and certain not least, become familiar with the companies you're interested in working for before you complete the interview. Video interviewing is no less important than being on the short list for face time with the

> hiring manager, so take the time to know how and why you're
> the guy or gal for the job. Remember, you're not that cool.

So there you have it. Video interviewing is here to stay, even if video resumes aren't. (I'll explain why later during online profiles.) If you prepare properly, nailing the virtual interviews can get you to that typical final stage of the in-person interview, and in some cases, the job. This, of course, is contextual to the role and level you're applying for, and whether or not it's a "remote" position or you'll work onsite. That means the virtual interview could be the final interview, and then you're hired. We hope.

Mindful Moment   Just as in an in-person interview, take the time to prepare for your video interview by understanding the role you are applying for, as well as do all the interview prep and tech check work that will help you shine in the midst of Q&A. An interview is still an interview and is critical to your hiring success. Don't screw around or act like an idiot just because you think it's a Skype call from Mom. Really.

Who You Know

Recognition

8

Building an Online Profile

Why the Resume Must Die

The reports of my death have been greatly exaggerated.

—Mark Twain

Okay, the resume is not dead yet, but I want it to die.

I understand that there's still a huge part of the career management industry keeping it alive, making it better and making it work for you, the job seeker. To all my friends in this industry, please forgive me, as I also understand it's probably not going anywhere for years to come. (And for those of you who are paying for professional resume and cover letter services, ask them if they can help you with your online profile.) I've had many recruiters tell me, "The resume is not dead. Trust me, it's not dead."

Again, I understand, but I still want the painfully ubiquitous resume to die a horrible death.

What's Wrong with Resumes?

Why a painful death? Because the resume is a self-serving piece of inconsistently formatted and fudged professional drivel that really doesn't help employers assess and hire for true quality of fit. Just ask any background-screening firm that does employment and education verifications. Remember that in Chapter 6, I said nearly 50 percent of all candidates distort or exaggerate information on their resumes. That's half of you. Damn.

Sure, the resume helps employers sift and sort to reach the short list, but it's a short list that's almost half fabrication, on average. And if you as the job seeker take that risk and blatantly lie or embellish your resume, and your prospective employer uncovers it, you are out of luck no matter what hot skills you have that they need.

Yes, many of us have stretched the truth at one time or another as it relates to our skills, experience, and achievements, but unfortunately embellishing the truth is still fabrication. It doesn't make it any better than an outright lie, especially if you're telling me you've been programming native iPhone and Android apps for the past six months, when you really only took an online course six months ago and helped to make one silly, farting app, one that isn't very good anyway because it sounds like a Yorkshire Terrier barking.

The other side of this is interesting, especially if you're an IT pro of the feminine persuasion. Silicon Valley has struggled to recruit and retain technically savvy women over the years, and even though you'd think that would be getting better than worse, between the years of 2000 and 2011, according to the Bureau of Labor Statistics, the number of women working in professional computing jobs dropped 8 percent, to 25 percent of the total, while the number of men climbed 16 percent. And according to Google's own data, some women who applied for technology jobs did not make it past the phone interview primarily because didn't flaunt their achievements, so interviewers judged them unaccomplished. These facts were referenced in a recent *New York Times* article about Google and the falling number of women in IT leadership.[1] So ladies, flaunt those achievements. (I know—interesting choice of word, *flaunt*. But don't look at me. Men should promote their achievements, and women should flaunt theirs?)

So what, then, do we use instead of this black-magic resume full of lies and deceit, or one that doesn't pump you up enough?

Look to LinkedIn

Your online professional profile, of course. The one you better have completely up to date on LinkedIn, the granddaddy and grandmamma of online professional networks, where thousands of recruiting professionals are scouring and sourcing every day. (And I'm not even talking about the majority of recruiting pros who search for other online information about you across the Internet and at other social networks.) And by the way, much of the same advice you get about building your resume applies to the online profile as well, which is

---

[1] www.nytimes.com/2012/08/23/technology/in-googles-inner-circle-a-falling-number-of-women.html?pagewanted=all.

why I mentioned earlier that you should ask your career management consultant about helping you with it. (Or, just keep reading my book. Thank you.)

LinkedIn is the primary place to have an up-to-date professional profile these days. There are others, one of which I'll cover later in this chapter, but first consider that LinkedIn has more than 175 million members in over 200 countries and territories.[2] Professionals like you are also signing up to join LinkedIn at a rate that is faster than two new members per second. Two members per second—do the math here—172,800 people sign up daily, and 63,072,000 people sign up annually. At that rate, if it can be sustained and the current members maintained, then it'll only take a few more years to hit all the billions of adult professionals working globally today (plus, those not working and looking).

This isn't a shameless plug just for LinkedIn; it's a greater call for managing your career online in a universally accepted standard format. It's a place where the peer pressure element of keeping one another honest in an online network/community is consistent over time; where your true skills, experience, and achievements position you in the best "truthful" light possible; and where your professional history is available to everyone you're connected with, many of whom you've worked with or for at one time, if not currently.

However, I get the fact that anybody can fudge an online profile just as well as they can a resume—or undercut themselves, too. Although it won't help you with the humble factor, there's a peer pressure element of keeping one another honest in an online network or community (two different things that we'll discuss later).

There are other, similar LinkedIn-like professional networks on Facebook, including BranchOut, which I'll discuss later in this chapter. If you're on more than one such network, it's important to be consistent across all of them or wherever you have profiles.

Granted, talent acquisition technologies, including applicant tracking systems (ATS) have been slow to adapt to the online profile; there's still the "click here" to upload your resume, which I know can be an inefficient pain in the butt. That's changing for the better as the overall candidate experience improves, however glacially. Ultimately, it will allow for easy integration of your online profile to the system belonging to your employer of choice. It will also bring the benefits of a search-optimized professional profile, which I will also talk about later in this chapter.

Let's get to building, shall we?

---

[2] As of August 2, 2012. http://press.linkedin.com/about.

▒ **Mindful Moment** Do you have an online professional profile on LinkedIn? Do you use the standard and easily updated format to promote and flaunt your skills, experience, and achievements? Or are you still cobbling together various iterations of your resume to then upload and email? Think about the benefits of having an online profile and read on.

Just the Facts, Jack. But First, the Story

I've seen dozens of resume formats over the years. Some sport simple, straightforward sections, and others have fancy schmancy formatting. There are many facets to context, even when it's cubic zirconia, which is again why I recommend the online profile. Since LinkedIn has set the standard here, this is what I'm going to focus on in this chapter. By no means am I a LinkedIn expert; I've got plenty of industry friends who are, though. But I am an online profile advocate because I know it works and is more efficient than today's resume alone. Yes, at the executive level it's a different story; usually there are bios and press kits and extensive resumes besides the online profile. As of earlier this year, LinkedIn has executive members from all 2011 Fortune 500 companies and its corporate hiring solutions are used by 85 of the Fortune 100 companies. So there you go.

There are a variety of online profile sections I'll cover in this chapter, but not everything. Just enough to get you started or for you to update your current profile. (Which you probably haven't touched since your last job search, right?)

Your Summary

Let's start off with your story. Yep, your story—what I think is one of the biggest differentiators for you and your career aspirations, currently employed or not. You know that section in your LinkedIn profile called "Summary"? Well, that's where we're going to start. Think of a universal, all-purpose cover letter, one that conveys succinctly who you are in the great world of work at this very moment. Remember, and I'm going to tell you this more than once going forward, you can and should update your profile summary at least once a quarter if you're gainfully employed and more regularly if you are actively seeking.

Many of my recruiter friends concur. Your summary is especially the place in your profile where you highlight your story:

- Why you are where you currently are.

- What your current role is and where it is.

- Where you came from briefly, in the context of your skills, experience, and achievements.

- What your professional goals are.

- What your professional (and even personal, since they're intertwined) philosophies are. (But that doesn't mean espousing your extreme political or religious views. I'm all for transparency, but save the rants for your late-night blog posts.)

- What your hobbies and other personal interests are (there are other sections for interests and volunteering details).

- A little personality feature, injected here and there (without going over the top).

Keep it scannable, though. Too long and it won't get read. You have only a few seconds of human reading time to capture, so keep it 200 to 300 words, max. Now, that doesn't mean you can't go longer, as in a traditional cover letter, but whatever you do, make it a readable piece, not a jargon-filled list of technical drivel. Yes, you'll get picked up in searches with the right keywords, which I'll discuss briefly later, but you still need the human sourcer, recruiter, hiring manager—whoever—to scan/read your summary and digest the professionally personal essence of you. Figure 8-1 shows an example of a LinkedIn profile and summary page.

Here's my summary. No judging or wagering, please.

For nearly 13 years, I've been a human resource and recruiting B2B software and services marketing strategist, business development and sales professional, evangelist, entrepreneur, analyst, advisor, manager, and writer.

My extensive knowledge of nearly 25 years in business development, marketing, sales, public relations, and more recently social media best practices, and my thorough understanding of the human resource and recruiting marketplace, has helped hundreds of B2B software and services companies grow their businesses on some level. I've increased visibility, thought leadership, and sales for most of the companies I've worked with and for.

I currently lead global messaging, product marketing, and go-to-market strategy for BraveNewTalent, the leading social platform where organizations build talent communities around relevant topics that attract, engage and develop their next-generation workforce from future, current and past employees.

Previously I was the Chief Strategy Officer at HRmarketer.com, an HR B2B marketing software and services firm. I'm also an advisor to JobEscrow, pioneers and inventors of the new "Employment Escrow" industry, as well as on the board of referalbon.us and co-founder of the TalentCulture "world of work" community that includes the highly popular weekly Twitter Chat #TChat.

I've been a top social influencer in leadership, human resources, talent management, and recruiting, as well as a prolific "HR business" blogger since 2004. I've authored multiple articles on marketing, business development, HR, recruiting, and leadership and am finishing a book titled Tech Job Hunt Handbook *to be released at the end of the year. I speak at HR and recruiting industry events, and I also moderate HR/ recruiting/marketing-related webinars and roundtables.*

Lastly, I'm a proud father of two beautiful girls and loving husband to my beautiful wife. I enjoy reading and running, and I write regularly about fatherhood, responsible parenting, and domestic violence awareness and prevention.

Now, if your profile doesn't have a "story" summary, it doesn't mean you won't be found and possibly even recruited, or that you won't stand out from the crowd. A short bulleted list of accomplishments is better than a stick in the eye, as my dad always used to say. However, when you share your story in the summary, you really stand out to potential employers.

Figure 8-1. Linked Profile and Summary Section. Courtesy of LinkedIn.com.

Your Previous Jobs, Titles, and Descriptions

This one's easy and pretty much the same information you've been embedding in your resumes for years—your current and previous employers, current and previous job titles, and current and previous job descriptions. Make sure your descriptions capture the most important points of what the company did/ does, what your role is/was, and any brief accomplishments you've had.

Your Specialties, Skills, and Expertise (Think Key Words)

For any of you who are SEO gurus, or at least know enough to be dangerous like I do, then you know to embed the right word combinations in your profile—those that are relevant to your tech role and industry and that are the most common terms searched for by employers seeking your skills and experience. This includes the specialties section and the skills and expertise section (see Figure 8-2).

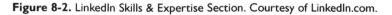

Figure 8-2. LinkedIn Skills & Expertise Section. Courtesy of LinkedIn.com.

There is also the ability to now to list previous work samples and projects in your LinkedIn profile, which details and accentuates your skills and experience. You can also showcase your blogs and the websites you contribute to by feeding them into your profile. You can highlight your volunteer work, the professional organizations you belong to, any special awards and honors you've received, and much more. Fill in all those sections as well!

Your Education (even If It's Incomplete)

Remember in Chapters 2 and 3 when I talked about going back to school and adding to your skill set? Well, make sure to tout that educational background in your profile, whether it's completed or not, or if it's still in progress.

Your Professional Headline

This is supposedly an easy one, but I recommend reviewing a few other profiles you admire (which means you look for them in your network or outside of it and assimilate what you like and what you don't like). It's the headline, right under your name on your profile.

Here's mine: *Director of Product Marketing at BraveNewTalent*

That's what I currently do and whom I work for, but it could've been "Experienced Producting Marketing Professional," especially if I were in the market for a job. Whatever you put there, make sure it summarizes who you are professionally, in a few key words.

And, of Course, Your Headshot

I don't remember where the heck I heard that men shouldn't smile in their professional headshots, online or in print, but that women should. (Are we back to the *promote* versus *flaunt* choice?) They say that men shouldn't smile because it's creepy. Are you frickin' serious? You know what's creepy? Not putting any picture at all in your profiles. That's creepy. And then adding to that remaining anonymous in your social network activity—when you're posting blogs anonymously, commenting on other blogs anonymously, tweeting anonymously, etc. That's really creepy. I certainly don't want to offend any of the fine folk in the Anonymous.[3] Really, I don't. But it's creepy, kids. Let me see the whites of your eyes. Please.

---

[3] Anonymous is a loosely associated hacktivist group. It originated in 2003 on the imageboard 4chan, representing the concept of many online and offline community users simultaneously existing as an anarchic, digitized global brain.

Anyway, the idea that men shouldn't smile in their online profile pictures is bullshit. See Figure 8-1—that's me smiling. If I'm creepy to you, then so be it. But I'm not. Really, I'm not. Let's have a group hug now, shall we?

Just make sure your headshot is professional looking, even if you appear casually dressed, as I do. It's contextual for what you do, the industry you work in, and what you're looking to do. If you're looking for IT work in a conservative company, which you'll know because of the research you have done (which we'll get to), then maybe you should wear a coat and tie, or a business suit if you're a woman (smiling, of course).

There's the argument that hiring managers will make discriminatory selection decisions based on what you look like, so you should instead choose to not have a photo. Listen, we're visual beings, and the fact is you're going to be seen at some point in the screening process. If your tech skills, experience, and achievements are what they're looking for, then that will shine brighter than any new tattoo you just had etched lovingly on your neck. Again, this is why you need to have a professional-looking headshot in your profile, and also look professional in your video interview and your in-person interview.

Preferably with a smile, tattoos and all.

Recommendations and Accolades

There's yet another critical element that can give you more credibility than the standard three to five references you offer "on request" for your resume. Those are the LinkedIn recommendations you ask your current and previous employers, colleagues, collaborators, clients, customers, mentors, teachers, and/or friends to give you, which you in turn should always reciprocate. You simply ask someone in your LinkedIn network to provide a brief but glowing recommendation of you and the work you've done.

How valuable are these recommendations? Well, that depends on what the recommendations say, who gave them, who's reviewing them, and so on. But the consensus is that there is some additive, subjective value to them. It tells the recruiters and hiring managers that you were liked, were a pleasure to work with, and accomplished many different things at the organizations you worked for (which you've already been touting). It's another part of the personality puzzle your prospective employers are trying to put together. Again, they're subjective and aren't truly valuable screening tools, but these recommendations are read and they can help differentiate you from other applicants who don't have recommendations.

And is it really that bad that you don't have any recommendations? Most experts say "not necessarily," since your skills, experience, and achievements will shine through and, it is hoped, get you the interview.

How many recommendations are too many? I laugh when hear career management experts say that people with over 40 or 50 recommendations are "awfully showy." What the hell does that mean? That's bullshit, as far as I'm concerned. I've got that many; I'm in marketing, for God's sake, and I understand the value of social networking in the 21st century. There are rough roads through the world of work these days, so smile really big and toot the hell out of your horn—as long as you back up the honking. Recommendations are a way to do that, to receive previous employer and peer validation that you can share on with other prospective employers and peers (even if you shared more than 3-5 in your executive resume).

On a side note, recruiters use recommendations to locate other applicants, leading them to connect to possible new sources of hires. Conversely, you can use the same tactic to get back-door introductions to other companies you may be interested in. Right?

Again, if you do ask for recommendations, reciprocate in kind. I can't emphasize that enough. Give recommendations to those who gave to you a recommendation. That's one of the ultimate returns of investing in professional "social" networking—your network's got your back and you've got your network's.

Oh, Yeah—You've Got to Connect

So, if you haven't already figured it out, and I'm sure you have, to get the most out of having an online profile on a site like LinkedIn (besides having a glorified electronic resume), you need to connect. That means searching and finding your current and previous employers, supervisors, colleagues, collaborators, clients, customers, mentors, teachers, and/or friends—and sending them an invite to connect. You'll be sought out as well, because we all have friends who are changing jobs, looking for jobs, getting promoted—you name it, they want to connect to share. You should do the same.

You've probably noticed that if you already have a LinkedIn profile, and have been contacted by recruiters, that many of the hiring pros have 500+ connections. Don't feel insignificant if you don't have that many, or even 100. It's more about creating a relevant professional network that will help *you* help *them* help *you* over time. So get connected and make the most of your online profile.

I always tell people to keep their windows of opportunity open, because they can never know what might present itself, no matter how happy they currently are. That's why I recommend you update your profile at least once per quarter.

Don't frickin' look at me that way. Just do it. Trust me.

A Word About Branching Out

Are there other professional networks out there like LinkedIn? you ask. Yes, there are. Although they are not as widely adopted as LinkedIn, and some have a different recruiting and career development purpose that I'll talk about in later chapters, there are other professional networks like BranchOut. BranchOut is known as the "LinkedIn on Facebook"—because that's what it is. They currently have over 30 million registered users and over 500 million professional profiles. *BranchOut allows users in more than 200 countries to leverage their Facebook friend network to find jobs, recruit talent, and strengthen relationships with professional contacts.*

Similar to completing a profile on LinkedIn, BranchOut gives you the ability to build a professional profile that can be separate from your Facebook connections. This is important because many Facebook users still prefer a separation of church and state—keeping their friends and family away from their "professional friends."

Also important to note is that you cannot simply import your LinkedIn profile to create a BranchOut profile. Why? LinkedIn claimed it cut off the application programming interface (API) because BranchOut violated their Terms of Service, which is probably the case. But the competitive nature of these firms is crystal clear; LinkedIn got the jump on things, but with nearly 1 billion registered users worldwide on Facebook, BranchOut is going strong, as well (as does Facebook—watch what happens with their Social Jobs Initiative and more in 2013). Whatever you choose to do, be consistent across networks with your professional online profiles.

That is all.

Mindful Moment   When putting your LinkedIn profile together, focus on your summary; jobs, titles, and descriptions; specialties; skills and expertise; education; professional headline; and of course, a professional headshot of you smiling. I want to see it, so don't try to pull a frowning fast one.

Wait, What?

I know, I know. You really need to polish up that prettily formatted resume. Again I say, throw it the hell away. The online profile is the future. Trust me. For those of you who already have an online career profile that you manage (as well as you employers who source and recruit online and value the online profile over the resume), please evangelize to accelerate change in the rest of the world.

In fact, the entire career management industry can help by sharing some of the best practices for the resume that can, and should, be applied to the online profile, as follows:

- Consistent standard layout for portability

- Concise professional summary

- Highlighted accomplishment relevant to the bottom line

- Timeline of professional activities, with any gaps accounted for

- Search-optimized profile with key words for which you want to be found

- Multiple online recommendations

- Regularly updated, whether looking for a job or not

My progressive HR and recruiting practitioner friends have pointed out on more than one occasion that most IT job seekers who frequent online professional and personal social haunts are more likely to manage their career profiles online. Amen to that. They know, as we know, that there thousands of recruiting and hiring professionals scouring the online profiles every day. Your professional connections could also be the back doors into the employers you're interested in working for, as well as get you introduced to those folks you don't know.

So do me a favor, oh digital native brothers and sisters, online savvy job seekers, hiring practitioners, career management professionals, and employers alike: share these recommendations with folks who may still write their resumes in longhand and then type them on an IBM Selectric III typewriter. Let's get everyone to know the power of the online profile. The resume is dead! Long live the online profile!

Mindful Moment Why do you keep creating so much work for yourself with the resume? You're an IT pro. Think about it. Online professional profiles are the future.

9

Researching Employers

Why the Hell Would You Want to Work There?

Some world views are spacious, and some are merely spaced.

—Neil Peart, writer and rock musician

Damn, I was wet behind the ears.[1]

That summer of 1981, the produce manager and the main produce clerk would tell me just how much every single early morning I came to work. My only saving grace was the sweet rock that blared from the banged-up radio with a makeshift hanger antenna; the first song I heard the very first morning of work was Billy Squier's "In the Dark."

Of course I felt this way; I was young and inexperienced and prior to this I had a paper route. In fact, I wasn't quite 16 yet when the non-union supermarket hired me to work in the produce department. I knew nothing about the market, the management team, my future co-workers, working conditions, perks—all I knew was that I'd be paid minimum wage, which was $3.35 per hour.

But I had my eye on the prize—my first car—a 1972 two-toned, red-and-white Chevrolet El Camino with 175 horses under the hood, my first and only muscle car. All summer long, I worked split shifts from 6 to 10 in the morning, and then again from 3 to 7 at night.

I wasn't fully aware that we were in a recession and unemployment hovered at 7.5 percent, and only a year and a half later we'd be at almost 11 percent

---

[1] Immature and inexperienced.

unemployment with nearly 11 million people out of work. What I did learn that year was that there were two symbiotic economic systems in California's Central Valley bread basket—(illegal) Mexican migrant labor that worked the farms, and the rest of us; the shadow economy and the legitimate economy.

The crossroads for me was our back dock behind the supermarket, where all produce deliveries were made daily. Our large and offensively snarky produce manager haggled, purchased, and rejected the orders delivered to that back dock. Usually it was the local farmers who delivered their goods, but sometimes it was the (illegal and legal) foremen who delivered the produce orders.

I learned from the latter that they labored in crappy working conditions out in the fields for very little pay. It depressed me a little, but again, I had my eye on the prize. (I did eventually get that El Camino, and I worked at the supermarket for more than two years.) I learned quickly, though, that even the legitimate economy I worked in, paychecks and taxes and all, wasn't so glamorous, no matter how much cool cruising I did in that beautiful car/truck. (What exactly was an El Camino anyway?)

I had a horrible boss who was an idiot, co-workers who belittled and bullied one another (me for the first few months), and rude customers who demanded I go in the back and get even fresher produce than I had just restocked the shelves with—and even after all that, being a teenager, albeit a down-to-earth one, I worked there for two years. I imagine some of you have stayed in uncomfortable work environments during the past few years, unless you were laid off, waiting for tech jobs to start heating up again and your particular skill set is in demand.

Stay Out of the Shadows

Nobody wants to work in misery, to nearly (or actually) cry after every long, strenuous day. Our work and personal lives are so tightly knit these days, that what we do is what we are is how happy we might or might not be. No one wants to work in a toxic environment; we want to love the work we do and hopefully enjoy the people we do the work with. This is why researching where you want to work next is so vitally important. You really must learn everything you can about a company you're interested in prior to getting a query, a call, or an interview.

You want to be happier, but stay away from creepier, in the sense that there's an ever-growing shadow economy out there today, including many entities that need talented IT pros such as yourself.

For example, maybe you've heard that anyone can set up a company with as little as $600, with no proper identification, a company that can then rent a board and faux investors. You can create a shell company that can be run, anonymously, and sell whatever products and services you want—all the while avoiding paying corporate taxes in the United States. This is the proverbial offshore tax shelter we hear about based in Belize or Seychelles or Cyprus or the Cayman Islands.[2]

Incidentally, according to recent economic reports,[3] the United States is the easiest place to set up a shadow company, with at least four states requiring no proper identification at all, which is against international law established by the United States and Europe.

There's a lot more going on in the shadow world than sham corporations, of course. There are, ahem, you know, some people who will pay you in hard cash under the table. Hey, work is work is work, while "legal" corporations pile up the cash in their "legal" bank accounts. In fact, it's been reported that up to 23 percent of global GDP comes from off-the-books transactions.[4]

You're thinking about it, aren't you? *Screw the legitimate job search, I'm offshoring to the shadow world and either launching or getting a job there.*

But don't go there.

All kidding aside, this is an unfortunate reality check: sometimes the best of business brands (you) will do anything they can to game an overly complex and outdated tax and regulatory system, as opposed to helping transform the economic climate into a more transparent web of interactions that improves global commerce and job creation.

I know it's tempting. Dammit, if it wasn't for those pesky, messy, meddling humans, the world of work would actually work flawlessly. We'd work together happily and collaboratively, without deceit, harassment, or discrimination. We'd all be accountable and personally responsible and have each other's backs, we'd have reciprocal respect with our leaders, and reality TV would not be a reality.

There is lots of money to be made in tech—both in the shadow world and the legit world—but what's money if you're miserable? Again, this is why the employer research is so frickin' important.

---

[2] You still must, of course, pay all taxes due the U.S. government.

[3] www.nytimes.com/2012/07/29/magazine/my-big-fat-belizean-singaporean-bank-account.html

[4] www.freakonomics.com/2012/08/30/how-deep-is-the-shadow-economy-a-new-freakonomics-radio-podcast/

Look for the Smudged Glass

In the "world of work" I've worked in and written about for the past 13 years, we talk all about not-so-happy knowledge workers in global corporate offices big and small longing for something else. Go figure, right? Two downturns later, a contentious political and stagnant job environment, and little if any pay raises (with the exception of a stellar few of you) and you've got us mad as hell. In fact, according to the latest Gallup Employee Engagement Index information,[5] 70 percent of American workers are "not engaged" or "actively disengaged" in their work, meaning that productivity and loyalty to the work and teams goes to hell. Also according to the index report, "Americans who have at least some college education are significantly less likely to be engaged in their jobs than are those with a high school diploma or less."

This means that many of you IT pros who most likely have some if not a lot of higher education in the form of college degrees and certifications are more likely to be unhappy and unproductive in your jobs. Maybe you've worked for crappy bosses and with crappy colleagues, working in *crappy conditions out in the fields for very little pay*, and you're ready to go window shopping. How do you do that? What used to be hearsay research via the gossip superhighway pre- and post-public Internet now has a lot of valid data behind it, and that data just grows and grows, as do the analyses and the way they're served up. It's easier than ever to peel back the onion layers on a company today online without crying.

I'll even go out on a "social" limb here and say that companies with good career opportunities and good workplace cultures are those that understand and embrace employment brand marketing, and have smudged glass doors. No need to scratch your heads, especially if you're a job seeker. Let me explain.

▓ **Mindful Moment**   There's quite a bit of "sketchy" in the modern workplace today, both in shadow and the legit. Even with tech booming, knowing how a company culture functions, and what its dysfunctions are, can make a huge difference in your daily happiness and productivity. Dysfunction doesn't scale otherwise and affects whether or not you want to work there, or stay there. Think about the time you cried after a long day of programming or sys admining.

---

[5] www.gallup.com/poll/155924/mondays-not-blue-engaged-employees.aspx

The Joys of Work–Life Window Shopping

Here's how to get some insights into a potential employer. First, take a look at the company's career page, Facebook corporate page, or any social point of presence. Wait, they don't have any? Then I say move along unless there's another professionally compelling reason for you to stay. I mean, corporate brands have struggled for the longest time to market their workplace cultures. If they feel like they don't need to do it, that workers should feel honored that they were phone screened in the first place, then interviewed, and then offered a job at below market value (except in the Valley), forget it. You don't want to work for a company like this. There are plenty of other employers, both old and new, that are offering much better transparent cultures that only want the best talent—you.

For the many companies that thankfully do have some marketing presence, is there anything on the page beyond job listings that gives you an idea of company culture? Look at the people in the pictures on their website—do they look like real people who really work for the company and not pretty model stock photos? Are there any video testimonials from real people who really work for the company, talking about what it's like to really work there? Does it feel condescending?

Have you seen the funny "Condescending Corporate Brand Page" on Facebook? It's a comical look at the thin employer brand that's pushed in the general corporate world, again with the happy stock photo models jumping in the air together because they're so damn excited to be working together.

Funny, but true. How many of these pages have you seen across sites online, including the company's own career site? I say if you're not going to keep it real with real folk, don't keep it at all. Wait, you're paying that much for your mobile application developers? Well, okay…

Hey, don't get distracted by the shiny objects. Stay focused with me. These career sites should also be mobile and social-friendly, which as you know means regardless of what device you're using, you can check them and their jobs out easily and then share them easily across your online social networks. Remember, happy (passionate and hardworking) employees make for great employment branding, creative employment branding, great customer service, and ultimately overall product and service brand marketing. So when you see it—and trust me, you'll know if it's for real 9 times out of 10—then that's really good.

Now, if the employers are spouting jargon-filled rhetoric about work–life balance in their job descriptions, run in the opposite direction. How many times have we all read this drivel and thought, "Yeah, I've heard that before. Working 60+ hours per week and you want me to work on Labor Day? C'mon."

No, it's more like finding the right employer that gets integrating our professional and personal lives, because that's the reality of modern life. Both worlds are highly intertwined, and it's only the mindful presence of being in each appropriately when sometimes we find Zen—that moment of harmonic convergence in our lives when all things family, friends, co-workers, employers, work, and life become one.

Like working in the backseat with my MacBook Air on my lap and the hotspot on my phone keeping me perpetually connected, with my wife driving and talking with my nephew in the passenger seat while my daughters squawk excitedly about Mr. Fredrickson's house rising up in the air via hundreds of multicolored balloons in the movie *Up*.

That's been our integrated reality for many road trips. But we wouldn't give it up for all the Zen in China because the intrinsic rewards outweigh the work–life imbalance we attempt to skirt—to enjoy what we do and love our family. Again, it's not even really about balance or imbalance—it's the highly integrated world of work–life we live.

If I'm your employer, I'm going to do everything I can to foster the emotional connectivity and encourage the internal motivational drive, as well as move the motivation needle externally with "rewards" when appropriate. But I want you to work hard, I want results, I'm going to focus on pay-for-performance, and if your position allows, I'm going to let you do it as you see fit (when, where, and how). I will be empathic and trust you, but I will not be a pushover.

And if you're the employee, you're going to demand flexibility in exchange for regular, quality output whenever, wherever, and however you're doing it. You want to take time off when you need it, regardless of the reason, and you don't want to be questioned. You want empathy and their trust and you will reciprocate. You want to to be pushed and pulled and challenged to learn as long as you're enjoying what you're doing in the context of what you're doing (and the company's thriving, of course).

That's what we need to read on the career sites and in the job descriptions. Let's find the employers that embrace the mindful workplace presence of frenetic Zen.

Earlier this year, Glassdoor,[6] a service I'm going reference again in this chapter, released its second annual Top 25 Companies for Work–Life Balance report[7] recognizing companies that offer the best balance between work and personal life. The report is based entirely on feedback shared by the employees themselves within the past year. The top five companies were MITRE, North Highland, Agilent Technologies, SAS Institute, and CareerBuilder.

Some of your best referrals come from your peers, right? So I recommend that you check out companies like these and others that get good reviews, because they're the ones that get it, at least most of the time. You use Yelp for food, don't you?

Mindful Moment   When window shopping for new employers, look for the real people and stories being shared about integrated workplace culture via creative employment branding across the career site to other social points of presence. They're out there, and the ones that really get it are the ones who'll get you. And the decent paycheck and benefits don't hurt, I know.

Press Your Face Against the Glass

Have you reviewed your prospective company LinkedIn and BranchOut profiles so you can see who you might know in the company, even if it's a second-degree contact you might be able to get introduced to? The cool thing is that most professional networks show you who the people are via their photos and avatars. You might even see someone you know, but didn't know you knew.

You should make the time to do this because it's still about who you know. Referrals are still one of the best ways to get noticed and maybe even get your foot in the door. In fact, you should research those organizations you're interested in via all your professional social networks of choice, including LinkedIn, Facebook (and BranchOut), Twitter, Quora, GitHub, Stack Overflow, and more to find out who you might be connected to directly and even indirectly and what it is they might be saying about the companies you're interested in. (Or what they're not saying—you know, read between the lines.) Even better, reach out to these connections and ask them specifically about the companies you're interested in. What are the recruiters and hiring

---

[6] An online social jobs and career community that helps employees, job seekers, employers, and recruiters find and share detailed information about specific jobs and companies across the globe.

[7] www.glassdoor.com/Top-Companies-for-Work-Life-Balance-LST_KQ0,35.htm

managers like (unless they've already been beating down your LinkedIn doors)? What are the pay and benefits like? What is the integrated work–life culture like? And so on.

Find out as much as you can from your connections about who influences the applicant-selection decisions and do your best to connect with those people and share your interest in said jobs. Don't overwhelm the contacts you know (and especially those you don't), but don't underwhelm them, either, by simply applying on the corporate career page—you know, the one with the pretty model stock photos offering images of faux Zen-like work–life balance.

Not everybody you find is going to be happy about where they work or have worked. In fact, we live between two worlds of business today—one where passionate, love-zapped, culture-centric companies focus on the internal and external customer and strive to create an emotional connection between employment brand, product/service and you, the career consumer. And then you've got the other one. This is the one we've been working in for a long, long time—the business as usual, non-transparent, top-down bureaucracy, one where customers inside and out usually run a slow second to productivity and profits. The one with the better alignment and balance is the one who understands and embraces marketing and that emotional connection.

And that brings me to the glass doors. Use sites like the ones I describe next, the latter of which has the "glass door" namesake, to research and learn more about the companies, professions, and industries you're interested in.

Mindful Moment   Remember, it's still about who you know. Use your professional "social" network connections to learn more about the companies and jobs you're interested in before you go through the arduous application process.

Your Career Search Yelps (and Gulps)

If you're familiar with Yelp, you know you can check out local businesses and read reviews from fellow consumers about what they think of those same businesses' products and services. The Internet has gloriously democratized our shopping behavior and that's a good thing. World-of-work websites like Vault and Glassdoor have done the same for those of us looking for work. These sites provide peer-reviewed company information for best and worst places to work—including the how, where, when, and why. They also include industry and profession rankings, resume and cover letter writing best practices (remember mine is the online profile), education recommendations, job listings, and lots of other career development information.

Vault

Vault is the older of the two sites I'm referencing, launched in 1996 (see Figure 9-1). Ever since, they've touted themselves as the place for career intelligence. First, you have to register to access the industry blogs and newsletters, the company and profession overviews, and the job listings. That's free, but to get even more intelligence, you've got to pony up about $10 per month for access. Either way there's tons of information, too much information actually, which is indicative of the data firehoses that drown us daily. If you know anything about the psychology and economics of scarce attention, you know that the more that's presented to us, the less we consume. Choose your career intelligence wisely with a site like Vault.

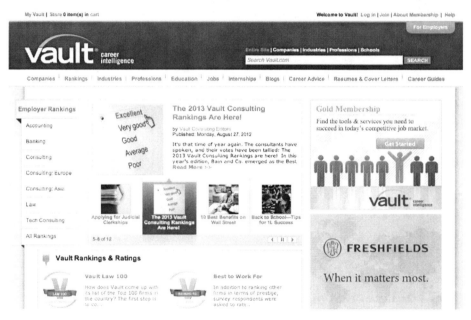

Figure 9-1. Vault. Courtesy of Vault.com.

Glassdoor

Glassdoor is a much newer career management portal, founded in 2007 and launched in 2008 (see Figure 9-2). What's interesting about this site, and why I like it as well, is that you sign up for free, preferably with your Facebook account, as more than likely it's integrated as a Facebook technology partner and logging in will make for a much better user experience. Once you sign in for the first time, you get full access to salaries, reviews, and interviews for one month. After that, you can get unlimited access if you simply post an anonymous salary, company review, or interview experience of your own.

A-ha! Yes, that's one way they build out their peer-reviewed information. Much of the same career development information is available as in Vault, including career advice from a great group of professionals (I used to write for the Glassdoor blog in full disclosure), but you'll also get interview reviews, which is really unique, giving you insight as to how companies run their interviews, what they ask, and what you should prepare for prior to having a video in-person interview. Also, when you sign-in via Facebook you get to see where your connections work and maybe get an intro or more like you can do when using LinkedIn and BranchOut.

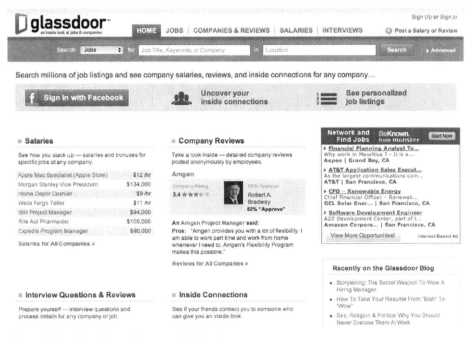

Figure 9-2. Glassdoor. Courtesy of Glassdoor.com.

Yes, we all want to see inside and understand what makes the companies we're interested tick, and the quicker the better. A job search is a full-time job in itself, and most of us don't have a lot of time to do research on the best places to work, so the more transparent and real a company's guts is, the easier the research and the targeting. Of course, there's no guarantee you'll get the job, and it'll still come down to who is the most qualified time and time again, but doing your homework can give you the edge. Going in blind can screw your chances.

Keep in mind that whatever peer reviews you read about what it's like to work in company X or work for boss Y aren't the most objective insights you'll ever read. Everybody likes to be liked, and even though these reviews are usually always anonymous, a squeaky clean review might not be all that it seems. That goes as well for the disgruntled employee who trashes his or her former employer just enough and in a non-threatening or completing head-bashing way to be made public. Emotions run high and low when you're in any given moment. Just remember what you thought of (or wrote about) your previous employer when you were laid off. Bastards.

One more thing might help with your own marketing tipping point—the glass doors you're looking through are two-way, so keep your online nose as clean as possible (see Chapter 6). You might have read here in this book and elsewhere that hiring companies aren't supposed to use the information they find about you in social media—but they do. In fact, most recruiters and hiring managers consider your social media presence in their hiring decisions—you are what you share online.

Keep it real, but keep it clean, especially when those snotty noses and salivating mouths are pressed up against the glass.

Mindful Moment   To get a firehose of great company, profession, industry, and career development information, use sites like Vault and Glassdoor. You'll get the insight and the edge you need when researching who you want to work for and why.

10

Leverage Your Network, and Their Networks

Move It or Lose It

> *More business decisions occur over lunch and dinner than at any other time, yet no MBA courses are given on the subject.*
>
> —Peter Drucker

Have you ever been to a Pink Slip Party? At these networking events, the recently laid off mingle with recruiters and employers.

These events became popular during the dot-com downturn in the early 2000s, and have continued ever since. Or maybe you've gone to Chamber of Commerce mixers, or career fairs, or tech conferences—all of these activities help to make up the greater body of business and professional networking. But it's all personal, all the time, no doubt about that.

Many of you have had career coaches or professional mentors throughout your IT incarnations, and I'll bet one of the primary world of work mantras you've had beaten into your bright but obstinate skulls (I'm with you there) is this one: "It's not what you know, it's who you know." Ack, right? Add to that, "It's not what you know, it's who you know and how you leverage, you know, who you know." And how you reciprocate—blah, blah, blah.

However, this is the very nature of networking, and it's not new just because of all things shiny social media today; it's a misnomer that social recruiting is

truly new, because we've been sourcing online pools since before the Internet was available to us all. Networking by its very nature is a highly personal thing regardless of context or physical setting, and our Rolodexes have been both the literal and figurative metaphors for our networks for decades.

Keeping the Drucker quote in mind from the start of this chapter, social networking truly came on the scene 40 years before we used the Mosaic client for earlier communication protocols such as FTP, NNTP, and Gopher, and then the Mosaic browser to publicly surf the Web and find online professional networks. Breakfast meetings, lunch meetings, and dinner meetings all allowed us to meet, network, and do business with one another while getting really tanked and higher than a drunken skunk. The AMC show *Mad Men* popularized the hyper-fiction reality that once was, but my ex-father-in-law lived some of that in the 1960s in San Francisco. How did people not pass out and sleep all afternoon before the dinner drinking—I mean meeting?

Trade shows, conferences, seminars, coffee shops, golf courses, open houses, supermarkets, movie theaters, churches, synagogues, mosques, parks, playgrounds, political rallies, the DMV—I could go on and on, but you get the point, right? Networking can and does happen in nearly every social "community" aspect of life. Nothing new there, except that now that face-to-face fire is fueled by the interconnectedness that online networks bring us today.

Computers went from filling a football field to a single room to computing on a single server the size of a flying toaster (remember those screen savers?), and managing data and communications has changed dramatically. In my lifetime alone, I've gone from using a rotary telephone and file cabinets full of paper to using a smart phone as a computer and storing terabytes of data in the cloud.

It's a crazy, cool science fiction world, and we live and breathe it!

When I worked at San Jose State University in the late 1980s and early 1990s, we were already online using email, managing a variety of interdepartmental data via the intranet and the Gopher protocol, and connecting and collaborating with an ever-growing network of other professionals at universities around the world. Then, of course, there were the online networking origins pre-Internet that included IBM's SHARE and UNIX groups, Compuserve, AOL, and the Yahoo! User Groups. Any of you "old school" techies out there know what I'm talking about. These were the new, hip, and cool ways of networking with like-minded professionals about a variety of topics—all in the comfort of our own rooms. Recruiters caught on quickly, jumping into these IT user groups and bugging the crap out of the network members.

Then came the roaring late 1990s and early 2000s, the new golden age of tech innovation, launching parties for businesses with a website but no model, champagne and caviar, and the glorious rising sun of boom to the darkness of nightfall bust. Applicant tracking systems were born to better track your technical asses. This was when I entered the HR and recruiting tech marketplace with a company called Tapestry.net. We touted talent communities and our own proprietary candidate matching algorithm that we called interested qualified applicants (IQA). Our talent communities (as we called them, something I'll talk more about later on) consisted of databases of software developers, IT pros, and bilingual Japanese professionals (which was the primary origin of the company). But they weren't really networked communities because there was only one-way communication with them—meaning we sent them job postings from our paying employers. Some applied, and we screened and presented the short lists to our clients. We served as a front end for the growing-but-new talent acquisition software market.

Lastly we entered the social and professional networking world we know today. This, of course, started in 2004 with LinkedIn, and then bloomed into Facebook, Twitter (more a communications channel than network, mind you), the Ning networks, Glassdoor, GitHub, Stack Overflow, Quora, Focus, and many, many others. Here's a funny little story. After setting up my LinkedIn profile years ago, which made me member number 1,760,099 (okay, not an early, early adopter, but today there are over 175 million registered users, so there), I then decided to join MySpace. Yeah, remember that little gem of a social network? Well, 15 minutes after I set up my profile, I was propositioned by a lovely young lady. Sure it was a business proposition of sorts, but not the kind of professional hookup I was looking for.

Today we're more connected with the world than we've ever been and with the rate of emerging markets coming online like in China and India, networking has never been easier.

So, now what?

Mindful Moment   The wonderful world of networking isn't new—we've been meeting one another in myriad social business situations for decades. And now with the proliferation of online networking, connecting to one another and leveraging each other is easier than it's ever been. How do you connect and leverage professionally online today?

First- and Second-Degree Burn Rates

In Chapter 8, I talked up online profiles and why you should invest your time there and not in revising your resume and cover letter. If you're not convinced of this, then best of luck uploading that resume into the black hole known as an applicant tracking system. You've lived in this world, so you know what it's like to apply and never hear back, even if it was an inside or contingent recruiter who reached out to you in the first place and convinced you to apply.

The traditional routes to getting a job have enough "process debt" (think technical debt) to shut down the U.S. federal government without the help of either hopelessly gridlocked party. You have to network with other professionals and organizations, communicate and collaborate with them, and work that network to get the "ins" you'll need. That doesn't even mean you'll get an interview, but you sure as hell aren't going to get them applying the traditional way.

In Chapter 9, I talked about researching the companies you're interested in working for—window shopping, as I called it. The points about seeing who you're connected with and where are worth reiterating here and expanding on further as they relate to leveraging networks.

Again I ask, have you reviewed your prospective company's LinkedIn or BranchOut profile so you can see who you might know in the company, even if it's a second-degree contact you might be able to connect with or at least get introduced to? The more you research and reach out, the more likely you'll expose yourself to what I'll call first- and second-degree burn rates—increasing the likelihood you find the right fireplace to stoke and call home whether you're actively looking or just a passive passerby wanting to keep those golden hands of opportunity warm.

You should make the time to do this because it's still about who you know, who they are, who they know, where they are, and where you are in relation to all of it. Listen, referrals are still one of the best ways to get noticed and maybe even get your foot in the door—in fact, even in this latest downturn, referrals account for more than 40 to 50 percent of all hires. You should research those organizations you're interested in via all your professional social networks of choice, not just LinkedIn, to find out who you might be connected to directly and even indirectly and what it is they might be saying about the companies you're interested in (or what they're not saying—you know, read between the lines). Reach out to these connections and ask them specifically about the companies you're interested in. What are the recruiters and hiring managers like (unless they've already been beating down your online network doors), what are the pay and benefits like, and what is the integrated work–life culture like?

Again, find out as much as you can from your connections about who influences the applicant-selection decisions and then do your best to connect with them and share your interest in said jobs. Remember, don't overwhelm the contacts you know (and especially those you don't), but don't underwhelm them, either, by simply applying on the corporate career page or sending your resume to jobs@company.com, especially if you want either of the two most basic job search needs: acknowledgment that you've applied and closure that you've either moved along the pipeline or not. I can and will repeat this mantra until the end of time.

Then again, don't spend inordinate amounts of time on the wrong networks. If you're looking for jQuery folks to connect and network with, check out sites like GitHub; save the cute cat and kid pictures and crocheting tips for the folks in your Facebook stream. I'm not making fun of either; my grandmother taught me how to crochet when I was 12, and I do like cats and kids.

Networking with the right people is critical, even before you see a job to apply for at a company you're interested in working at. It's also important to let everyone you know that you're seeking a new job opportunity. Your own network can and will help you make connections that you wouldn't have imagined otherwise, which is why having a targeted list of companies at the ready might help you network into them and discover those inside the organization who can help.

Working with Recruiters

By the way, recruiters love to connect with people on LinkedIn, which might or might not be a good thing for you. On the one hand, I've heard from many "wanted" IT pros over the past year who are incessantly hounded by LinkedIn recruiter InMails (unsolicited e-mails), causing them to delete their profile. This is probably an extreme response, though. The same goes for you networking with recruiters; don't pummel them with requests to help you find a job. Just as in all networking, connect with the recruiters, and get introduced to them, see if there's synergy there, and see if you can help one another.

That is why it's important at this stage to talk a little bit about working with recruiters. I have many good friends out there who are recruiters and damn good at what they do, and they do what they say they do. There are also a small contingent of recruiters who are just looking for their next commission check and could not really give a shit about you and your future.

Recruiters in this tech market can be a godsend, however. They can help you traverse the wild west of IT hotspots, show you what companies to look at, introduce you to key people, open up extensive networks up to you, and help you negotiate better salary, benefits, and perks (which I mention again in Chapter 16).

Maybe you already have recruiter friends, both internal recruiters and third-party recruiters (recruiters who work on commission on their own or via a firm), who you've worked with in the past or will work with again. Whether you have or not, here are a few tips to consider in the early stages of networking with and ultimately working with recruiters:

You're the boss, baby. So be the boss. Remember, recruiters can be valuable allies in the war for you, but be clear and concise from the beginning about what you're looking for, the kinds of companies you want to work for, whether or not you're open to relocating, what your skill sets are, and your strengths and experience. Don't waffle too much or they might not want to help place you. If you're looking for a stretch assignment, then practice your pitch as to why before you share it with a potential recruiter. Because they're most likely talking to many other candidates at any given time, sometimes for the same tech positions you're interested in, it's important that you seep into their consciousness and be top of mind when the right positions come up.

Vet them. Ask for references and try to find other candidates they've placed that you can talk with. Were they sold placements? Were the candidates happy with their working (and personal) relationship with the recruiter? Do they play nice with others, especially the hiring managers you want to speak with? Just as they and the employers have done to you, search for them online and see what you can find. Check out their LinkedIn profile as well. If they write or blog about IT recruiting, read what they've written to see if it gels with you and your professional outlook. The more you know about them, the less likely that you'll be played. And trust me, a lot of folks get played out there in the world of work. Don't be one of them.

You gotta like them. A little. Yes, it is a business transaction between you and the recruiter, but you've also got to have some personal connection and rapport with this recruiter. They're helping you get your next gig and you want it to be the right one, so having some appreciation of one another is important. If it doesn't work out this time with the job the recruiter is trying to place you in, if you've got a solid relationship, there's always the next time. Like any and all networking contacts, keep in touch with them and they'll keep in touch with you. You don't have to be Facebook friends and share kitten pictures, but don't be a stranger either once you've networked or worked together.

Get Out of the Office

Now, if you're a social introvert and prefer the online environment, then so be it. But don't convince yourself that you don't need any professional connections to move around the IT world today. Remember, it's not about numbers—you don't need hundreds of connections, just the relevant ones. No man or woman is an island, no matter how good you are at what you do; being able to connect and network with others is a sign that you're socially able to have relationships, and the world of work is all about relationships, which brings me back to my point about it all being so frickin' personal.

Indeed it is. What used to be the in-person first- and second-degree burn rates via all the networking activities I've already listed, has transformed itself into online networking, which has then come full circle to fueling the face-to-face fire.

But really, you have to get out of the house and the office. You do. There is fresh air and the sun and there are the men and women you've met online to meet in person and have intelligent, soul-enriching conversations with, or just to shoot the shit with, at various events and in-person activities that just might get you your next job. You then bring those business cards back with you and connect with these people in the appropriate professional networks and start all over again.

Here's my recommended online networking and job-search checklist:

- Create an online profile on LinkedIn and leverage across other professional "social" networks.

- Find the networks where like-minded IT professionals flock, share, and learn. Don't join them and spend all day online talking shop, cats, and kids, however.

- Connect with previous employers, peers, colleagues, consultants, and friends.

- Check out their connections and companies and research those you're interested in getting in front of—the proverbial back doors.

- Ask your network about the other connections and companies you're truly interested in getting in front of to put a plan together of how.

- Ask your network for introductions and referrals.

- Reciprocate when your networks ask you for help.

- Go outside and meet these people in person. Please.

It works, but you've got to invest the time online and in person. Nature abhors a vacuum (remember that from middle school science?), so don't be a recluse and wish that a great new job would magically appear to give you a lap dance. Be professionally personal and network, network, network.

Mindful Moment   To leverage your network means you have to have a network. Over the years you've worked with and have become connected with many like-minded IT and business professionals. Connect with them online and in person to grow professionally and find new opportunities.

From Networks to Talent Communities

That's the way it begins—change—the movement from one state to another, from a static status quo state to a hopefully more progressive and productive state. It's like moving from flat two dimensions to a vibrant three.

The change begins in small groups, the sharing of new knowledge of what can be done that hasn't been done before and the return of that "change" investment—hence the importance of networking. The new knowledge fills the room, some of it permeating each exposed pore, entering the bloodstream and flooding our brains with possibility.

I spoke in the summer of 2012 with a smart group of HR and recruiting practitioners at the Northern California Human Resources Association

(NCHRA) Santa Cruz Region meeting. My presentation was on social recruiting with a focus on talent networks and communities, the long tail of recruiting and quality over quantity—of change and what can be.

Most of the attendees were from smaller companies in the Santa Cruz area, but what was striking (and not surprising) was the fact that when I shared some recent research on social recruiting, which claimed that over 90 percent of employers would be engaged in it this year, everyone looked at me as if I just said we'd be riding magical unicorns in the big screen release of *Everybody's Doing It* in 3-D. I mean, applicants apply, they get screened, interviewed, and hired. Get the butts in the seats and all that.

Of course the reality is that although about half the room confirmed they use LinkedIn for professional networking, sourcing, and recruiting (get on your online profile if you haven't already), only three had Facebook company pages and no one—and I mean no one—used or even understood what Twitter was. Well, there was one attendee who said he kinda used it. Kinda.

We then discussed the realities—that half the room prohibited most access to social networks during work hours. One HR practitioner even proudly said her company banned Facebook and Pandora during work hours. Oh, man. Don't kill my music. Mercy me. Am I right or what?

But none of the attendees balked at my from-the-hip truths (one recruiter in the room nodded away and winked at me):

- There are a gazillion people on social media today.

- Recruiters do source and recruit using social media.

- Candidates do use social networking tools to search for jobs.

- Companies are still of mixed opinion as to recruiting value.

Yes, companies are still mixed as to the recruiting value of professional social networking, which is why I've written about talent communities the past two years, interviewing various HR and recruiting practitioners and vendors about them, speaking about them, dreaming about them (yes, really), and living and breathing inside one in particular—TalentCulture's #TChat Twitter Chat[1] since November 2010—and now working for a talent community platform company called BraveNewTalent (see Figure 10-1).

BraveNewTalent allows you to sign up for your own profile for free, or import your LinkedIn profile, and start connecting with other professionals,

---

[1] Twitter Chats are organized online discussions around specific topics or industries conducted on Twitter via a named hashtag Twitter stream that is easily followed in Twitter clients (#TChat, for example, which is all about the world of work).

organizations, and more important, IT, business and a myriad of other professional topics. You can learn and share knowledge, find mentors, and become a mentor (more on mentors in Chapter 11), investing in your career development and making you more valuable today and tomorrow.

But I digress. You should've seen the looks on the NCHRA attendee faces when I explained Twitter Chats. By the way, do you know what a Twitter Chat is? Just checking.

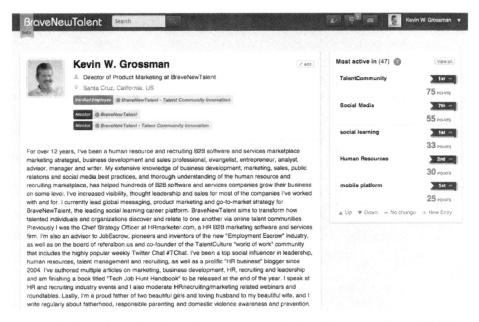

Figure 10-1. The BraveNewTalent talent community platform. Courtesy of BraveNewTalent. com.

Much of the social recruiting and talent network mainstream as it stands today relates to recruiting you for a company—the term *talent community* has been bastardized to date; as I mentioned earlier in this chapter, the company I worked for nearly 13 years ago said they were one, when they really weren't. But true talent communities can and should also form inside of companies with existing employees, and alumni, and their networks, both inside and out—a mass of hub-and-spokes circles within circles within circles that even the most progressive employers can only dream of maximizing return on.

Most everyone in the meeting agreed that the three-dimensional "unicorn" in the room is the fact that a talent community is only a community when those who belong collaborate, commiserate, and connect with one another regularly for what can amount to infinite combinations of reasons—including sharing original and curated content and learning from one another—but not necessarily applying for jobs outright. This, of course, can happen in existing social networks, other platforms, and software systems that help create talent communities, and a combination of all in between.

But the most common reality is that we usually end up with a two-dimensional network model, sourcing active candidates from a smattering of job postings and creating a database of people where occasional, hopefully relevant company and job information is shared with them. There's just no true "community" inside.

You know what I'm talking about. When you're looking for a job, you're looking for a job. Right? Why the hell would you want to stay and play?

But work with me here—what if you could network with other professionals and organizations, as well as learn about various relevant topics, sharing your own knowledge about those topics, all of which will help you grow and stretch yourself, which in turn makes you more valuable to your current employer and prospective ones?

What if? It's time for a bold new approach called talent communities.

Wait, you really don't know what a Twitter Chat is?

However, to be fair, many would argue (even me at times) that the major social networks of Facebook, Twitter (#TChat, duh), and LinkedIn can be talent communities. Closer to home for you, all the major job boards including and especially Dice (see Chapter 13), have IT-specific communities you can join, network in, and glean technical insight from, just as you can do at BraveNewTalent (although BraveNewTalent allows organizations and professionals to share relevant content inside, push it out to their other networks, and pull other content back in again—the "other content" I mentioned and closed networks). There are seemingly an infinite number of technical user groups online globally, regionally, and even in your local area that you can join. Just search for "Linux User Group" or your IT flavor of choice—and voila! Lastly, there are also other talent network and community services that are employer-specific that you could indirectly become a part of or be asked to join by your current or prospective employers like TalentCircles, Jobs2Web, Taleo (now Oracle), Kenexa (now IBM), and many other applicant tracking systems on the market today.

Just make sure you're making them work for you, and not the other way around. Talent networks and communities are like any networking you do— the return is only in the reciprocity, meaning always pay it forward to get paid back.

▓ **Mindful Moment**   Have you ever thought of your online networks as communities? If so, what made them so? Do you share with and learn from one another? Do you find that this ongoing activity helps you become more valuable as a current or prospective employee? And really, you don't know what a Twitter Chat is?

To Learn, to Know, and to Do

In a sense you've already been connecting, communicating, and collaborating via all the "talent" networks I've highlighted to date and many others I haven't. So in a sense, you've already participated in talent networks, some with community learning activities that truly make it community. You can share and learn in most of the online networks—the only problem is that you're siloed in these various social points of presence and you have to jump in and out from each one to participate in each one; there is no central diffusive hub. That's changing, though, with platforms like BraveNewTalent (so much for subtle, right?).

Conversely, most of the HR and recruiting technology industry that's touted as talent communities are nothing more than databases of you, the job seeker, getting job broadcast after job broadcast and maybe the occasional webinar, but rarely the opportunity to connect and learn from other professionals, which is what I think is the most valuable contributions your networks make, besides helping you get a job, of course. Usually the platforms are nothing more than a crazy maze of bad roads.

Consider this: The U.S. Interstate Highway System construction was authorized in 1956 by the Federal Aid Highway Act. More than 55 years later its network includes nearly 50,000 miles of highway and about one-quarter of all vehicle miles driven in the country use this system. Add to that thousands and thousands of miles of other byways and bad roads and you've got a lot of endless driving going on.

Along the way there are a myriad of rest stops, fast food restaurants, gas stations, hotels and motels, run-of-the-mill and eclectic points of interest—you name it. Along most major thoroughfares you'll find plenty of places to stop and "refuel," but there are times where there's a whole bunch of nothing and you better be sure you've got enough fuel in "all tanks." Add to that extreme hot and cold weather, accidents, and commuter gridlock and you're along for one helluva ride.

The highways and byways are a means to an end; we're not driving them for the journey, just the destination. Most of the time at least, unless it's a first-time vacation road trip experience—like your first true job hunt. Or even the next one, or the next one.

Like an M. C. Escher maze, the routes through social networks to job boards to career sites to applicant tracking systems are as endless as the miles and miles of bad roads we travel every day. Most career search drivers just want to get on and off, and yet we don't really help them do that; we don't provide them with a Zen-like GPS so they can get to where they're going and apply for that dream job—you know, the one advertised on the big, religiously gaudy billboards along the highway: "Jesus is really sorry about the candidate experience. Have some fries and a Coke. Or a Pepsi."

True talent communities give us plenty of quality rest stops that allow us all to learn from one another and share our experiences—the good, the bad, and the in between—understanding that we all travel the many of the same roads and we collectively and collaboratively fill the potholes and repave our sanity as we traverse the world of work, which, remember, is quite personal.

To learn, to know, and to do—this is how we development ourselves and make our skills, experience, and achievements come to fruition and become more valuable. This is the social heart of networking. Companies that are getting it right are giving us learning-land rest stops complete with collaborative refueling stations, gamification options, testing and assessment centers, white boards to share insights, virtual face-time communications, and whatever else you can think of to have them get to know you and vice versa.

Happy driving, kids!

Mindful Moment   The social heart of professional networking creates a talent community of learning and sharing that includes the entire organization ecosystem—new applicants, current employees, alumni, contractors, service providers, and customers. And yes, helping each other find new and exciting opportunities. But the intrinsic value of a reciprocal networking really does increase the value of the moving parts—and those are you, you, and you. You'll find mentors and make yourself mentors, which is what I'll discuss in the next chapter.

CHAPTER 11

Mentors and Professional Associations

Walking in Their/Your Footsteps

I am not a teacher, but an awakener.

—Robert Frost

In case of personal Armageddon, flee to the sea. That's all I've been able to think about these days each time I run from my house to the ocean and back again, usually about 4.5 to 5 miles, three times per week. I think about it because along the way I witness the destitute, the disenfranchised, the drug addicts, the mentally ill, and the miserably lost—the entire spectrum of fringe, from those who have chosen to live this way to those who have not.

Some are camped out in their cars, moving from space to space, sometimes just one space over to adhere to loitering and parking regulations. Others walk listlessly along the water, rifling through public and private trash cans for food while scanning the ground for change and smokable cigarette butts. And then there are those I can't see, but I know are there—those camping in the creases, crevices, and cliffs in and around Santa Cruz. As I run along the water, I note at times that I'm less than five feet from the cliff edge that drops off to the cold Pacific below.

The fictionalized images from novels, stories, and movies about the end of the world come to mind vividly, but these individuals are real, and their stories real. To those who have experienced more recent personal Armageddons, who have lost most if not everything during the past four years, and who have given up on finding work, on getting back on their feet, and on staying relevant and marketable in the world of work—in life for that matter—I empathize. I do. It's tougher than it's ever been to stay gainfully employed over the long term. We're all competing with five generations now for fewer full-time jobs in a world where being a generalist is as ubiquitous as a quick keyword search in Google or Bing, meaning you've been scrapped for automated efficiency. Pack your things and begin the exodus to the sea.

But even the sea brings red tides of danger for those without hope, especially those camped out on the cliffs. Job report after job report includes a recurring theme: "The changes don't account for people who stopped looking for jobs."

There are red tides that produce natural toxins, that suck the air from the sea, and that can kill marine and coastal life. The red tide of inaction in this constantly changing world of work is sucking the air from adaptability, driving many to the fringe, even those in the IT hot spots.

As I've written this book, I can't help but think about why I run, about why I stretch my older self with cross-training to shave seconds off my mile times.

It's for the same reasons I've stretched myself professionally, taken chances, failed, failed again, succeeded (a little), pushed myself to learn new skills and to remain relevant and marketable in an ever-connected global economy.

And I'm not talking about going back to school, not in the traditional sense. I'm talking about self-educating via reading, listening to, and watching relevant content found online across multiple social and professional networks, publications, blogs, and more (Chapter 3), or to "skill-up" as we're saying at BraveNewTalent these days. We're also skilling-up in the associations we belong to as well as the volunteer work we do.

And even more important to skilling-up, it's about the networks we keep. I've reached out to my network to be mentored, and in turn have been a mentor to others.

It's not the cliff that bothers me the most while I'm running. It's the rising red tide without mentors to shadow our paths.

In case of personal Armageddon, stretch yourself and ask for help.

Which is why I'm writing this book, volunteering to help job seekers, and participating in career panels, as I've mentioned elsewhere: I've experienced career development and management angst as much as the next person. I've become an informal mentor in a sense, not for the sake of saying it to make me feel better, but to do something that makes others feel better, and hopefully help them figure out how to get an "in" somewhere, somehow, some way.

It doesn't matter what age, position, or experience level one is at; we all could use mentoring in our lives from an early age on, outside of our immediate family and friends (although I hope you have as well). When I began to hit the skids in the last year and a half of high school, after being "on top" in grades, student government, and sports, one of our high school counselors befriended me and told me to cut left when everybody else was cutting right. He mentored and counseled me in a way that no one had done before; he kept it real as they say, at the same time encouraging me to stretch myself in the direction I wanted to stretch. Writing was a big part of that. He's the one who inspired me to be a mentor throughout the rest of my life.

Fast forward to another high school career panel in 2012. Keeping my old counselor and friend in mind, we treated the class nongenerationally and talked with them straight. At one point, the three career panelists concurred that being passionate about what you do is one of the most important tenets of the world of work, ever. I added that today we're not only loyal and committed to the work that moves and schools us, but also to the people who are part of that committed work—because that's the work that moves us to do greater things for the world. That's the work that makes it easier for startups to start up and for established companies to grow—creating new jobs and replacing some of those lost over the past five years, including full-time, part-time, flex-time, contract, and project work, and any combination of those that you can imagine. That's the work that transforms technologies, processes, communities, and the very heart and soul of the world.

"Follow your bliss," one young man said, wearing a vibrant blue and black striped tie and Polo shirt combo. The room filled with nods and smiles. Right on, I thought. This career panel was put on by an amazing local organization called Your Future Is Our Business (where my wonderful wife worked early this year). YFIOB is a community-based 501(c)(3) nonprofit organization dedicated to fostering business–education partnerships that benefit students. Their mission is to support young people in Santa Cruz County in making informed educational and career decisions.

The two classes of high school students we spoke to—and this included a panel of me as marketing/tech guy, a midwife (who was actually the backup midwife for our second daughter's birth), and a physical therapist and athletic trainer—were all very attentive as they asked us serious career development questions. I find it silly that those who long to label are scrambling to figure out just what to call the generation born in the mid-1990s and later. As far as I'm concerned, it's silly and pointless, although one thing is clear: They'll be the most tech-savvy generation from birth than any other previous.

And they are. They were amused that my high school had a computer lab of one computer, and that I had learned how to type on an IBM Selectric III typewriter there. They now have magic gadgets that even Steve Jobs hadn't dreamed up yet.

Afterward, the young man who had said, "Follow your bliss," came up to me and began asking me questions about getting into video game programming and telling me how he is already programming on his own now. I told him to keep learning and doing, because doing is knowing is growing. "So do," I said. "And keep rocking those ties, Mister."

This is why we are all Generation Now—each of us is a lifelong learner and mentor longing to find our bliss and to be committed to the work that moves and schools us and the world. Amen.

■ **Mindful Moment**   Mentoring is all about paying it forward—helping to nurture and guide someone's aspirations as you were nurtured and guided. Who's been a mentor to you and why? Who have you mentored and why?

The Informal and the Formal

Much of what I've already shared has to do with informal mentoring, which really does make up most of the mentoring in the world of work and life today. This is yet another extension of all the networking I talked about in Chapters 9 and 10—the very process of connecting with like-minded IT and business pros and talking shop could develop into an informal mentoring relationship.

Informal Mentors

Please note that I am not a mentoring expert; I only know what has worked for me over the years. To share with one another what's worked in your career and definitely hasn't is a very powerful social learning and bonding activity. Mentors in your life could also come in the form of previous teachers, professors, parents, family members, old friends, new friends, online connections, previous supervisors, colleagues, clergy—whoever in your universe has had a positive impact on you and your life decisions.

In the broadest definition, mentors are supportive individuals who devote time to someone else (other than their own children). Even though mentors can fill any number of specific roles, they all have the same goal, which is to help others achieve their potential and discover their strengths. In our context, that means your career development and management.

Mentors help us define and reflect on our professional goals and then suggest ways for us to achieve them. Mentors helps us traverse the highways, byways, and bad roads of job searches and give us insight on the tough questions about what we want to be when we grow up—and we're always growing up—and get greater perspective on the various facets of the IT industry of which we're fond and that puts food on our tables, and sometimes a nice car in the driveway. Mentor and mentee (the recipient) relationships can even help you eventually land a new job, a promotion, or that lateral move across departments. Mentors can also be an open ear to bend when we need to bitch about our boss or whatever has gotten us down in the daily grind.

Mentors can also be your friends, maybe even your lover or spouse (like mine), but it's important to note that you'll need to pick professional mentors whose expertise, beliefs, and attitudes are right for you and where you want to go. (Don't sleep with your mentor, unless you marry them and plan to have children. You heard it here first.)

You should consider mentors who have good reputations at your current company, or the company they work at if they're online connections. Remember, you can read their online recommendations and even contact the mentors' connections for references. Yes, references. Even informal mentoring is important work and can have a profound, hopefully positive affect on your career. Also, consider mentors outside of IT if you're looking to get an outside perspective on your career path, or if you're interested in expanding your business knowledge in finance, operations, marketing, sales, customer services, whatever the interest. The value to glean is counterbalanced by the value you give—mentees can mentor, too.

Whether you're approaching the mentors or they've approached you, or you're the mentor approachee, here is a checklist to consider as mentor and mentee:

- Understand each other's expertise, beliefs, and attitudes to ensure some level of synergy exists.

- Set realistic expectations of what you want out of the relationship and how often you'll try to meet. This can include tutoring, job shadowing, career exploration and development, role playing, and other similar activities.

- Try to meet in person when and if possible, or at least virtually online via Skype or Google+ Hangout so you can have that all-important face time.

- Of course, phone calls and emails are fine, especially when you want to share recent challenges or accomplishments.

- Shooting the breeze is fine, but you should have an agenda at the ready; we're all really busy and you want to make the most of your time.

- Make sure to send each other opportunity and connection recommendations when appropriate. Remember, you've got each other's back.

Formal Mentoring Programs

Most companies have some form of formal mentoring program in place. Many call it the buddy system or job shadowing, but in the end, it's institutionalized mentoring—which doesn't mean it's bad, by the way.

Participants in formal mentoring programs are usually matched based on skills, experience, and job competencies—the mentee being the one who needs help acquiring the skills, experience, and job competencies. In a world where we still parachute folks into their jobs and then let them find their way out of the jungle, we need jungle-friendly mentoring programs. Compared to informal mentoring, formal mentoring programs can be measured and progress more consistently tracked.

But you can go out and have lunch or maybe even a beer with your mentor. Just remember, no sex.

Formal mentoring programs also help create a workplace culture of open learning and growth, which in turn increases productivity and delivers to the bottom line. And if we have any shares involved, profit sharing, quarterly bonus plans, or the like, we'll truly care about making it work. I know, I know—money isn't everything, but it's a big something we live on.

Like the informal mentoring described earlier, you as mentee can learn a lot about the inner workings of your business, like how to traverse the jungle realm, who else to go to for answers and support and to learn other parts of the business, and those unspoken rules that need to be understood quickly to be successful. In formal mentoring programs, your mentors are usually senior staff and management, and they know more about how to manage your career paths internally. Stick to them like glue, baby.

Lastly, I challenge you to pay it forward—to become a mentor someday, formally or informally, especially if you've never been one. For me, the rewards have been great and the tangible value has paid huge emotional, psychological, spiritual, and yes, even financial dividends.

■ **Mindful Moment**   Most of our professional and personal lives involve informal mentors—those individuals from any and every facet who give us guidance and advice and what we should be doing and how we should go about doing it. Also, many companies offer formal mentoring programs where you're assigned a mentor on joining the ranks, which in turn helps you traverse the inner workings of the business, learn more about different parts of the business and how you fit in, and increase your value to your colleagues and the company.

Join the Professionals

Besides the formal and informal mentoring that can enrich you, there are many professional IT associations out there today. If you're not already a member of one of them, you should consider it. These professional associations can be local, national, or global, and usually have annual membership fees. The returns can be powerful in the form of networking, mentorships, enhancing your career, and increasing your industry knowledge with ongoing education and certifications. Adding associations to your resume and online profile can help you stand out with prospective and current employers as well.

Most of us would agree (I hope) that professional networking and developing relationships are important, so much so that it means investing the time and resources to recoup your return. Joining professional associations can give you a sense of security and trust. Professional associations also put on their own networking events, giving you yet another opportunity to connect with your peers.

Most associations also conduct local or national conferences, giving you the opportunity to participate and learn about the latest and greatest in your career development, learn "best practices" and new ideas, hear from the thought leaders in your field, and meet with your peers. Professional associations give you yet another opportunity to find a mentor who can help you with your career development and management, or for you to become one yourself.

The career resources available in many associations can be a huge boon for you. They usually have job listings online or in print available to members only, as well as a multitude of tips about building a better resume and cover letter or—better yet—online profile, and job search strategies that include interviewing and salary negotiating techniques. These associations can also have subject matter experts (SMEs) who are available to answer your specific career-related questions. These could be in the form of seminars and webinars, or they might offer training or certification classes both in person and online.

Here are 10 professional IT associations for you to consider. By no means is this an exhaustive list, so I encourage you to find others relevant to your part of the profession.

Association for Computing Machinery (ACM)

The ACM is a membership organization for computing professionals, delivering resources that advance computing as a science and a profession, enable professional development, and promote policies and research that benefit society. Membership dues are $99 per year and there are student dues available. Find out more at www.acm.org.

Association of Information Technology Professionals (AITP)

The AITP is, of course, an IT-focused professional association. Its goal is to provide a community network for IT business professionals that includes education programs for advancing technology and business skills, leadership development opportunities, networking, peer mentoring and knowledge sharing, and online resources. Membership dues run approximately $100 to $150 per year for both national and local chapters and there are student rates available. Find out more at https://aitp.site-ym.com.

Association of Software Professionals (ASP)

The ASP is a professional trade association of 1,000 software developers who create and market applications such as desktop and laptop programs, software as a service (SaaS) applications, cloud computing, and smartphone apps. ASP was formed in April 1987 to strengthen the future of try-before-you-buy software as an alternative to conventional retail software. Its members, all of whom subscribe to a code of ethics, are committed to the concept of shareware as a method of marketing. Membership dues are $99 per year and student dues are available. Find out more at https://www.asp-software.org.

Computer Professionals for Social Responsibility (CPSR)

CPSR is a global organization promoting the responsible use of computer technology. Founded in 1981, CPSR educates policymakers and the public on a wide range of issues. CPSR has incubated numerous projects such as Privaterra, the Public Sphere Project, EPIC (the Electronic Privacy Information Center), the 21st Century Project, the Civil Society Project, and the CFP (Computers, Freedom & Privacy) Conference. Originally founded by U.S. computer scientists, CPSR now has members in 26 countries on six continents. Dues are $75 per year and there are student dues available. Find out more at http://cpsr.org.

Institute of Electrical and Electronics Engineers (IEEE) Computer Society

The IEEE Computer Society is for computing professionals about technology information, inspiration, and collaboration. By making the most up-to-date and advanced information in the computing world easily accessible, the IEEE Computer Society is the source that computing professionals trust to provide high-quality, state-of-the-art information on an on-demand basis. Dues are $99 per year and there are student dues available. Find out more at www.computer.org.

National Association of Programmers (NAP)

The NAP is an association dedicated to programmers, developers, consultants, and other professionals and students in the computer industry. Their goal is to provide information and resources to help give members the competitive edge in today's fast-paced, ever-changing computer industry. Dues for certified members are $199 per year and student dues are available. Find out more at www.napusa.org.

Network Professional Association (NPA)

Established 1991, the nonprofit NPA is an organization for network computing professionals. NPA founded the widely acknowledged and the industry's only international Awards for Professionalism, which honor individuals for their outstanding achievements in network computing and meeting the values of professionalism. Dues are $125 per year. Find out more at www.npa.org.

Society for Technical Communication (STC)

The STC is the world's largest and oldest professional association dedicated to the advancement of the field of technical communication. The Society's members span the field of the technical communication profession and reach across every industry and continent, with members in almost 50 countries; membership is continuing to grow rapidly outside of North America and Europe. Dues are $215 per year and there are TC professional dues available. Find out more at www.stc.org.

SVForum

The SVForum is all about innovation, entrepreneurship, and leadership within the Silicon Valley ecosystem of individuals and businesses participating in emerging technologies. SVForum connects annually with more than 12,000 engineers, technologists, and entrepreneurs, at more than 200 events, covering a wide range of topics from emerging technologies to product launch, and beyond. Dues are $145 per year and there are student dues available. Find out more at www.svforum.org.

Women in Technology (WIT)

WIT is a not-for-profit organization with the mission of advancing women in technology—from the classroom to the boardroom— by providing advocacy, leadership development, networking, mentoring, and technology education. With nearly 1,000 members in the Washington, DC, area, WIT strives to meet its vision of being the premier organization empowering women to be architects of change in the technology industry. Dues are $95 per year. Find out more at www.womenintechnology.org.

Mindful Moment   Do you belong to a professional IT association? Joining one can provide powerful returns in the form of networking, mentorships, enhancing your career, and increasing your industry knowledge with ongoing education and certifications. Associations can be local, national, or global, and usually have annual membership fees. Adding these memberships to your resume and online profile can help you stand out with prospective and current employers as well.

12

Zero In on the Company

Be a Tricky Dick

Son, sometimes you couldn't find your ass from a hole in the ground, but I love you.

—Richard E. Grossman (My Dad)

Yep, that's my dad. Pop, as I affectionately called him over the years. I use past tense here because he passed away this summer after a brief but aggressive battle with stage 3 melanoma, and this book is partly dedicated to him; he was one of my biggest mentors, besides being my dad. With his stellar work ethic, Pop taught me much over the years about the world of work, responsibility, flexibility, what it means to be persistent in the face of adversity, and the lifelong value of a smile.

A master of levity, Pop injected humor and silliness into most everything he did. He infectious smile and laughter propagated to many others in his radius, the scar above his lip glinting under light like polished glass, a scar that came from years of repetitive punches to the same place as a child and then as a cop (and yes, he returned most of those in kind and then some). The scar added a richness to his character, like biscuits soaked in honey and butter—you could never get enough.

This all came from a law enforcement veteran of 32 years. Anyone who ever worked with him shared the same sentiment—from the most hardened cops and criminals (who he called his customers), to literal strangers he'd meet on the street, in the store, at the campground, in the post office, and in the doctor's office. Everyone experienced his sunny disposition, his goofy humor, and his viral smile.

He inspired me to do the same—to be silly, to embrace life and all the people in it, to give life and all the people in it a second and third chance, and to laugh in the face of adversity. At the same time, he also inspired me to tackle life, punch it, and pin it to the ground, even if I grew up not finding my ass from a hole in it.

My dad was a mechanic in the Air Force. After serving, he returned to his hometown of Porterville, California, where he became mechanic foreman for the local Chevrolet dealer. This was back in the 1960s, when you could practically listen to a car and diagnose its problem. After that, he went in a completely different direction and became a police officer. That's where he spent the rest of his career, complete with a short stint as a police captain in the South Pacific and then eventually a detective in charge of the forgery and fraud division at the Visalia Police Department (my hometown), from which he happily retired.

He was known as Tricky Dick among his fellow officers because of his supposedly unorthodox Columbo-esque[1] investigation techniques using more "emotional quotient" street smarts and smiles instead of faux bumbling. I remember Pop getting up at the ungodly hour of 4:30 a.m. to go to work every work day and then getting home and working into the night after dinner, with dozens of file folders, police reports, photographs, and piles and piles of paper-based evidence strewn across his desk and on the floor next to the desk.

"Why do you like what you do?" I asked one time.

He shrugged and smiled. "Because I like chasing people across paper."

"Cool. How do you do what you do? That's a lot of paper."

He removed his glasses and rubbed his eyes. "I've got to know as much as I can about each and every one of my customers in order to catch them. I need to know where they work or worked, where they shop or shopped, if they're junkies or not, if they're gamblers or not, what exactly their scams are and to what end. I need to know everyone they know—their family, their friends, their enemies."

Pop had one of the best arrest records in the department. Banks and businesses loved him for the money he saved them and helped them recover. And, Tricky Dick to his core, the more information he had on his "customers," the easier it was to map out the messiness they left behind.

---

[1] *Columbo* was an American detective mystery television series, starring Peter Falk as Columbo, a homicide detective with the Los Angeles Police Department.

Humans are horrible decision makers and we're inherently messy, no matter how smart we think we are. It's like the gambler's fallacy where we'll put one more dollar into the slot machine because this time we're gonna hit it big, even though we know the house wins most of the time. It's the pleasure centers in our brains that we're working on satisfying 24 hours a day, seven days a week, 365 days a year. Emotion trumps logic every single time; we trip and then we fall, but we get back up again to make the magic happen, because like I wrote in the beginning of this book, ain't no one gonna do it for us. The magic only comes with practice.

We're also inherently open and hungry for positive attention, even if we think we're private. That's also true when it comes to investigating your prospective employers, recruiters, and hiring managers. They will be digging up information on you and your "real" experience, and you can do the same on them as well. Even the biggest recluse wants to be liked. Everybody does. Don't look at me that way.

Why the lengthy story of my dad, Tricky Dick? You really need to be just like him if you want to get that job. Follow the job and company "across paper" and get to know them in depth. Jobs are like perps—the more we chase after them blindly with a shotgun, the more elusive they become and the less likely we're going to hit the target. But the more we know about the jobs, the better we understand them and know where to aim and when to shoot. Knowledge is a powerful weapon and gives you the line-of-sight into the jobs and career paths you want. Be prepared when called on.

I miss you, Pop.

Mindful Moment   So you've made it to the final stages of the job search and your tech skills and experience have attracted a company's "hiring" attention. They want to meet with you now. Sweet. It's time to start your due diligence. Yes, the job search can be a full-time job, but now it's time to be a detective and uncover the clues that will help you get the job.

Get to Know Them

You've been doing your research, you've got them in your sights, and now you've got their attention. Maybe it's one company or maybe it's ten (it depends on what you got, where you are, and a little magical timing to tie it all together). Maybe you've been phone screened, maybe you've had a virtual or recorded video interview (Chapter 7), and now you've gotten the email and the call that they want you to come in to interview. You're in the final stages of the job search. A lot of what I've already covered in this book will help you tremendously at this stage. So let's review.

Remember all that rigmarole about building out your online profile (Chapter 8) and then connecting and networking to past and present employers, colleagues, and friends? At this point, you've probably already done that, as well as connecting online with some of the folks in the early screening processes at the companies you want to work at, most likely a recruiter, an HR person, the business owner, the hiring manager, or some combination thereof. My rule of thumb is that if you've met them in some capacity during the job search process, then connect with them online. You'll not only find out more about them and their connections (if they accept), but you never know when you might call on them in the future for opportunities. I didn't say Facebook, I mean professionally like on LinkedIn, or in the membership association you belong to (see Chapter 11).

Wait, do you mean you didn't connect with them? But that part only takes a few seconds. Yes, they have to accept your connection request to be officially connected, but please do that right now. It's kind of the new common courtesy of professional networking today and will give you the ability to connect with them easily, see their networks, and potentially grow your own network while discovering even more opportunities at the same time.

Trust me, the long-term benefits for you are exponential, whether you get the job or not, and especially if you make the time to nurture those relationships over time. These connections on the inside could at some time move on to other opportunities, which could in turn lead to other opportunities for you.

I digress. Get to "know" those who've been screening you to date and understand what similarities you share with them. It's these commonalities that connect us emotionally. Likability is a simple fact of life and even with all the messiness and poor decision making, if you share common interests, then use them to your benefit. If you're both runners, then prepare to talk about running. If you discover they have children, and so do you, then prepare to talk about your children. If they used to work at IBM, and so did you, then prepare to talk about your experience at IBM. If they used to work under Sue, and so did you, then prepare to mention it—but do not trash talk about Sue or anyone else related to Sue when you're actually there talking about Sue. Even if the hiring manager gets messy, do not fall into that trap, no matter how much you might like one another.

By the way, do you know how savvy recruiters know when you're in the throes of a job search? It's not what I would've thought—when we update our profiles with the latest and greatest. That can be part of it, but it's when you're connections spike, meaning when you're adding people to your network. Most of us actually update our profiles after we're hired. I bring it up only because this gets you noticed in a way that could bring about other opportunities that you never imagined. Keep every window open.

Go Outside and Feel the Burn

And then there's the part about going outside, to see the very people who might be hiring you before they hire you, or other friends and confidants who can fill you in—just like your online connections—on the influencers and hiring folk you need to know. Maybe you've been coding until 4 a.m., but get yourself out there and find out more about prospective employers that might want you before you sit down for the final dance.

Duh, right? I know. We're all really busy and that's the beauty of online networks and connections. We don't really have to go outside. We can IM, text, stream, Facebook, LinkedIn, Twitter, and G+ each other until we're blue in the face. We can even still email each other. (Remember when our fearless leaders thought that email would be the demise of business?)

But if you are like me, and I'll bet that's the case, your online connections should fuel the face-to-face fire. You want to feel the burn of each other's presence. Remember, there are physical cues that could be helpful to you when asking about hiring manager X and your contact Y is being too generous. Live face time also trumps live virtual video chat time, as we talked about in Chapter 7. It's also still better than just the online chatter.

That face-to-face fire is what melds relationships, too. You might not end up getting the job, but the time you've invested in research and relationship building is invaluable. The relationships you've taken the time to build online via your professional "social" networks foster real-time gatherings for break-fast, lunch, and dinner, in coffee shops, on golf courses, at fitness centers, at gadgetry stores, at happy hours, at conferences and expos, in airports, in train stations, at bus stops, and in carpools—you name the physical venue and make time to be there.

Maybe you're still hesitant to go outside, but think about the recruiters who are recruiting you. You know, the ones who have spammed you and called you out of the blue with offers of magical powers and golden treasures unimaginable. I know, I know—there are many very good IT recruiters out there, too, and I'm good friends with some of them. My point is that recruiters worth their salt aren't afraid to get out there and find, connect, market, and sell. Granted, their very livelihood is dependent on the very same research and relationship-building skills I'm advocating for you—yes, your very livelihood is dependent on it as well. There are so many parallels between recruiting, marketing, and sales. Get outside.

Did you know that *recruit* comes from the French word *recrute*, which literally means new growth? Those same recruiters who have survived the two downturns we've seen in the past 10 years aren't afraid to find out as much as they can about you and your immediate professional connections. The best of the bunch are highly aggressive and not afraid to employ guerilla tactics in identifying and screening the best IT talent they can find.

And don't forget what I just wrote about in Chapter 11: the benefits of professional association memberships. If you're already in one of those I outlined, or others I didn't, that's another rich resource for you to find out more about the companies interested in you. Remember, professional associations put on their own networking events year round and sponsor numerous other events, as well as giving you ongoing direct access to members for yet another opportunity to connect with your peers and ask them lots of pointed questions.

These are the relationship realms that create new growth and give you the inside scoop. Feel the burn, baby.

Guerrilla Tactics

It always sounds so excitingly aggressive when you use those words, doesn't it? No, I'm not talking about X-raying websites or hacking into databases. What I mean really by guerrilla is to go beyond the usual when researching your prospective employers. Yes, you might glean enough of what you need to know prior to your final interview stages via your online connections and few face-time meetings, but if you want to know more about the company you'll be in the final interviewing stages with, then you'll have to dig a little deeper. And by the way, when you arm yourself with a little more knowledge about the business you might be working for, you better position yourself contextually as it relates to your future role and where it fits into the greater business realm.

Remember in Chapter 9 when I talked about the career sites? Again, take a look at your prospective employer's career page, Facebook corporate page, or any social point of presence. Is there anything on the page beyond job listings that gives you an idea of company culture? Look at the pictures of people on the company website. Do they look like real people who really work for the company and not pretty model stock photos? Are there any video testimonials from real people who work for the company talking about what it's like to work there?

Speaking of videos, if you go to YouTube and search for the employers, you'll probably find of bevy of employment brand videos (or at least a few) and employee testimonials that again, however subjective they most likely are, will give you some more information for your interview arsenal. For the more creative companies, you'll probably find some hilarity as well.

Revisit Glassdoor and Vault. You might have already used those sites to read company reviews, and manager and executive reviews, all posted by current and previous employees. But don't forget that Glassdoor also has interview reviews—people sharing their interview experiences from various companies. Subjective as they are, you might get some potentially valuable insight.

Of course you can simply do a web search for the companies you're interviewing with and scour social media sites for company comments and sidebars. If you're going to work for a well-known brand, say an airline or a health care company, you'll most likely find lots of smack online about these companies. Customer service is the bane of many of them today, because they're still so poor at it, and all things social have given us the platforms from which to spew forth our universal distaste. So who knows what you'll find, but there might be something of value for you to use.

Another place for you to check on the company websites is their resources, news, and press pages. Here's where you can read (and watch and listen to) their latest thought leadership pieces, white papers, articles, infographics, podcasts, videos, presentations, company announcements, product and service launches, new hires, industry trend announcements and much more. (You can also find a lot of these doing web searches and finding such content beyond the company websites. Think SlideShare[2] as well as the other "social" sharing sites we've been reviewing.)

You can also read about the various news entities that are covering the companies online; most companies show that in their "news" pages, and those mentions will also come up in web searches. Public companies will regularly share earnings reports and investment and investor news on their websites. Startups and privates sometimes share investment and investor information online, usually to attract investments, but at least you'll get a sense of who's investing in whom if you're familiar with the venture capital and private equity community. Of course if you follow the stock market, you can check company earnings as often as you want online at sites such as Yahoo! Finance[3] and CNN Money.[4]

Speaking of companies filing to go public, if you're a truly a finance geek, you can check out S-1 filings and addendums to filings online. If you're not familiar, an S-1 is a filing used by public companies to register their securities with the U.S. Securities and Exchange Commission (SEC). The S-1 filing contains the basic business and financial information on companies that want to sell shares and have public investors. Investors can use these filings or "prospectuses" to

---

[2] www.slideshare.net

[3] http://finance.yahoo.com

[4] http://money.cnn.com/data/markets/

evaluate possible investment opportunities prior to a company's initial public offering (IPO). You can use EDGAR,[5] the Electronic Data Gathering, Analysis, and Retrieval system, which performs automated collection, validation, indexing, acceptance, and forwarding of submissions by companies and others who are required by law to file forms with the SEC. How exciting is that. No, really.

Another resource you can use to research companies is Hoovers.[6] Hoovers is a huge database of company, industry, and individual information that includes about 85 million corporations and other entities and 100 million people, covering 900 industries. You can access it for free for basic information, but if you want to dig deeper, you'll have to pay the database piper.

Another similar resource that focuses solely on technology companies is CrunchBase.[7] CrunchBase is a free directory of technology companies, people, and investors that anyone can edit (additions and edits go through an approval process). They tout nearly 100,000 companies, 131,000 people, and 8,000 financial institutions.

Context Is King and Queen

You might have heard over the past decade that content is king. That might have been true at some point for a short time, because knowledge is the currency of the 21st-century economy and valuable content goes a long way. Look at all the content you can consume during your company research: cue the firehose and open wide. Add to that all the conversations you've had with colleagues, insiders, recruiters, hiring managers, and friends who give you a holistically subjective workplace culture overview (which is very important).

But remember, scarce attention and rote memorization of company clutter doesn't necessarily arm you with the presentation skills you'll need to win over your prospective employer.

That's why *context* is king and queen. Synthesizing everything you've learned, visualizing how you'll then fit into the role within the organization, the business value you'll bring to the business today and tomorrow (which we'll talk about in Chapter 14), and how your skills and experience can be best applied to their current IT initiatives and why they'll help drive the productivity, efficiency and the bottom line: that's what matters if you want the right deal, a regular paycheck with growth opportunities.

---

[5] www.sec.gov/edgar.shtml

[6] www.hoovers.com

[7] www.crunchbase.com

Think again about the shotgun analogy. I've been using this in marketing and PR for years—the fact that so many companies load a piece of promotional content that they've spent a lot of time on, only to close their eyes and shoot without thinking through and researching exactly what they wanted to do, why they wanted to do it, and who they wanted to target.

Your window to capture anyone's attention while making a memorable connection is pretty darn small. If you've ever read Malcolm Gladwell's book *Blink,* you know that some of our best decisions are made in 20 seconds (think rapid cognition). Twenty seconds. Damn.

Here are three things to consider with your own personal marketing:

- *Content.* Of course we start with you and your consistent personal brand. You want your whole-brain marketing messages—your skills, experience, and the way you're positioning yourself online and in person—to quickly engage and entice and motivate potential employers intellectually as well as emotionally.

- *Placement.* What's the context of your personal marketing? Are you targeting the right audience with the right pitch? Remember, your short-term and long-term personal marketing efforts are not one size fits all. Going in cold is never easy, which is why everything we've talked about with networking and researching and plenty of prep is key. How you use any other activities to spark interest and conversation definitely needs to be tailored to your employer audience.

- *Structure.* Are you optimizing your personal brand for your prospective employer's experience? Is it easy to access everything about you that could help you get the job? Can they easily have a conversation with you if they want to know more—are you making it easy to contact you? Do your personal pitches have clear calls to action for what you want them to do and why you're so valuable to their organizations?

Think like a contextual content marketer. Really.

Prepare for the final stages and the final interviews (more in Chapter 15) with the new/old three world of work Rs:

- Reach Out (to your networks)

- Research (the companies)

- Reverberate (to make the most of your networked impact)

▨ **Mindful Moment**   Here you are—in the final stages of the job search with a prospective employer. You've been screened and scrubbed, and now they want to meet with you in person. Even if you've done a little preliminary research about the company, it's time to do a little more on your primary contacts, other company insiders, and even deeper info about the company itself via financial reports, press releases, company thought leadership, and more. Synthesize and contextualize why they need you and what you will help the company do.

Where to Go and What to Do

Redemption

13

Cool Tools for Getting a Job

Is There an App for That?

Any sufficiently advanced technology is indistinguishable from magic.

—Arthur C. Clarke

Except that magic kinda peters out when you've been up all night and now it's 6 a.m. and you've got classes that you're already struggling in starting at 7 a.m. You're struggling in those classes for the same reason you are staying up all night—playing video games.

My downfall? The original Legend of Zelda[1] for Nintendo when I was in college. Oh did I love playing that game. Every. Single. Night. Fortunately for me and my grades, that was the last true video game I've played since. Nope, no Xbox, no PlayStation, Farmville, or Bejeweled or any of those other silly Facebook or online games. Bejeweled? C'mon.

Okay, there is the Nintendo Wii below our cable box and the Rock Band console in the hall closet, but still. Oh, and when Angry Birds came out it had a Pavolvian Zelda effect on me, but no matter who tries to tell me it's beneficial to my work in [enter your line of business here], I still say it's only a great way to let all the life stressors of the day roll away into a mind-numbing, highly addictive, slingshot world of vengeful ball-bearing birds and thieving chortling pigs. Please, no integrated work–life lessons here.

But can you imagine playing video games in your job search? Maybe you've had this experience where the game itself is a screening and recruiting tool.

---

[1] http://www.zelda.com

Games That Lead to Jobs

The good and fun news is that there is more redeeming screening workplace value in gaming for you as external new job candidate or internal transitional candidate in the world of work today. That's particularly true when we're talking about making the screening part more fun and "engaging" for you. (I know, there's that buzz word again—how many times have you heard the recruiters and HR use that with you of late?)

As I talked about in Chapter 12, the value of using video game content to screen and recruit you depends on the work being screened for—it's all about the context and what you're being measured for, what skills they're screening you for, and what experience they want to see come to life inside you. Not being recruited to a company as a double-sided-ax-wielding dwarf in the now-ailing Second Life site where you can be whatever you want to be and hold meetings, or each other (kinda like a sexualized Dungeons & Dragons, which I also played back in the Zelda days, by the way). Being recruited to your company because you're testing my skills at coding Javascript, along with having a little fun? Absolutely. Don't you think?

According to the Entertainment Software Association:[2]

---

[2] http://www.theesa.com

- The average game player is 30 years old and has been playing games for 12 years—is that you?

- The average age of the most frequent game purchaser is 35 years old—is that you?

- Forty-seven percent of all game players are women. In fact, women over the age of 18 represent a significantly greater portion of the game-playing population (30 percent) than boys age 17 or younger (18 percent)—is that you?

Wow. I never would've guessed that last one, but it's cool. And as a talent-acquisition and talent-management evangelist, I totally get how gaming helps to screen and assess. In fact, social gaming to screen and recruit savvy IT pros like you has become popular in skills assessments and online testing. Companies are programming in the test-taking "fun factor" that improves your attention and engagement. It also—hopefully—further strengthens the "true" results of the tests.

I can't tell you how to win the games because so many of them present varying creative scenarios to test your core technical skills, your communication skills, your collaborative skills, and much more. The results will always be unique to you, and if the results mean measurement is done correctly and objectively, then you'll get a fair shake if you performed well (under pressure).

What's amazing is that I've watched how naturally my young daughters have taken to our iPods and iPads, launching and playing all the toddler learning games, videos, and interactive stories all on their own. But they are not just playing them—they are working with them and learning. For example, in one of the word-builder games, the application sounds out the word and then the individual letter sounds on the touch from the scattered letters that spell the word. This is pretty simple, yet extremely powerful and, yes, engaging. Imagine yourself playing these adult-skill games—how cool would that be versus the ol' logic problems sometimes presented to you during interviews (see Chapter 15)?

This is what IBM does. And Siemens. And Marriott. And L'Oreal. And the military. And many more companies that are launching entertaining social screening and recruiting games for you to play, and then if you get the job even initially trained and hopefully retained by. The analyst research firm Gartner[3] predicts that by 2014, more than 70 percent of 2,000 global organizations will have at least one "social gaming" application, which can range from recruiting to mastering a skill to improving employee health. How much fun is that for

---

[3] http://www.gartner.com

you all? We've certainly come a long way from hand-to-eye coordination with Pong, haven't we?

Here's my formula (thanks to my lovely daughters):

Career Management Gamification + Engaged Talent Communities
= Highly Qualified External and Internal Applicants and Hires

Because unless they're playin', you may not be stayin'. And soon many will be playing. Have fun. Heck, some of you might even be involved in creating these screening and recruiting video games, giving "gaming the system" a whole new meaning.

Be the Operating System

Let's play video games a little bit longer, shall we? Way back in July 2002, the United States Army launched its America's Army[4] game. It has since become one of the most popular computer games in the world (according to the Army—and other recruiting thought leaders). The Army also then created a multimillion-dollar U.S. Army Experience Center located in Philadelphia where potential recruits explore different army bases and occupations using video games.

According to America's Army website, players must adhere to the Rules of Engagement (ROE) and grow in experience as they take on challenges in teamwork-based, multiplayer, "force versus force operations." Like in the Army, accomplishing missions requires a team effort and adherence to the seven Army Core Values—loyalty, duty, respect, selfless service, honor, integrity, and personal courage. These are integral to being successful in America's Army, which in turn lead to improved sourcing and recruiting into the Army. Screw Call of Duty—the Army's got it goin' on.

Something that might be closer to home for you is IBM's CityOne game.[5] CityOne gives players the opportunity to improve industries such as banking, retail, energy, and water while providing city solutions worldwide in an online game. Players guide industries inside cities through a series of missions. Imagine a Sims-like game where players help green-up the environment by making critical decisions to improve the cities. How? By hitting revenue and profit goals, and increasing customer and citizen satisfaction, all on a limited budget. The key takeaways for IBM and you? Players learn about business process management, service reuse, and cloud and collaborative technologies that keep city organizations and systems more agile. In the same breath, IBM might identify you as a potential job candidate for any of their related divisions,

---

[4] http://www.americasarmy.com

[5] http://www-01.ibm.com/software/solutions/soa/innov8/cityone/index.html

or identify a current employee that should be elsewhere in the organization. Again, that's the purpose of these games: to identify skilled professionals, like you, in a variety of reality-based scenarios that are creative and fun.

Or, there's always *Celebrity Apprentice,*[6] a train wreck for a cause.

Many assessment companies today, in all flavors and sizes and platforms, now offer employers the ability to generate social games on the fly via the Web and mobile devices that quiz, test, and evaluate personal and team-building strengths, cultural fit, emotional intelligence, and a myriad of other hard and soft skills. All in the name of challenging you to challenging fun. Good luck.

■ **Mindful Moment**   Have you ever played a video game in a job search to evaluate your skills and experience? If you haven't yet, you will in the near future. More and more companies are implementing social gaming in their screening and recruiting processes, which makes it more fun and interactive for you. No, not Angry Birds either. I don't care how many HR thought leaders use the game as an analogy for performance management. Egads.

And Then There Are Waiting Rooms from Hell

Or, more precisely, they might be the waiting rooms *for* hell.

Don't look at me—*they* built them—the companies you want to work for. They wooed you in through their career site or the jobs posted elsewhere online, leading to a weak-but-saturated section of their warm and fuzzy employment brand, promising a brave new world of work. They provided overscripted and overproduced employee videos, and sometimes compelling job descriptions that promised competitive pay, flexible benefits, maybe some telecommuting time and open vacation time, and equipment and development allowances. You took the bait, uploaded your resumes or your LinkedIn profile, and then completed the application process.

These waiting rooms are, of course, well-branded with their logo likeness and taglines, and have hanging on the walls the LinkedIn, Facebook, Twitter, G+, GitHub, Stack Overflow, Quora, Focus, and many other social and professional network logos, all lit up like Hamm's beer signs from the 1970s with the rolling images of calmly moving rivers and canoes and tents up on the bank. You felt at home, and at peace, and you really thought you'd get that call.

---

[6] Donald Trump's reality TV show where stars compete in business tasks and win money to donate to their favorite charities.

But then nothing happened, and you grew impatient. Then you got really angry when the nothingness compounded and you finally bailed for supposedly greener pastures (and other online applications elsewhere).

Of course, I've been talking about the proverbial applicant tracking systems (ATS) and other similar CRM databases that have been around since the late 1990s, sucking us in ever since and trapping us forever. Even if you think you know how to game the ATS with keywords, it still doesn't mean you're getting out of the waiting room black hole anytime soon. For both the active and passive among us, at least we'll have automated job notifications, right? How cool is that? Not very.

My point is that much work has gone into the same old mousetrap when it comes to getting you to apply for jobs online from the company career site, a job board, or a social network—only to be sucked into the database and never be heard from again. That's the black hole experience, from where no light shall ever return. You might have heard about this from your recruiter friends, but not many companies do a good job at searching through their own existing applicant databases. Again, this goes to the point about the black hole.

So although ATSs have had more sparkly light-sucking functionality over the years, making them cooler tools for companies, for the rest of us they're just tools. Figuratively speaking, of course.

However, even if you're getting into those companies via the back door from peer or recruiter referrals, most companies are going to want you to go through their hoops; they want to capture you in their databases so they can keep sending you jobs to apply for if you don't get them the first time.

Think about it this way: A big part of the employment journey is the front end, so the front-end research you do, as well as the "candidate experience" of applying for the job, will certainly give you an indication of how much this employer wants you. The crappier the experience, the less likely the hiring process is going to be any better, much less the job itself. The more light shone on the experience, the more likely the companies will start feeling the backlash, publicly, and finally do something about their overall world of work culture.

For the second year in a row, the Candidate Experience Awards[7] has done just this—surveying actual applicants from hundreds of companies, and asking them how their candidate experience was. According to the CandEs, which is their short nickname for the awards, employers have the opportunity to benchmark their candidate experience against that of other companies (which

---

[7] http://www.thecandidateexperienceawards.org

is good for you), and they have the opportunity to participate in at third-party survey of their employment candidates (you) to see what they really think of the company's process.

Thank goodness.

The 2012 awards, announced in October at the 15th annual HR Technology Conference & Expo, had more than 17,000 responses. Mercy. Winners (and companies you should check out for opportunities) included the following:

- Automatic Data Processing, Inc.
- Achievers
- AT&T
- Boston Scientific
- Capital One
- Cliffs Natural Resources
- Deloitte
- Deluxe Corporation
- Hyatt Corporation
- Intuit Inc.
- Mayo Clinic
- Pacific Northwest National Laboratory
- PepsiCo
- Sage North America
- Sapient
- Wall Street Services

Dante's Job Board Purgatorio

So if the company's own job site is a potential waste of time, then what about the ubiquitous job boards?

We've already covered online profiles, professional "social" networking sites, and company research sites that can give you the insight you need on the companies and individuals you hope to be working for and with.

But job boards? Really? Many in my industry have claimed that job boards are dead, just as many have claimed that the resume is dead—both claims being unfounded (even though, as you know, I want the resume to die). Nobody gets a job via a job board any more, right?

According to some of the latest research from Internet recruiting pioneers Gerry Crispin (one of the creators of the Candidate Experience Awards) and Mark Mehler of CareerXroads,[8] over 20 percent of external company hires came from job boards—the more than 16,000 job boards in business today. Compare that to not quite 4 percent of hires coming from social media and 28 percent coming from referrals (which, yes, in turn, can spring from social and many other sources).

So job boards aren't dead, although there hasn't been that much innovation in career seekers for decades. Then what's so cool about job boards? Well, Purgatory's on the way to Paradise. When we went mobile, that is.

Many of us are connecting via smartphones and tablets today—these are the main points of contact that we want to be contacted on. That's not a surprise to most of us. What might be surprising, though, is that according to a 2012 World Bank report,[9] about three quarters of the world's population now has access to a mobile phone and the number of mobile subscriptions in use worldwide, both prepaid and postpaid, has grown to over 6 billion—and nearly 5 billion of those are in developing countries. The same report, titled "Information and Communications for Development 2012: Maximizing Mobile," stated that more than 30 billion mobile applications—what we lovingly call our apps—were downloaded in 2011. Some of you probably developed at least, what, a billion of them?

A much smaller but valuable subset for you are the mobile-friendly versions of job search apps from a variety of job boards and services, making it easier and more convenient to do the following:

- Search for relevant IT jobs.

- SMS or text for relevant IT jobs.

- Set up automated alerts for relevant IT jobs.

- Apply for relevant IT jobs by uploading your resume or submitting your LinkedIn profile (a work in progress via mobile devices and tablets because resumes, cover letters, and related work samples aren't kept on those—unless you're storing in the cloud).

---

[8] http://www.careerxroads.com

[9] http://www.worldbank.org/en/news/2012/07/17/mobile-phone-access-reaches-three-quarters-planets-population

- Be sent application reminders to apply via your laptop or desktop and not your mobile devices.

- Review your application history for relevant IT jobs.

These could be native app downloads for Apple and Android products, or browser-based apps that are configured for mobile rendering via Javascript and HTML that don't require a download (not all are created equal, by the way). The following is a short list of job boards that are IT specific or have a robust IT jobs database—but more important, they have mobile apps for your job search convenience.

Dice[10]

Dice is one of the biggest career sites for technology and engineering professionals today, with more than 80,000 IT jobs to search from and a variety of tech talent communities you can join, absorb relevant content from, leave comments about, and learn more from about everything from cloud computing to Ruby on Rails.

Monster.com[11]

You might have heard of this monster of a job board. Monster.com is a global online employment solution site for people seeking jobs and the employers who need people. It's more of a solution site because it has gone from a "job board" to being a global provider of job-seeker, career management, recruitment, and talent management products and services. And they've got an IT resource talent community called Inside Tech.

CareerBuilder.com[12]

CareerBuilder has been around longer than Monster.com and claims to be the largest online job site in the United States. And yet like Monster, CareerBuilder has had to diversify its products and services to stay viable in the recruitment market, including job seeking, career management, recruitment, and talent management products and services. It has also launched CBmobile Ambassador, a mobile employee referral app that can help you search for jobs, refer jobs to your personal or professional networks, and share job openings via email or text message. One of a gazillion domains that CareerBuilder owns, Sologig is

---

[10] http://www.dice.com

[11] http://www.monster.com

[12] http://www.careerbuilder.com

a site they made their own and relaunched over five years ago. It is really more of an I.T and engineering job portal than a talent community.

Indeed[13]

Talk about another monster of a job search site: Indeed has more than 70 million unique visitors and 1.5 billion job searches per month. Indeed is available in more than 50 countries and 26 languages, covering 94 percent of global GDP.

Simply Hired[14]

Simply Hired is a job site with more than 30 million unique visitors per month (according to its website), and the company provides job seekers free access to more than 8 million job openings from company career sites, newspapers, and job boards. Simply Hired also connects employers and candidates via its pay-for-performance recruiting solution.

LinkUp[15]

LinkUp is cool because it only aggregates jobs from company websites, indexing more than 22,000 company websites and job listings daily. This way, the jobs on LinkUp are technically always fairly current (dependent on the company websites, of course) and shouldn't contain any fake jobs.

Beyond.com[16]

Beyond.com touts itself as a career network that connects job seekers and employers through 70 career channels and 3,000 industry and regional communities, including some that are IT and engineering focused.

You've also got recruitment tech companies that provide other companies with "quality mobile recruitment solutions"—say that five times fast now. Two of the most progressive are JIBE and Jobs2Web. Of course, unless you're applying to companies who use companies like these, you won't experience the fairly seamless flow from mobile touch point to applicant tracking system. Sorry, I can't help you there.

---

[13] http://www.indeed.com

[14] http://www.simplyhired.com

[15] http://www.linkup.com

[16] http://www.beyond.com

But for what it's worth, JIBE does integrate with all of the major ATSs, including Taleo, Kenexa, iCIMS, Jobvite, Peoplesoft, ADP Virtual Edge, and Silkroad—as does Jobs2Web. So if you're applying to companies the traditional way, whether that's via mobile access or your laptop/desktop, depending on the company, you're bound to hit one of the above ATSs.

But Wait, There's More

Hope comes in the form of two sites: GitHub and Stack Overflow. I talked of them a little in Chapter 2 and will expand more here because they're both really the technical community sites de jour these days. Many of you have probably taken a dip in their knowledge-sharing pools.

It's pretty amazing how we can collaborate on software development projects online today. Since its launch in 2008, GitHub has amassed over 2.4 users and over 4.1 million repositories (software development projects) according to its site. "Git" refers to a very fast and efficient distributed version control system for collaborating on software development, and GitHub is just that: a web-based hosting service for software development projects that use the Git revision control system. There are paid plans for those who want to create private repositories and free accounts for open source projects. GitHub creates a technical community where an entire ecosystem of folks from all over the place can share code, develop cool stuff and learn from one another.

In GitHub, you can create your own profile that lets you know what's happening in the community. You'll see an ongoing list of Open Source projects hosted at GitHub. And remember my whole rant about how the resume should die in Chapter 8? Well, GitHub profiles are being shared as the new online technical profile, much like many professionals already do with LinkedIn (although, again, many of you are tired of getting "hit on" by recruiters on any professional social network). GitHub also holds regular "meet-ups" in cities globally, because we all know how important face-time is to solidify the online relationships we've started. Kind of like network dating without the awkward intimacy expectations.

Then there's Stack Overflow: a "question and answer" programming site for programmers. Like you. The site was launched in 2008 by Jeff Atwood and Joel Spolsky, and the name was chosen by the readers of Coding Horror[17], Jeff Atwood's programming blog. Stack Overflow prides itself from being scam-spam free, even though it's completely free (unusual for a site like this to be both). What's cool about this site (if you haven't already experienced it) is

---

[17] http://www.codinghorror.com/blog/

that it's run you and your programming peers. You're free to edit anything and everything inside it like a wiki, sharing your programming insight with many like-minded others, regardless of what programming language or what operating system you use.

I'm a big proponent of true online community, so Stack Overflow makes the grade here. They regularly appoint moderators from within the community, and sometimes they even hold moderator elections if there's enough participation. You can register for free and if you're interested, you can earn "reputation points" or "karma" and "badges" to win cool stuff. Yep, gamification is baked right into the Q&A platform for your participatory pleasure. Lastly, all the user-generated content is licensed under a Creative Commons license.

We're Still Fighting Black Holes

This brings us full circle to the fact that you as job seeker come up short in the end. The companies who are developing cool job search technologies are really building better black hole waiting rooms from hell to trap you in. Maybe I'm being too hard on them, because there are millions hired every year who have traversed the highways and byways of back-end tracking systems to then actually reappear all aglow in the front end and land "plop" in a seat in an office or at home, working.

Then again, the hiring companies are paying the money for these cool tools. You, however, are not. That's the business reality of job search. And two downturns into this new millennium, you're not going to be paying for any direct job-seeking tools beyond career management folks who help you prep your resumes, your cover letters, and your elevator pitch. No, most of the job-seeking tools available to you are free, as they should be, in markets bullish or bearish. Every single recruiting technology I've seen since the rise of the ATS has been about getting to the short list of supposedly qualified candidates quicker, faster, and better, not about getting you to the job quicker, faster, and better. Applicant-to-job matching algorithms have certainly improved, and you can sign up for a myriad of new services, for free, that claim to get you to the right job quicker, and to introduce you to networks of networks of networks—a referral free-for-all.

And that's again why all the company, job, and people research I've written about as well as the networking, networking, networking is so important for you. Hiring is a human endeavor. No amount of cool technology will ever change that, even artificial technology—something I once touted when I worked for Tapestry.Net. Even if you know how to plant the right keywords in your resume, CV, or online profile—and I'm talking about search-optimizing them so the systems sorting and filtering on specific IT skills and experience will bring you up out of the black hole depths—you want to get the call so you can separate yourself from the screening layer.

There is one bright spot I see in the talent tech landscape as of today, though, that's appropriately called Bright.[18] It's still early for the company, but for over a year and a half they conducted one of the largest resume-to-job description studies in history. Their study included more than 2.8 million resumes, 8.6 million job seekers, hundreds of recruiters and HR professionals, and a team of 15 data scientists and engineers. The data from their research was then used to build the Bright Score, which launched in the summer of 2012.

The Bright Score looks at hundreds of features on a resume quickly, allowing them to analyze and score a holistic view of you, the job candidate, in the time it would take a human evaluator to absorb at most a couple of words (hmmm … I've heard that before). They claim to immediately identify the candidates who are fit to move forward in a search, something that could only be matched if a recruiter spent an hour on every single resume (which I know they don't—it's more like 30 seconds per resume). They claim to have calculated a billion Bright Scores with a comparative accuracy of 93 percent when tested against human evaluators.

We'll see. Hiring is still a human endeavor, which complicates things further. And that takes us back to the black hole waiting rooms. There are those who talk about the candidate experience, those who talk with others about the candidate experience, and those who experience the candidate experience.

The latter would be many of us (along with millions of others), although I've done the first two as well. Almost two years ago I had gone through a high-level job search with a well-known firm in the HR B2B marketplace. Considering that they should know better the best practices of recruiting and hiring, I was left with inconsistent acknowledgment and no closure. Even thought I didn't get the job, I was led to believe that there were other opportunities. And then nothing but crickets chirping in the night.

Right after that experience I wrote about how employers owe us, the applicants, at least two things regardless of the position level being applied for:

- Acknowledgment, simply that you've applied and we acknowledge that. Thank you.

- Closure, simply that you are or are not qualified for the position, that you are or are not getting the job, there are or

---

[18] http://www.bright.com

are not other opportunities available, and we acknowledge all these things in a consistent and timely manner. Thank you.

Two things. That's it. I'm sure many of you agree.

But this dysfunction is not really a function of technology. It's a dysfunction of human ineffectiveness and process inefficiency that has remained mostly unchanged for decades when it comes to screening, recruiting, and hiring.

The experience just outlined was an active job search. But what happens when it's a passive person being tapped? That would be me as well (along with millions of others). The past few years I've been "tapped on the shoulder" by a few known HR/recruiting B2B tech brands. Most of them were incompetent communication fests that led to more questions than answers.

And then nothing. Again, crickets chirping in the night. You've just got to be louder than the crickets to be seen and known. Leveraging the job search technology to be found is only the first step. Once you've been found, then it's time to let your skills and experience shine, again leveraging your network and being prepared when you get the call to talk job shop with a prospective employer.

You can help make the candidate experience more fruitful for you.

Employers are working on improving the experience as well, from the very first point of contact to the final interview. If they tap you on the shoulder, just ask them professionally (firmly, but nicely) to please speak in complete sentences and finish their story, hopefully the one that ends with you getting the job.

Thank you. There's an app for that. It's called the human brain.

Mindful Moment   Do you apply for jobs via job boards? Keep in mind that they're not dead. Twenty percent of hires made today still come from job boards. What's made them easier to deal with is the mobile technology permeating every aspect of our lives today. Granted, many of you still go in to the applicant black hole when you apply, but alas, don't give up hope and don't stop leveraging the little hipness you're given. Video games and job boards—that's what you get—so work them as well as you do your networks.

From Best Practice to Business Case

The Blue Ocean Gospel

Don't tell me the moon is shining; show me the glint of light on broken glass.

—Anton Chekhov

They won't call you just because you think you're all that and a bag of tricks. Really, they won't. Even after they've screened your resume, cover letter, online profile, blog, and shared ideas across open-source sites, and even if you've got the IT and business skills they're looking for. If you're not making your business case, you're not getting the job. Being a jack-of-all-trades generalist and a best-practice-touting man or woman about town doesn't hold the same cachet it used to have.

For decades after World War II, employers embraced generalists across a wide variety of roles and industries, even in some IT roles, because they wanted employees who knew a lot of little things. Not that they'd ever need all that widespread-yet-thin knowledge, but if they did, they'd have the upper hand and competitive advantage. Or so they thought.

Knowing a little about a lot of things didn't necessarily solve the business problems at hand, though. The other decades-old issue of executive management keeping the top-down, hierarchical "do what we tell you when we tell you" method in place also no longer solved the day-to-day and long-term business problems. The powers that be didn't have all the answers, and they discovered that their front-line employees across departments and divisions were making the pain of the nonagile business quite known, dramatically affecting revenues and the bottom line. We counted on labor to improve productivity and efficiencies a lot more then, and the headcounts proved that. And headcount moved in both directions, depending on the need: downsize after downsize, then staff up after staff up.

Until this decade, that is. The millions of jobs that were wiped away during the last five years are not coming back like they have in previous downturns. Political economics aside, software now runs the world. You've heard this already many times of late and you live it: Software runs everything from our favorite electronics to our appliances, our cars, our planes, our trains, our power grids, and our enterprises—software runs the world. With these programmed efficiencies and better people-management processes, generalized skills are just not needed like they used to be—the generalist has been coded and automated.

Even with emerging markets like China, India, and South America, those jobs and generalized skills that were once outsourced from here to there, and not being optimized with the same advances our economy has been experiencing, are now experiencing the early stages of the same changes. This means as the level of skill sophistication heightens around the world, the lower-skilled jobs that were outsourced to emerging markets are now being automated there as well, forcing the costs of skilled labor up. And specialized manufacturing is going to where the skilled tech artisans are. This is why you're seeing tech manufacturing jobs grow again in the United States.

You know the ThinkPad, right? You might even have one. Lenovo could surpass HP soon in the global PC market and Lenovo will actually start manufacturing at its new PC line in Guilford County, North Carolina.[1] For those of you who haven't heard, the Google Nexus Q has "Designed and Manufactured in the U.S.A." etched onto its bottom.[2] Are Foxconn's days numbered?[3]

This world is changing really fast, kids; faster than in any time of our previous history on this glorious, and sometimes miserable, world, a world revolving around a still-vibrant star in an ever-expanding dark matter universe.

---

[1] http://www.newsobserver.com/2012/10/01/2383480/lenovo-expanding-in-guilford-county.html#storylink=misearch

[2] http://articles.cnn.com/2012-06-28/tech/tech_mobile_google-nexus-q-usa_1_foxconn-andy-rubin-android?_s=PM:TECH

[3] http://www.nytimes.com/2012/09/25/technology/foxconn-plant-in-china-closed-after-worker-riot.html

▓ **Mindful Moment** Millions of jobs aren't coming back to the United States or Europe. You've heard that enough, I know. But software now runs the world, from anywhere and any time, automating many of the nontechnical tasks globally, leaving most of the IT work to the talented professionals such as yourself. And manufacturing, especially for many electronics and automobiles, will be happening in the United States (again), and already is.

Be a Specialist

We've made some pretty special things over the years, haven't we? The latest tech booms have resulted in software development, social networking, cloud computing, mobile computing, nano-technology, robotics, solar power, power grid engineering, wireless technology, digitized media, inductive charging (also known as "wireless charging") that uses an electromagnetic field to transfer energy between two objects. (That Apple won't embrace yet, which bums me out.)

But I digress. This has all been a good thing for you technology professionals— if you've truly got the specialized skills that are helping to solve real-world problems yesterday, today, and tomorrow. This is why I've been harping on going back to school and upgrading your skills—those skills that are highly marketable today. Now, knowing a lot about a few things that make the greatest impact on the organization you want to work for is where it's at. I'm a big fan of the "blue ocean strategy,[4]" creating new business markets where there were none before, without immediate direct competition and the potential buyer segments as seemingly endless as the sea itself. It might sound like a lofty goal for the individual job seeker, but creating a specialized business case of who we are and who we can serve and new business paradigms we can breed in our wake, makes us more likely to differentiate ourselves in the marketplace. That's better than being lost in yet another ATS.

Whatever the IT role, we're in the age of the highly specialized specialist with nothing but opportunity in front of you all. For those individuals who not only have the skill sets employers want and need today, but also those who position themselves in the best employable light, that helps the organizations you're interested in glean applicable insight to their business problems. That's the big difference between having the right stuff and selling the right stuff; the difference between speaking best practice and making the business case.

The most successful companies today are the ones who hire and apply those business cases—the specialized matrices of leadership at all levels and in all

---

[4] http://www.blueoceanstrategy.com

roles. No, this ain't socialized human capital, just plain ol' capitalism with an evolving free market foundation. That gets smarter and smarter, more productive and efficient.

Mindful Moment   You as a technical professional know that the only way to remain relevant and marketable is to specialize—to know a lot about a focused area of expertise that solves the right business problems. Talking IT best practices is not the same as making the business case of why you should be the one they hire.

Define It Specifically

Earlier this year, a dear friend of mine asked for some resume advice. She's in a career transition and wants to open herself up for a related—but a little bit of a stretch—move. I'm no resume-writing expert, but I do understand the importance of making your business case in keyword-rich storytelling.

She had written "qualification" statements such as these:

- Dedicated and hard-working, with an unmatched drive to produce results.

- Continually recognized for an outstanding work ethic with positions of increasing responsibility.

- Strong communicator with the ability to work independently or in a team environment.

- Proven history of self-motivation and eagerness to take on new responsibilities.

Now, by no means am I making fun of her; she's a very intelligent and sought-after business professional and these are all admirable qualifications. However, they're nonspecific best practices, and although they convey her strengths, they don't really tell me exactly:

- What results she actually produced and how they impacted the business.

- How her work ethic prompted increased responsibility.

- How her independence and collaborative skills impacted the business.

- How her initiative impacted the business.

This got me thinking more and more about the differences between talking best practices and making the business case of why you should be hired. Listen, you might have the hottest skills west of the Mississippi and you could be in the warm embrace of recruiters schmoozing you to steal you away to paradise, but those recruiters might be thinking only about their payday. If they aren't positioning you not only in the best but the right business case light and touting the problems you'll help the organization solve, then you might find your friend the recruiter gone like a ghost.

During my tenure in the magnificent HR/recruiting marketing realm, both on the vendor side and the practitioner side, my colleagues and I spouted best practices over and over again to our "buyers"; that they should just buy "because."

Each of us is a business in practice; we're either a startup (whether new to the job market or exploring a transition) or we're an established business (already have a job and a career path).

We're looking for our "product" to be purchased, to be acquired or invested in (you can choose your own analogy here). We market ourselves with our online profiles (and if you insist, our resumes), with our referrals and references, with our appearance, with our hopefully on-target interview responses.

The general best practice marketing will only go so far, though, unless we convince our potential "buyers" of their short- and long-term return-on-investment (ROI). True, it's more difficult to make the business case when you're a brand new startup with limited, if any, results to date, but that will come with time, and the more you work on the direct experience spin, the quicker indirect generalities will fall away like failed business models.

Being bold and taking risks can come with making the business case as well. In fact, my dear friend is expanding her existing career—by starting her own business soon.

Right on. From the figurative to the literal career path magic. And from general best practice to career business case and you're in ... the door at least. There are no guarantees you'll get the job, but no matter what you do, don't stop making the case.

Some of you might be asking, "What about the gaps in my history? How do I make a business case with that?"

Consider this conversation that I had almost 12 years ago when I worked briefly as an internal sourcer and recruiter for a recruiting software and services company.

"If there are employment gaps or stints shorter than a year, screen 'em out."

"Why?" I asked.

"Because that means there are deficiencies, problems, or they're flaky job jumpers and can't be trusted. We've got clients to service with viable candidates with continuous work, and that means at least one year per job," the client services manager answered.

I frowned. "But, what if our matching software identifies them as viable candidates? Shouldn't we still keep them in the short list until they're screened further?"

"No, screen 'em out."

"But that doesn't make good business sense until they're at least phone screened."

The manager laughed. "Are you serious?"

Yes, I thought. I am. The irony is that in China and India, it's common for professionals to move from one job to another in shorter time spans, leaving one company to then boomerang back at a much higher rate than in the United States.

Mercy—we can be so short-sighted and backward in the United States. Only during the brief dot-com window did we see techies spring from job to job when demand was high, specialized skills came at a premium, and generalists were hired right off the street. (The hiring manager I was speaking with earlier must've missed that memo.)

I thought it was unfortunate then, and I think it is unfortunate now, that we still hold these gaps and job hops against job applicants, especially those who have been out of full-time work for any length of time, even if they've cobbled together part-time or project work just to stay alive. (Remember Chapter 4? The contingent workforce is on the rise.)

Sure hundreds of thousands of jobs have been added in 2012, and IT is hotter than ever in most metro regions, but it's still not a great market considering that hundreds of thousands more have walked away from their job searches.

Maybe there are those of you, like me, who've walked away from full-time jobs and experimented with entrepreneurial endeavors and self-employment and contract work, and might even continue to do so. That results in the riddling of your resumes and online profiles with slight disfigurements that can be quite misleading.

Here's my advice to you job seekers who have any or all of the above in your work history: Tell a story, keep it real, and make your business case.

Mindful Moment   Generalizing your qualifications that you're hard-working, experienced, and a strong team player isn't enough. Unmeasurable generalities won't differentiate you from your competitors, the other folks vying for the same positions. You must be specific in the telling of your story—sharing what results your IT skills and experience produced and how they affected the business.

And Then Sell the Story

I can't help you with backward employers whose HR pros, recruiters, and hiring managers don't look beyond the bullets on the paper, but you can still help yourself in the telling. I've been a writer throughout all previous professional incarnations, and still am, and although I'm learning every day, I understand a little about the mojo of good story.

For starters, do you know that section in your LinkedIn profile titled "Summary"? That's something I already talked about in Chapter 8, but it's worth mentioning again and again. The summary is an opportunity for you to do more than just say I've done blah, blah, and blah, because that's one of the first things folks scan when they're looking at your profile, besides your picture. (And yes, it could be your "summary" atop your resume, if you insist.)

Use the professional "Summary" sections across all your online networks to immediately highlight the following:

- Your career objective(s) and what you love to do.

- How your previous and current experience validates your career objective(s).

- Your results and accomplishments and how they could benefit a future employer, partner, or investor (hey, you never know), even if you're not "in the market."

- Your personal interests and how those round out your world as well as for a future employer, partner, or investor.

I try to update mine regularly, whether I'm looking or not. Write economically but make sure not to be too vague; specificity and the right keywords are critical for you to be found and get read. Use your voice and keep it real.

In addition to the preceding suggestions, the following are for those of you who still craft and send cover letters, which is most likely many of you, because it's our opportunity to truly home in on a specific role, sent along electronically with our resumes, profiles, or some combination thereof. Like the online summary, the following are long-established practices from many of my career management friends:

- Always include a cover letter with your resume or profile; it helps you stand out versus simply "applying" for the position.

- Customize the cover letter to the job you're applying for. Remember all the research you did in Chapter 9? Make sure the hiring manager on the other end gets that you're serious.

- Incorporate the three whys—why you're interested in their organization, why you're interested in the role, and why you're the one to bring the right problem solving to the role and team.

- Keep your cover letter to one page. You'll have the opportunity to share greater details of your work in other contexts via show-and-tell interviews and more.

- Proofread, proofread, proofread—and then have someone else do it. It's not just for spelling and grammar, which much of the English-speaking world is getting worse at, but it's also to ensure you're addressing the right contacts and companies. Nothing kills a job search quicker than addressing the wrong person.

It's really a never-ending story, this job search journey we take, one that you should review and revise regularly at least every few months to ensure you're making your business case. Because no one's going to make it for you.

Mindful Moment   Make the time to fill in any gaps in your job experience and prep your pitch and your story. It's a never-ending story, your job search, and you need to take the time to make the business case and talk ROI turkey. Do it in your online profile and your resume and your cover letters and your interviewing.

Breaking Best Practice Down Further

I've been in marketing a long time, particularly in B2B marketing, where I've helped hundreds of companies make the business case to other companies. Rarely do the companies have only one sole buyer; there are many different buyers and influencers to convince, and it's no easy task when there are one or two holdouts, no matter the number of champions you have inside.

The job hunt is similar to B2B sales. As I've already mentioned, each of us is a business in practice; we're either a startup, or we're an established business. Companies are looking for our "products" to be purchased, acquired, and invested in. It takes time to make your business case—it's a longer term sales cycle for many professionals today—and you've got to educate your "buyers" across multiple touch points over time, including using case studies (your previous accomplishments in the workplace). Then you must wait as they seep into their mindset until "Bam!"

Segue to personal marketing communications and business development. The fact is, the buyers and influencers of your B2B company—Me, Inc.—are busy zooming around the world of work and their lives and rarely stop to give you a moment's notice.

Marketing yourself is about creating and sharing valuable shiny objects that get your "buyers" to slow down and stop long enough at the intersection to have a "live," engaging conversation about your business case, not necessarily to shock them abruptly into stopping, although you want them to stop nonetheless.

Now, how many conversations does it take to make the business case and close a deal? Mr. Wizard I'm not. (Although that would be an interesting case study if I were.)

Whatever the case, I'm not suggesting that you do a SWOT analysis,[5] and spend an inordinate amount of time developing your personal brand and crafting your messages and pitches—the job search can be painful and tedious enough already, exposing you to social situations you might always struggle with. However, I do recommend you take the time to do the following:

- Create a succinct, one-sentence marketing message of who you are (even if it's a little jam-packed): I'm a human resource and recruiting B2B software and services marketing strategist, business development and sales professional, evangelist, entrepreneur, analyst, advisor, manager, and writer. (That's me, by the way, for those of you keeping score at home.) This is something you can use in your primary online profile, your other professional and personal profiles, as a headline to your

---

[5] A SWOT analysis is a strategic planning method used to evaluate the Strengths, Weaknesses/Limitations, Opportunities, and Threats involved in a project or in a business venture.

personal blog, in your cover letters—basically anywhere you're pitching yourself and you want to leverage the proverbial yet consistent soundbyte: I am me. Hire me.

- Showcase your accomplishments with real-time results. Making the business case means highlighting how you've helped improve the previous organizations you've worked for. Faster time to market, increased revenues by X, reduced system downtime by Y: whatever the specifics are, tell them in a tight-knit story with the payoff being the results. Show them in fact, in the written word, in audio or video formats, the stories of your professional exploits by using your profiles or your blogs. Heck, bring them in person to show at your interview (laptop, tablet, flash drive). Just make sure your stories are true, consistent, and validated by your references. Profile yourself in a way that makes you unique, a blue ocean market unto itself; the employer who takes a dip into your warm water will swim unfatigued forever.

- Speaking of those ... again. Like the vetted case studies businesses use for marketing purposes, the career path accomplishments you craft in easily delivered stories and varied formats must be verifiable. Make sure you have your references and referrals at the ready to validate it all. Really. As I revealed in Chapter 6, people make things up all the time to further their careers, and no sooner than that misinformation is revealed, your career aspirations at that particular employer are most likely dead in the now bloody Red Sea, lost among the chum of your fellow competitors bleeding out their professional lies. You will need others to validate your business case, so make sure there won't be any skeletons in your accomplishment closet.

Like I said, move from best practice to business case and you're in. At least in for the final interview. That's what we'll talk about next.

■ **Mindful Moment**   Highlighting your previous accomplishments in consistent detail is critical to your job search. Think like a B2B marketer. Knowing that your message will take time to seep into the mindset of your buyer, the hiring manager and employer, the influencers like management and HR and possible colleagues, besides the referral champions you might have inside. Create a one-sentence marketing message, showcase your ROI in various mediums, and make sure your references will validate them.

Interviewing, Part 2

Winning the Hearts and Minds with Face Time

When you go in for a job interview, I think a good thing to ask is if they ever press charges.

—Jack Handy

Good God, how I miss "Deep Thoughts by Jack Handy," from *Saturday Night Live*.[1] Anybody remember those?

I'll bet the above quote is funny to many of you, while at the same time revealing the wonderfully painful experience known as the in-person job interview. The one where your mouth is dry, your forehead and hands are slick with sweat, and you say and do quite inappropriate things.

And the interviewee hasn't even entered the room yet. (Rim shot, please.)

Years and years (and years) ago, when I worked for San Jose State University, I was out to lunch with my boss one day. While this wasn't an interview for a new position per se, it was an informal interview for a promotion within the program in which I worked. He had asked the week before if I wanted to go to a well-known Japanese restaurant in the heart of San Jose's Japan Town. I joked that I didn't eat sushi (at the time, anyway), and he half-smiled and told me that there was more to Japanese food than sushi.

What I didn't tell him is that I had never eaten at a Japanese restaurant, so I really had no context other that what I had seen in movies and on TV, and from my friends who ate sushi.

---

[1] http://www.deepthoughtsbyjackhandey.com.

So there we were, at first keeping it casual and talking about life and college, of which I was still in at the time, when our food order came. I had ordered a bento box with tempura shrimp and vegetables, and he ordered sushi, of course.

We moved the conversation along to the business at hand, with him asking me pointed questions about why I wanted the promotion. He asked, "How are you going to balance the role with your classes?"

Before I answered, which was my first mistake, I stared curiously at the dollop of green paste nestled in the far corner of my bento box, which was my second mistake. He noticed and threw out another question. "You've had wasabi before, right?"

Now, what do you think I answered? C'mon. I had never been to a Japanese restaurant before, so why would I?

"Absolutely," I said.

And he just sat there and watched while I took a spoonful of wasabi and plopped it into my mouth, as if this were exactly how you were supposed to eat it. He burst into laughter, and had to cover his mouth from projecting ice water all over the table.

I chewed and swallowed, and within 2 seconds, every taste bud in my mouth imploded and every blood vessel in my nose exploded. Rivers of tears flowed freely down my face. I couldn't breathe.

"Are you all right? I thought you said you'd eaten it before," he blurted between weighty guffaws.

I must have drank 15 glasses of ice water; our waiter just left two pitchers on our table. My boss kept laughing and I stopped eating, and we never got beyond the wasabi incident.

And, no, I didn't get the promotion, but that's not the point. (My boss was forced from his position a week later and everything changed in our department. Isn't that the way it always is?)

Of course, the moral of this story, as it is with many similar stories, including incidents you may have experienced in interview situations, is that you should not try to be something you're not. I don't care how great an actor you are, or how much a smarty pants, do not try to be something you're not. Doing so will bite you in the ass; and at this stage in your job search, just getting face time with your potential employer means that you want nothing to bite you in the ass except for, maybe, the uncomfortable seat you are invited to sit in.

▓ **Mindful Moment** Have you screwed up during an interview? Said something stupid? Did something stupid? Put both feet in your mouth while trying to explain how you singlehandly coded the entire Facebook platform, but then got shafted when it came to kudos? C'mon. Don't be a doofus. Keep it real.

Get to Know Me

The interviewing dos and don'ts have been shared since the beginning of modern workplace time, all of them decades in the making. As I pointed out in Chapter 7, more and more companies are using a mix of recorded and live virtual interviews, as well as in-person interviews—which doesn't necessarily complicate things, at least for those who are comfortable on webcams on both sides of the hiring equation. But it does indicate that our Internet connections have gotten bigger, better, and faster; our technology has gotten smaller, and is integrated into our lives much more cohesively. Combined, these make it easier for companies hiring teams dispersed around the globe or down the street to interview viable candidates without involving travel, traffic, and scheduling madness. If you've ever done business around the globe, as I'm doing now, you know what I mean. Who needs sleep anyway?

But, of course, there's still a place for the live, in-person interview. Particularly for engineering teams. The startup culture prides itself on having its early teams, which usually are made up of in-house engineers. This helps to solidify product development as well as cultural cohesion. Can you still get that job virtually? I know a lot of folks in the HR/recruiting space who would say yes, and I feel that way too, especially those of us who've been working more remotely than not for years.

But the process of in-person interviewing to hire local isn't unique to the Valley startup culture. Many enterprises prefer to have their IT teams onsite, working together around the globe. It was only about five years ago when HP's experiment of allowing their IT folks to work remotely was dismantled, and everyone was pulled inside again. Sure, there's something to being close to the systems and servers, without issues of layered firewall remote access. Companies working on locked-down military and other sensitive and secretive government contracts have no choice in that regard. That's why employers relocate the brainpower they need, and why in-person interviews for the short list in certain technical, managerial, and CTO positions will always be used.

Then again, engineering teams working together globally are virtually connected all over the world, though they may be hired locally. No matter where you end up working, you'll more than likely still have an in-person interview with your future boss and team. Remember, whether you'll be working down the street or around the world, hiring always has been and always will be a human endeavor. We prefer live, face-to-face meetings to live streaming whenever possible—usually in one-on-one interviews, group interviews, and relaxed social settings—to ensure a cultural fit.

I Can't Say It Enough—You're Not That Cool

So, after Tapestry.Net went belly up in 2001, and I did some consulting for about a year, I started to apply locally for product marketing positions at technology companies. One of those applications was for a marketing position at the Santa Cruz division of a tech company specializing in defense, homeland security, and other government markets worldwide. Back then, just as most interview experts continue to tell you, you have to prepare for your interview. And like then, the recommendations still don't go further than to do some cursory research and reading, and to reread the company's "About Us" pages.

That's not enough.

In the tech world, none of us has charisma needed to compensate for a general lack of knowledge about the company you want to work for. IT pros need even more than general knowledge. Anyone applying at a technology company, or applying for a technology position in any type of industry, needs a deep dive. Hiring managers worth their salt know that you're not going to understand the r business underpinnings of the company, but you'd better know more than what's in the "About Us" message.

That wasn't my problem; the company's information was quite clear. I just didn't prepare enough. Period. I gave the position description and the "About Us" a cursory read, and I went into the interview thinking I'd be all right. They eviscerated me—the entire interview team, which included four individuals, all of whom I had known would be in the room. One question at a time. I'm surprised I wasn't drenched in sweat by the end of the interview. It was horrible, and when I left, I tried to convince myself that I had a chance in hell.

Which I didn't. And I was never called by the VP of marketing again.

Winging it isn't the best interview strategy if you're really interested in the job and in working for the company. This is why I've emphasized that you do your due diligence and research the company, the position, and the players prior to even getting the callback for an interview. The employers are doing their research on you—every little bit they can.

Remember, it's also not just about what you know as you go into the interview; it's also about the *context* of what you know. Meaning, how are you going to take all your skills, expertise, and knowledge and apply them in the role? How are you going to help move the business dials in the right direction? Chapter 14 was all about making your business case and projecting your positive return for the company if they hire you. That is what's going to elevate you above your competition.

And lastly, if you know who's going to be in the room, learn a little bit about each of them beforehand. Connecting personally with the interviewers can make all the difference in the final selection process, especially if you've already made the skill-and-expertise grade. Employers want to hire the best talent, sure, but we also like to work with those we like.

So be likeable and be prepared.

Good God. Shut Up.

Do let them talk some. Really. Actually, more than just some. Nothing kills an interview faster than a "rambler." That was another interview problem I had: trying to compensate for not being prepared and thinking that "charismatic rambling" would suffice. Some of it did help me connect with a few of the interviewers, but that wasn't enough. I could tell halfway through the interview that I was talking way too much—but sadly, I didn't shut up. Blah. Blah. Blah.

Most interview experts agree that you should answer the questions fully, yet succinctly—putting your responses in the context of how you're going to solve problems and help the company. Conversely, don't answer in short bursts of nervous word strings, meaning that you shouldn't answer with a simple yes or no—or yes or no with a few qualifying words on the end. Those answers make it difficult for your interviewers to get to know you and to judge if you're the right person for the position.

Prior to your interviews practice listening to questions and focusing on responding concisely, going off on as few tangents as possible. You have no control over how interviewers approach the question asking; they could be ramblers themselves or stunted talkers (not much editorializing beyond the question).

And, good God, *listen*. I can't emphasize that enough. No matter how nervous you are or how much is on the line. Listening is the most important part of a quality reciprocal communication. You may glean something that will help you seal the deal, whether you have more interview rounds to go or not. So, bring a note pad and take notes. The old-fashioned way. Actually, write in long-hand or some short-hand that you can read. But write.

Some of you technophiles may be asking yourself: "Hey, why can't I use my laptop or tablet? I used them in college to take notes. What's the big dif?" Kids, if you're writing down your notes, you're much less likely to get distracted by your email or your social networks, or an instant message that comes in. And your future employer can see that you're paying attention and writing, not distracted. However, there may be instances when you're talking code shop with your interviewers and it's encouraged that you have your laptop out to compare notes. You'll know when it's appropriate and when it's not.

Listening is critical in the moment *before* you answer any question. You want to make sure you understand what is being asked and why. So do not be shy if you don't understand the question or the context. Getting clarification conveys the impression that you're listening and that you're in the moment, that you want the job. You can't do much about a poor interviewer (which you will get, and probably have had, including many horror stories), but you can push that interviewer to be clearer. (I know, what the hell is it with: "If you were a line of code on server in the cloud, which one would you be?")

And Don't Forget to Relax

If you're plagued with nervousness during any interview situation, try to focus on the questions, not the interviewers' personalities. They are asking you questions that *will help you get the job*—depending on your answers. The better prepared you are about the job, your relevant skills and expertise, your business case, the company, the hiring manager (if you know ahead of time), others who might be on the interview team, the better. In my late teens and early 20s, I used to suffer from severe panic attacks. If you've ever experienced them, you know that even 30 seconds of a panic attack feels like a frickin' lifetime. What helped me long term was relaxation techniques that slowed my heart rate, lowered my blood pressure, relaxed my breathing rate, increased the blood flow to my major muscles, and heightened my concentration, among other benefits.

Some relaxation techniques include:

Visualization. This was one of the first techniques I learned to help me relax. What you do is create images and a story in your head that takes you on a peaceful visual journey to a relaxing place or situation. Visualization can include using as many senses as you can to take the journey as real as you can. Years before I lived by the ocean, I imagined relaxing at the ocean and, mercy me, did that help.

Progressive muscle relaxation. This technique is all about focusing in on a specific muscle group, tensing it and then relaxing it again. Usually, you start at your toes and work your way all the way up to the top of your head. Focus on slowly tensing and then relaxing each muscle group. It helps you become more aware of physical sensations and mindful of being in the moment. Sorry to get all Zen on you, but this works.

Lastly, and this should go without saying, especially if you are a nervous type, when you're in the interview room, do not check your cellphone, your email, your texts, or Foursquare or Facebook. Do not eat or drink (unless otherwise sanctioned by the interviewers). Do not do anything but the interview.

Again with Just the Facts, Jack

This goes without saying as well, but needs a reminder: don't make stuff up. Ever. If you don't know the answer, don't invent it. Tell them you don't know the answer. Don't make shit up.

And make sure you can answer any questions about what you've used to market yourself—your skills, experience, knowledge, hobbies, and so on. This is why it's important to be consistent across your social and professional online presence.

You might be asked to work through some technical problems in real time, putting your expertise to the test. Scenario-based interviewing happens quite frequenting, and may even include skills assessments and tests while you're in the office. Maybe you'll be asked to do some coding or to triage a network system problem. Who knows? Whatever it is, you better be prepared to put the money you want where your mouth is.

More than likely, you will be tested during the interview or in ensuing interviews (if there are multiple events). Stick to what you know, and don't try to fudge what you don't, especially if you're given a whiteboard test and asked to solve a programming, engineering, networking problem—especially if it's live, in front of God and everyone. Or, it may be a simulation test, in which they sit you down in a room and in front of a terminal and give you a business scenario they want you to try to solve. This test is not so much about whether or not you solve the problem but, rather, about how attempt to solve it—the paths you take, the resources you use, the questions you ask, and so on.

What About Gaps?

If you've got gaps in your professional history and you're asked about them during the interview—which, if your interviewers are any good, they will—don't evade the question nor say you didn't do anything in those gaps. We've all got our stories, and there are reasons those gaps exist. During the Hirewire volunteer sessions I've mentioned earlier in this book, that's a question that comes up each time, especially for those reentering the workforce after a personal hiatus and those who have been out of work longer than six months.

So put your story together prior to the interview. Be able to look them in the eyes and tell them you were taking care of ailing parents, or sick children, or your own sick and/or injured self; or that you were laid off and have been looking for work ever since, and you've had X number of interviews to date and Y number of offers (if true, of course). Whatever the story, be prepared to manage the gaps and all else in between.

Stand up Straight and Look Me in the Eyes

Nonverbal communication can make or break your interview. Think of how disappointing it is if, when you're welcomed into the office, you don't shake the interviewer's hand. Cultural considerations aside (I'm primarily talking about in the West), in the United States, hand-shaking is a business social norm that has not gone out of style—as far as I'm concerned. This goes for both men and women. Be the one who reaches out first.

What Are You Wearing?

My long-time rule of thumb is this: when in doubt, dress traditional business nice. That's it. That means a suit or sports coat and nice slacks, and a tie if you're a man, and business dress or pants suit if you're a woman. If you haven't asked your network ahead of time, the recruiter, the hiring manager, or anyone inside the company where you're going to interview, and you're not sure what to wear, then default to business nice.

Regional differences do make a big difference, though. If any of you have lived and worked in the Bay Area and Silicon Valley, you know that culturally this area has had a long-time digression from traditional business wear—at least in the startup subculture and the long-time tech companies. I've been in meetings and even interviews with folks wearing a decent buttoned shirt, even a nice polo-type shirt, jeans, and even tennis shoes (not me, but everything else); these have been the dress du jour for men, and casual pants and blouses have been for women.

But not ratty T-shirts that say, "My other phone is not a Nokia." Or tube tops or cut-off jeans or ripped jeans with gaping holes or tank tops or Elmo pajama pants (which I have, a gift from my girls), or anything else you would only feel comfortable wearing at home while eating nachos and playing video games or watching rom-coms.

But as you move outward from the Valley and pure California tech plays, the rest of the United States—and even the world—gets a little more formal with the business dress codes. Even if ties aren't required for men (unless it's crazy Hawaiian shirt and hat day—I have no idea what that means), jeans are probably frowned upon. Sports coats, however, are not. Plus, if you're interviewing for any IT management or executive role, you most likely will be dressing traditional business nice.

Another thing about interview clothing: wear clothes that are comfortable and that will breathe. Remember, interviews can be stressful events, and when the heat's on and you're pummeled with questions (that you prepared for, of course), you want to stay cool. So don't wear the wool sweater vest or the silk shirt under your sports coat. Cotton breathes; polyester not so much. And when it's cold in the office, which is possible depending on where you live and time of the year, don't wear clothes that you might visibly shiver in. If you don't have the right clothes that'll keep you comfortable during the interviews, then spend a little money. This investment will go a long way toward your marketability.

And don't forget that how you carry yourself can make a big difference in how you're perceived. Try not to slump your shoulders with your head down staring at the carpet as if you're perpetually looking for an escape. Do your best to stand up straight and act comfortable and that you're meant to be there. Remain calm, and confident throughout. Focus on the task at hand—answering the questions in a way that positions you as the best candidate. Make eye contact with everyone you meet, from the receptionist to the interviewers to the possible future colleagues. Now, I mean natural, confident eye contact. Don't be a freak and make googly eyes at anyone or stare like a stalker on steroids. Just make natural eye contact with people, and when acknowledging questions or comments.

Squash the Smack Talk and The Potty Mouth

Listen, if you're interviewing for a job for which you and the interviewer have mutual contacts—that either (a) you've both worked with or for, (b) are also interviewing for the position, or (c) are just people you know in the industry you're in—do not talk smack, no matter how much you might be goaded by the interviewer. Do not do it. Ever. There are no do-overs.

What constitutes smack? Badmouthing your former boss or company, or sharing less-than-flattering gossip about former colleagues. Listen, I worked with a few proverbial "dicks" and "bitches" over the years, but I learned early on what can happen if you vent to the wrong people. It'll take only one person to share what you shared to come back around and bite you right on the ass.

You've got to keep a lid on that trash talk because it can be a karmic backslap, no matter how much you might trust your interviewer. If you really feel you say these things without repercussion, then do so on your own time, when you're out for drinks with the hiring folk. But even then, I wouldn't.

"It's a small world after all," and, you really need to check yourself, especially if there are any existing business relationships that could be beneficial to you that you didn't uncover in your interview prep. Stay focused on the task at hand, which is to position yourself in the best light possible, making the business case and convincing them you're right for the job.

And I don't care how hip and fresh the company is that you're interviewing with—skip the "F" bombs and other less fresh language. Cursing doesn't portray you as the fine communicator you think you are; it can actually ex-communicate you from the personable connections you're trying to make with interviewers. Let the hiring manager curse like a trucker (no offense to truckers). Keep it clean, and talk hip and fresh tech shop.

Twisted Logic

Everything's been pretty tame up until this point. Now you must also be prepared for the technical testing and the logic games during the interview.

Wait, what?!?

Yes, many of you have already experienced it. After the initial "paper" screening and phone screening, maybe some gaming to test your problem-solving skills, and then a programming or networking or some kind of preliminary IT testing, you get called in for the interview. There's always more fun to be had during live interviews, such as real-time logic tests, coding and other related technical tasks on whiteboards or computers, group interviewing, in-person simulations, and more.

Yeah, you knew it wasn't going to be just straight questions about your skills and experience, right? They've got to know you can do the work, which is why you'll be pushed even harder when you're there in the office (remember your visualization exercises, please).

Take the logic tests as an example. Many tech companies are known for their ability to test your logic, to test your ability to work "out loud." Google has been one of the most written about, as have Apple and Facebook and many other technology companies. But any firm, whether traditional tech or other industry hiring IT pros, may draw on technically challenging logic questions to test your skill in fending off—or employing—Jedi mind tricks during the interview.

For example, have you heard of this one? *"What are dangling pointers?"*

Don't look at me. I had no idea. Do you know?

What I learned is that a dangling pointer is a pointer to storage that is no longer allocated, meaning no longer available. But, they are still nasty bugs that creep up much later and can crash a program way beyond the time they were created. They're more like small inputs that are much more likely to fail on bigger, more complex inputs, making them difficult to locate. Engineers must know something about these dangling pointers because they can fry the most complex parts of a service.

And how many light bulbs does it take to answer a logic question? Too many. But let's say I have 100 numbered light bulbs lined up in a row, and then I switched off every other light bulb so that all the even-numbered light bulbs are now turned off. And then I switched on every third light bulb so that any light bulb that was off is now turned back on, and any light bulb that was already on is now turned off.

Are you following? I'm not. But let's keep going. Then I do the same thing for every fourth bulb, and then every fifth, and so on. How many light bulbs are turned on after 100 passes?

Are you frickin' kidding me? Not even the hint helped me. The answer (of course) is just ten bulbs, all of which are perfect squares.

Wait, what?!?

The trick is to review how many light bulbs in the row have an odd number of factors—meaning that the first bulb has an odd number of factors and the second has an even number of factors, and the fourth has an odd number of factors. This means (supposedly) that one and four will remain lit. The ninth bulb will also have an odd number of factors, so it will remain lit.

I do not understand.

So the deal is that all the lights that are going to be on are perfect squares because they have an odd number of factors: one, four, nine, sixteen.

Right? Are you following?

So, after 100 passes, you can go up to 10 times 10, or 10 squared. That means you'll have ten perfect squares: 1, 2, 3, 4, 5, 6, 7, 8, 9, and 10. According to the solution I read, these correspond to the 1st, 4th, 9th, 16th, 25th, 36th, 49th, 64th, 81st and 100th bulb, which will all remain on. And that means there will be ten total light bulbs that stay on.

I'm so completely lost. Please help me.

Hey, the good news is that, after all that brain work, it's pizza and beer. If you're really in the final running, the hiring manager and other team members may want to take you out to lunch, for coffee, or pizza and beer—somewhere outside of the office in an open social setting to see how you mesh with everyone else. I can't help you with the cultural fit, but just be yourself. They know and you'll know pretty quick.

■ **Mindful Moment**   Interviewing isn't rocket science, so let's review. Do your research. Be prepared. Don't blather. Listen, take notes, and answer their questions. Stick to what you know, back it up, and don't bullshit. Exude confidence; shake hands and look them in the eyes. Please dress appropriately for the interview. Don't talk smack and make no "F" bombs, please. Plus, be prepared to be tested further on a computer or a whiteboard, to be interviewed by more than just the hiring manager, and to be given logic tests and brain twisters to see where your head's at. Good luck.

Always Follow Up

Once the interview is over and you've thanked the interviewers, looked them in the eyes, and shook their hands, it's time to go home. And wait.

But that doesn't mean you just sit and wait, and don't do anything else. You should always follow up with those you have interviewed with and those who are making the hiring decisions. Send them a thank-you note telling them again, briefly, how interested you are in the job and why you think you're the most qualified applicant. And tell them you look forward to hearing from them.

And then wait some more.

And then when you get that offer, make sure you know how to talk turkey. Or negotiate for them.

A Word about Salary

As I wrote in Chapter 4, second to receiving or giving performance feedback (which you haven't done yet because you haven't got the job yet), or getting the new job (which you're about to between here and Chapter 16), negotiating your pay is the most uncomfortable thing to do in the world of work. Ever.

But it's not for everyone. Much of what I wrote in Chapter 4 about negotiating pay for contract work is applicable for permanent positions as well. Remember those two things I've learned?

- Most employers are looking to pay you the least amount possible.

- Most employers want to increase the scope of the work while continuing to pay you the least amount possible.

Such is life and many of you I'm sure have experienced it. There are those of you who look your prospective employers right in the eye and say, "I want $XXX,000 per year because of Y and Z, and not a penny less."

And in response, there are those employers who look you right in the eye and say back, "Well, the position wasn't budgeted for $XXX,000 per year, so I'll throw in more days off, and some stock options, because of your excellent y and z, but not a penny more."

Damn.

Then again, remember there are the rest of us who shoot either way too high or aim way too low. And today's economy it makes it even more difficult with companies increasing base IT salaries modestly at best—or skyrocketing some salaries in regions like Silicon Valley for the best of you.

So to review one more time, think and act like a seasoned marketing and sales professional. Do your research. Understand the scope of the job and the potential pay scale relative to where it's located, and you can do that easily with various free salary sites like Glassdoor.com, Salary.com, and Payscale. Document your professional accomplishments from your latest and greatest roles. You've got to make the business case as to how your past experience and/or current position success has impacted the business—or will impact it—and why the company should invest in you further. And lastly, make sure you build in a little negotiating wiggle room. Remember, if you shoot too high, you'll insult and amuse the employer and the negotiation may be short-lived. But if you aim too low, then you've wiped out your margin and any chance of going back up. It's more sales art than science.

Mindful Moment   Negotiating salary is a painful affair for most professionals. How comfortable are you? If you are comfortable then you play the game like a seasoned marketing and sales pro like I referenced in Chapter 4—you do your research, make your business case, and you build in wiggle room to negotiate downstream, because upstream ain't happening.

The Onboarding Battle and Beyond

Predator or Alien vs. You

The best way to appreciate your job is to imagine yourself without one.

—Oscar Wilde

Right on. You got the job. Can you believe it? Aren't you excited and relieved? After all that stressful soul-sucking and heart-wrenching—and sometimes enlightening and elevating—research, networking, screening, testing, simulating, interviewing, twisted logic, whiteboarding, pitching, proving, and negotiating yourself to the your now-new employer, you're ready to kick some IT ass.

But wait—you've got to onboard and acclimate first, deal with a stress of another kind, to prove yourself day after day after day to other humans you'll be working with. It's not like you're going in cold, though. You should have a little jump on the matter, since you more than likely met the primary day-to-day players you'll be working for, reporting to, and collaborating with. You know, those wonderfully pesky, messy, meddling human beings.

And here we go. I've said it before and I'll say it again—if it weren't for those pesky, messy, meddling humans, the world of work would actually work flawlessly. We'd work together happily and collaboratively, without deceit, harassment, or discrimination. We'd all be accountable and personally responsible and have each other's backs; we'd have reciprocal respect with our leaders, and reality TV would not be a reality.

We can dream, can't we? I mean, you've been hired and now it's time to be onboarded and get the employee handbook thrown at you. If you're lucky enough to get one thrown at you. Just as I've written earlier, you have to own your career management and development when you're job-searching. But you've got to own it on the job as well, no matter how accountable your colleagues and bosses are.

The Formal Yet Messy Process

Consider this: In 2011, more than 40 companies paid out more than $60 million in settlements or unfavorable court judgments after the EEOC brought systemic discrimination cases.[1] There are those, of course, who say that this

---

[1] www.goerie.com/article/20120819/BUSINESS05/308199983/Workplace-bias-under-fire.

kind of law enforcement hampers business growth with burdensome regulations and policies.

Right. Let's not forget the real reality TV of a group of really smart people who wiped billions of financial assets off the face of the earth only a few years ago. Nor maybe that idiot you used to work for who, to again quote my dad, "Couldn't find his ass from a hole in the ground." My point is that accountability isn't baked into our DNA, but basic survival is. Unfortunately, we'll do everything we can to fire the pleasure centers in our brains. Screw the pain, baby. Nobody wants that. This is why, as so much neuroscience research of late shows us, good people make really crappy decisions.

Like one of your new co-workers hitting on you because you've been so friendly and it feels right for him to do it. Or another employee leaving racist notes in your locker because she feels you've been getting preferential treatment, and it makes her feel good to do it.

This is why many employers, especially large enterprises, have formal onboarding processes. This is why new employees are assessed and employers put you through background screens. This is why they're supposed to throw the employee handbook at you. This is why we have frickin' rules and regulations. This is why we have policies on use of social media. This is why we have sexual harassment and discrimination seminars and workshops, and why we have acknowledgment forms to sign (and that really don't help anyway, but it feels good to do it).

I really wish it didn't have to be this way, that companies big and small could onboard their new employees more freely and effectively, applying agile development techniques, buddy and mentor programs, business cross-training and immediate immersion in the workplace culture so as to promote connection, communication, collaboration, and business success—some of the feel-good stuff I've spouted in the pages of this book.

It's necessary to have formal onboarding processes in place because of the very issues I've mentioned above. Most of us don't have to worry about these situations; the harassment forms we sign off to acknowledge we've read them are really for the next guy or girl, not you or me. But the compliance side of getting a new job isn't what's going to *keep* you in the new job—it's just going to keep you and your employer from potentially messy litigation.

It's the necessary evil that hasn't changed lives for the better. And what's also part of the problem, which has led so many people to be "primed and ready" to look for new employment sooner rather than later, is an onboarding compliance-focused process that fosters faulty employee engagement. Too many new hires are parachuted into their company jungles, left to find their way out and around among the Predators and Aliens.[2]

Hey, you're hired. Please fill out this paperwork. Here's the employee manual. Here's your brief orientation. Here's your supervisor. Here are your colleagues. Here's your first week's worth of training.

Good luck.

Now, of course, it's not that simple in real life, but not too far from the truth, either. How did we get here? More important for you, how do you stay there?

You stay there by doing a lot of what I've already outlined in this book—taking ownership in your career development every single day. Employers should make employee engagement and retention priority number one. You can help them do just that.

You're loyal to the work first of all. And then your colleagues and the teams you're on, and this is what drives your retention, so are management and development. Otherwise, if people don't want to be there, they won't stay long, and then it doesn't matter anyway. *That includes you.* When you're a hot commodity in your particular IT space, you're definitely going to be more easily wooed by another employer who claims to have just the right hip, fresh culture for you and your skill sets.

Right. Here we go again.

Engagement and retention start with your first experience with the employer's brand, whatever that may be, and not on day one of your job. It continues throughout your tenure with that employer and even beyond, if and when you separate. And for more and more of us these days, all good things still do come to an end. Even after they come to an end—the first time—there may be an opportunity to return to that employer (as I have done in my past) and try out the sequel.

Onboarding is critical. Onboarding is treacherous. Onboarding can help you dramatically early on, and it can trip you up horrendously as well. The important time frame is the first six months: what am I gonna be doing? HR, recruiting, and career management folks tout the following as "best practices"; they can help you make the business case for keeping you around. In fact, these are onboarding questions and beyond that you should be asking during the final interview process, before the negotiation is over and you take the job.

---

[2] For those who aren't sci-fi fans, the Predator and Alien franchises are favorite "alien vs. human" movies.

Who Are the Kingpins and Queenpins?

More than likely, you were introduced to some level of management during your interview process, at least to those whom you'll be supporting, reporting to, or department and/or division you'll be in. If you were hired in a supervisory and management role, with a team underneath you, then for sure you were introduced to key leadership.

This is stuff you gotta know; people you gotta know. You probably knew some going in, if you did your backstory research prior to the final interview stages, but now that you're in, you *really* need to understand the power structure.

You need to be seen to be known. You need to make yourself seen, and then be known for what you do, not what you don't do. So, if you haven't been introduced to the leadership team yet, then by all means ask for that during onboarding. Yes, the larger the organization is, the less likely you'll be rubbing elbows with the leadership team, but that doesn't mean you can't ask to meet them. Companies that recognize that accessible leadership helps with engagement and retention (there are those damn buzz words again) provide opportune moments when you can meet the elite. Because the very essence of sound leadership means being accessible to those they lead.

In smaller companies, this is a little easier, and you'll probably see the C-team with regularity, depending on the size of your office space and whether you're onsite more than not. Heck, in some of the newfangled companies, everybody's out in front of everyone else, sharing big open spaces with maybe a room or two for closed-door meetings when needed. This includes your leadership team, your teammates, and any subordinates if you're a supervisor.

So don't be shy—ask to meet see the whites of your leaders' eyes.

And Why Should I Care?

Because these are the people who can and will make or break you.

But even better than that, these are the people whom you can and will make or break.

You feel me? You see, even the most philanthropic not-for-profit still has an operating budget that includes securing tech talent like you, paying you a salary and, you hope, benefits, so you'll help the organization fulfill its social mission. They still have to secure funding from outside resources in the form of grants, donations, and the like, which means keeping the knowledge base intact in order to function. And for-profits are no different; they need their employees to believe in what they're building and selling.

But if you're not getting regular access to leadership, if you feel your voice isn't being heard in the organization when you have valuable input regarding IT processes and systems, then you're going to start falling out of love with your work—as well as falling out the door.

Now, there's a big difference between quality time with your boss, or your boss's boss, bending his or her ear to talk shop and share an idea or two, and camping out in your office or at your desk or in your car because you think you've got it all figured out and they've got it all wrong.

I can't help with you the latter. I've had employees who have gone overboard, even been borderline crazy, and then anything and anyone they come in contact with suffers. No, I can only help those of you who truly want to make your workplace a spot where you're digging some level of it every day. And that means meeting and getting to know your company's leadership so that they get to know you, what you do, and why what you do is meaningful to the business.

We all need champions across the hall and across the lines of business. That's why you should care.

There Is Air-Conditioning, Right?

As already noted, the onboarding jungle can be a hot and sticky place to be dumped into. However, the hippest tech companies, like Facebook, immediately get you breaking stuff if you're a programmer, and that's cool. The hack culture in and of itself is an empowering one, telling each new employee to step up and *do*, that there's no time like the present to fail and learn and make it all better.

HR isn't very good at the hack culture; by its nature, it really can't be any good at it. Remember, it's the one entity that must be accountable for the messy, pesky, hack-ridden folks we all are—the ones who can cost a company a lot of money in litigation. We have to regulate ourselves, to protect ourselves from one another. I wish that weren't the case, but it is. No bones about it. So even getting to hack away from the get-go still means there will be some semblance of consistent new-employee orientation and training. You may not listen very closely during it, whether it's one hour or one week, but you're sure as heck going to be asked to sign off on the fact that you are a messy and pesky human being who may screw up at some point and cause a ruckus that we, as your employers, need to be protected from.

Take advantage of this formal orientation, though. You may not meet all of the leadership team, but you will meet HR as well as other peers who will help you traverse the first weeks of jungle trudging. This is also where you'll have a cursory look at what to do and what not to do (culture policies, social media policies, etc.), understand what non-comp benefits you have (free lunches, education allowance, equipment, etc.), and get a company overview, however hot and dry (or humid) it may be.

You're only going to get the air-conditioning if you pay attention and sign off on the waivers. That's just the way it is.

Please Insert the Ruby on the Rails Here

Maybe it is a hackathon from the get-go, or maybe not. But either way, there will be some form of training schedule for the first few weeks. The frequency and duration of training will vary from company to company and industry to industry, but some training you shall have. If for some odd reason you don't get it, request it.

The training I'm talking about involves the bigger business picture. It's not about what you already knew coming in; that's why they hired you. It's about what the context of "you" will be in the business and your learning beyond the formal orientation you received in day one or week one. How do all the tech parts work separately? And how together do they either build stuff, break stuff, maintain stuff, or monitor stuff?

Beyond meeting and knowing who the leadership team is, you'll, of course, need to meet your peers and co-workers; you'll learn and understand what the different engineering and systems teams are doing for the organization and how you're all supposed to work separately together.

For example, in my current company, we've got two separate engineering teams working on two parallel software platforms, one that will eventually be retired and that's being used to experiment with features and functionality, and the other that will become the new platform—bigger, faster, better. There are also front-end and UX engineering teams focused on each platform. They all meet regularly to ensure that the left hand knows that the right is doing; each new team member who's added is immersed in cross-platform training and immediate building-and-breaking-stuff work. This helps to ensure product integrity and also solidifies the workplace culture. If you're not feeling the team-building and training love from day one, I'd raise a red flag or three.

Work It with Cross-Training

I'm a big advocate of making the "world of work" stick to you in your new incarnation. I hope that, at some point, you're cross-trained across various roles and departments, beyond your technical expertise. This isn't about your new employer turning you into localized bench strength for other respective positions; the company should have that baked into its talent strategy already. Especially if you're in a large organization.

This is more about furthering your holistic knowledge of the business and the roles you and your colleagues play—how each facet affects the other. If you know that your next line of code will affect finance and procurement in a way that will improve their ability to better manage the company's money and sharpen the purchasing decisions that are made, which in turn affects your ability to continue to code effectively, then you get clearer understanding of the why of your business.

If it's not offered, recommend or ask for cross-training. It could be in the form of formal training sessions, periodic retreats, informal lunchtime sharing, or a multitude of variants. The goal is for you to understand the greater context of your role with your new employer, increasing your value over time, growing your business problem-solving ability, and opening you up to possible other positions and roles internally (see Chapter 17).

The employer wanted you for your specialty, though, and how your specific skill set and experience will help address IT issues and creative time-saving, cost-saving, and money-making solutions. For decades, employers looked for jack-of-all-trades folks to solve problems in the enterprise, and that included IT. But since this latest downturn, software and process efficiencies combined with productivity increases (doing a lot more with a lot fewer folk) have led to the age of the "specialist" across roles, departments, and divisions.

So know that you've been hired for your specialization, and then learn on the job and be cross-trained so you make your skills that much more valuable and sticky.

Me and My Shadow

Another onboarding process I hope your new employer envelops you in is some kind of shadow system or buddy mentoring system. Maybe when you were hired that was the case, and you were assigned a peer who helped hack away at the jungle growth to shed light on just where the hell you were, who the hell you were, and why the hell you were there.

Many large enterprises have institutionalized "buddy" systems, while most of the small organizations have not. I helped create some form of job shadowing at a few of the firms I worked for, giving new employees both a mentor and some form of cross-training to learn the broader business strategy. You may get some of this in the engineering teams you're on, or it may be sanctioned and managed by HR and/or the learning and development professionals in your organization.

In a sense, it's like pledging a sorority or fraternity. You're assigned a big brother or big sister, or else you aggregate informally to help get through the onboarding (hopefully sans the hazing), especially that first team lunch where you can let your hair down a little (some literally and some figuratively) and get to know your peers. Or, equate it more directly to a Big Sister or Big Brother program for wayward IT pros who need quality peer-to-peer interaction in order to survive the quantum physics of a potentially Dilbertian society.

"Me and my shadow, taking the high road . . . "

Reviewing Your Performance from Day One

It's like a bad high school movie—one clique picks on another less-popular clique. But in this movie, it's not the popular kids who taunt the geeky ones. No, in this movie, the still-popular kids are your infamous traditional "Annual Performance Reviews" and the geeky aberrations are the still-rare progressive few pushing to change the system. But as with the perennial popular kids of lore, these not-so-bright performance-review knuckleheads are given a C average by those they review.

Too many professionals I've known over the years, in both the trenches and leadership positions, have given their own performance-management processes and systems a C grade or lower. It's time for some remedial attention—attention you can push for from day one, when you're told what the review process is like, how often you'll get to "check in" with your new boss or bosses, and opportunities for peer-to-peer interaction and development feedback. For the geeky aberrations driving the above changes, awareness is always the first step. But as I've already mentioned, there's a difference between "best practice" and "business case."

I've been conducting and participating in traditional top-down annual performance reviews for years; and for the most part, we get the process and how it works, technically speaking. What's the problem, right? I mean, if we all understand how we've performed during the previous year, along with setting goals for better performance in the coming year, maybe getting a reward in the form of a tiered pay raise is worthy. In that case, C grade or not, unless I can document negative effects of this process on my employees, our productivity, and our revenue, then changing the process is just a nice-to-have.

Nice-to-have versus a must-have; that's what I mean by best practice vs. business case. You can talk all you want about performance management best practices, but we're friggin' busy here trying to run a business.

That's the point, though. You need to receive regular performance feedback week to week and month to month. It doesn't even have to be a formal process, as it is usually in large companies. In fact, there are companies without formal performance appraisal systems that have reported lower turnover, higher employee morale, and stronger relationships between managers and employees, among other benefits.

Maybe this is the company you just joined. Lower turnover and higher productivity can be measured, as well as the impact on revenue. The point is that you need to have ownership and understanding as to your individual and collective contributions to the company—meeting critical software development deadlines, rebuilding entire network systems to be more reliable and cost-efficient, testing system usability, and ensuring a tight QA ship. These all help make the ongoing business case to remain happily employed (and, we hope, rewarded) and give gumption to geeks shouting, "We need more weekly one-on-ones and one-on-manys and many-on-manys and mentoring and 360s and collaboratively training and continuous feedback loops."

If you grew up playing sports as I have, you've heard the phase "Give it one hundred percent." Well, you want that reciprocity as well. You need to be reminded why you love the work you do and how it's making a difference in the business.

And that's my whole point here: regular one-on-ones with not just your immediate supervisor and/or team members but also with your peers and other cross-divisional workshops. These all help to give greater workplace cultural stability, performance feedback, and contextual traction as to the why, once again, you took the job.

The key is frequency. Once a year, at your annual performance review, isn't going to cut it. I've held one-on-one's with employees once a week, even if it's only 30 minutes or less. It's a time for you to reflect on your role and performance and to talk shop as much as it is for your supervisor to talk at you. Heck, it could be for a few minutes in different locations over time. For more formal meetings, the frequency should be monthly at a minimum, preferably for 30-60 minutes.

Having the face time can make all the difference, from onboarding to ongoing development. So if you're not offered it from day one, ask for it from day zero.

Mindful Moment Getting the job is fantastic, but now you have to survive the jungle onboarding process. How do you do that? Well, you get to know your leadership team (and they get to know you), pay attention during any formal orientation processes you may have, be present in any ongoing greater business training activities they may put you through, request to be cross-trained if isn't offered, request a peer mentor or "buddy" to help you along the way if it's not a formalized process (or pick one yourself), and push for regular one-on-one's. Face time is where the magic happens and how you find our regularly your impact on the business.

Internal Mobility

Let's Play Nation Ball

I don't view having too many good players as a problem.

—Billy Beane, Oakland A's baseball coach and
inspiration behind *Moneyball*

Internal mobility—it's a recent workplace buzzword, but an important one at that. Especially for those of you who employed and looking to grow and expand your skills and reach inside your organization. You know, like getting a promotion of transferring to another team or department for a new position you've had your eye on.

So per Billy Beane's quote above, what's also important is where those players are playing, how they're playing together, and if they're playing better together in the right positions because they're expanding their knowledge and value to the organization as a result of crossing-training, stretch assignments, even new roles.

You don't want to be thinking, "I don't want to be out here doing nothing. It's dangerous."

This was said by a 14-year-old boy in Chicago who should've been in school, but wasn't because of the 2012 Chicago Teachers' strike.[1] The same goes for you, not wanting to be in there, in your new job, doing nothing. It's dangerous to your development, mobility, and longevity.

---

[1] www.nytimes.com/2012/09/13/education/chicago-teachers-strike-enters-third-day. html?pagewanted=all.

You might've heard the quote, "An idle brain is the devil's workshop," which comes from H. G. Bohn's *Handbook of Proverbs*,[2] published in 1855. Its origins lay in the belief that hard work keeps people focused and out of trouble, whereas laziness breeds evil deeds. But with the latest in neuroscience research, we now know that our frontal cortex has much smaller windows of focal strength during the course of the day. We need idle periods, or breaks in thought, to allow our minds to rest and revitalize, letting what we've absorbed during those "focal spikes" to reengineer our synaptic pathways. That doesn't mean that teenagers—or employees—should be roaming the streets unchecked, with no formal or informal learning and without growth options in place, however.

If you're lucky, you're working for a progressive enterprise that understands how people truly learn, adopt, and adapt—and it is doing whatever it can to incorporate this view into the workplace, from day one to exit interview. But chances are, you're not.

As I've written repeatedly, we've got a lot of "process debt" to deal with. Similar to "technical debt," which is the layers of outdated programming code that we just overwrite instead of starting fresh, process debt is the accumulation of change-management attempts made in the workplace. Our decades-old learning and development processes haven't changed much, even in the light of recent research on how the brain works. Employers still throw the Employee Handbook at their new hires, make them sit in day-long training seminars where most have already checked out half way, and then silo their employees in self-branded promotional kiosks with limited if any exposure outside the imaginary but quite real "information control" firewall to valuable content from informal learning channels. Meaning, those employees are "doing nothing out there" while preventing you from doing anything inside, and that's dangerous for your employer and for you.

But we have access to *informal* learning channels, both inside and outside that imaginary firewall, via smart phones and tablet devices.

The democratization of learning and the potential of social mobility are here to stay. And employers and employees alike need to embrace the short bursts of quality peer-to-peer interactions and actionable insights. By letting you and I do what people have been doing for thousands of years—sharing knowledge across brand-agnostic open networks as opposed to orgs jamming self-serving job and brand info down your throat, the same companies can then channel the powerful mindshare and elevate the enterprise to one of empowerment and improvement.

---

[2] http://books.google.com/books/about/A_Handbook_of_Proverbs.html?id=9ZXiOwAACAAJ.

In other words, help me get better so I can do better by you in more than one place.

"I don't want to be out here doing nothing. It's dangerous."

The good news is, you and I are not "doing nothing." The danger lies in employer resistance, not in employee idleness. So either find that progressive company to work for or make your own way in the world.

The Constant Need for Roster Changes

Going back to the Billy Beane quote that began this chapter, consider that a team never has too many good players. Everyone else is looking to land those good players so that they can replace their expendable team members, their not-so-good players.

For example, after I left a particular job many years ago, the company kept the head of that department. the "team captain," for another decade. That was, they kept her until she became a pariah (which she kind of always was), and was asked to leave.

At another company, we kept a combination "expendable team member and pariah" for seven years before we finally released the person back into the wild.

I'll get to my nomenclature in a minute. The fact is that no one likes to be fired, but unfortunately, too many employers hold on to the one thing that holds their businesses back—the wrong talent in the wrong place. And they hold onto that wrong talent for far too long. Instead, they need to understand where the right talent is and where it, needs to go.

I'm not just talking about those who, after tedious training, patience, and futile remedial "this is why we hired you" chats, continue to perform poorly, but also about the crappy bosses your employer hired and/or promoted to manage you and your peers.

The reality is, no matter where you work, if you're one of the talented and happy employees who help maintain a great company, a company with super products and/or services, and with a strong bottom line, some of your not-so-good teammates will occasionally have to be fired. If you've ever managed teams, you know what I'm talking about. If you've even worked with sub-par peers, you know what I mean.

Who are these not-so-good folks? They are the people who, after exhaustive training, coaching, mentoring, and counseling, still cannot do the job. And that includes front-line IT people and management (and, mercy, have I worked with some crazy-doozies in the past). The problem is that too many companies are pretty damn bad at letting go of people when they just can't do the job; instead, they're extremely relieved when those people leave on their own accord. But, far worse, these companies are also pretty damn bad at identifying who needs to be moved up (and when) to maximize the corporate culture and raise productivity.

It's still an extremely tough job market right now—with the exception only being those with hot tech skills—so why would any subpar pariah leave a job if the employer dances around and says "you're doing a great job"? The subpar wouldn't, of course, and doesn't. Unless the person were truly miserable, crying after work every night, and even then maybe not.

Then there's the whole fear-of-litigation problem. I worked with a company who's CEO and VP of Human Resources had been working painstakingly for almost a year to build a case for terminating an employee, and they were still no closer to making the final decision than they were the year before. Meaning, their legal advisers told them to keep building the case.

I know—you don't have any control over what management does or doesn't do when it comes to subpar co-workers mindlessly blocking your IT development and mobility. Unless you're management and you *can* do something about it. Either way, you've got to be a go-to guy or gal; you've got to be the one who's picking the teams or being picked. Remember, there's danger in idle resistance—you've got to make your own way.

Nation Ball Is the Real Work Game

Ever play nation ball? I really loved the game when I was growing up. It was a two-tiered dodge ball variant that really rocked with fast-paced action, mystery, misery, intrigue, redemption, success, failure, and ultimate victory. It's just like the workplace. Your workplace. Whether there are 25 employees or 25,000.

In nation ball (as in many games of my youth), there were usually these players:

- **The Team Captains**. The playground leaders who always picked the teams.

- **The Go-To Guys and Gals**. Those who are always picked in the first few rounds of team selection.

- **The Expendable Crew Members**. Those who had some nation ball skills, who aspired to be the go-to kids, but who were known for getting picked off early on.

- **The Pariahs**. Those who stood on the sidelines because they were never picked. If they were picked, they were the first to go. Always.

This was the hierarchy. HR was made up of the teachers and playground aides, the watchdogs, who only cared about maintaining order and compliance. There wasn't a lot of T&D going on to facilitate better nation ball skills (or tetherball, or four square, or hopscotch, or kickball, or you name it).

It wasn't about "everybody's a winner" and "everybody gets to play." You either fought to be a go-to or you remained expendable. Or you were a pariah, and then forget about it. Right or wrong, those were the rules of the playground—and they are probably the unspoken rules at your company today.

Yet, with all the talk of employee "development" and "engagement" and "retention"—as well as the need for your employer to hold on to you, their best talent—you'd think that wasn't the case. But the business of IT is crazy-fast these days across industries, and there's limited time to help the expendable team members, not to mention the pariahs, especially when you want to stay in business. So the pariahs are ignored; the focus is on the go-tos.

Are you a go-to?

Management always goes to the go-tos first. The people who go above and beyond. They get to work early and work late. They get things done, finish projects on time, help grow the business, and own the knowledge capital of their organization—and can also include management.

The go-tos are the ones who get the inside moves—who have the internal mobility. The go-tos are the top talent your company wants to retain. But the very company that wants to keep you also jeopardizes its business in the way they treat you—they could lose you someday.

Yes, there's a ton of chatter about go-to folks having to do much more with much less, and maybe wanting to jump ship no matter how cold the water is. But, damn, look at those productivity numbers.

What do you do? You push yourself to be a go-to and you push your employer to treat you right. Oh, and watch out for the—

smack

. . . ball.

Rain or Shine

Yes, we will play nation ball, rain or shine. We have to; we gotta eat, and we gotta be go-to's. Whether we're happy or not, rain or shine. But, damn. Long term, you want to be happy because you just got this frickin' new job. So if you're sitting there chatting with nine of your colleagues, are you already one of the seven who are "actively disengaged"?

As I referenced in Chapter 5, *71% of American workers are "not engaged" or "actively disengaged" in their work, meaning they are emotionally disconnected from their workplaces and are less likely to be productive.*

Because many of today's IT jobs are seriously complex and constantly changing, it takes serious skills, focal strength, and sheer doing. Combine that with unhappiness at work and you've got a volatile mix that can taint the brand, your peers and colleagues, and new applicants.

No one likes to feel unappreciated and worked like a dog, especially when management believes they're doing right by you and your brothers and sisters, expecting your "Amens" to be loud and clear every time you walk through the office doors. And yet, there's no cross-training, no ongoing informal development opportunities, no encouragement to stretch yourself for intrinsic and extrinsic rewards. No wonder you're emotionally disconnected with the lovely taste of bile in the back of your throat.

If you're one of the motivated go-tos, then even in a stagnant mobility environment you may find other opportunities your colleagues can't, which would at least keep you on board while others are jumping off the ship, or maybe even sinking the ship (including management).

Maybe.

Or maybe you're in the right environment now that does offer the multiple moves inside. Rain or shine, right?

Either way, here's again what I recommend: Push your new employer for empowered employment from the inside out. Request that you want more responsibility managing your internal career path or paths, with their assistance of course, and that you want to be aware of other opportunities throughout the organization as well as ways to get there.

Let's Review All the Right Moves

I'm going to repeat a little of what I said about internal mobility in Chapter 5 and expand on it. Keep these examples in mind as you examine the willingness of your current employer or a prospective employer: how willing are they to provide cross-training opportunities, career development and mobility of any kind?

- **Lateral moves**—when you're unhappy with your current position and need a change of scenery without leaving all together.

  This one can be tricky, however. Especially if you're in a difficult position with a difficult boss and/or co-workers. If it's a serious situation that is affecting your day-to-day activities inside as well as when you go home, then you definitely need to talk with HR and get the situation dealt with. If it's not as serious, but serious enough to impact your career path, then keep it about your career path and other roles and skill sets you want to explore. Make it about you, not about them.

- **Ladder moves**—the traditional career climb to the next best thing internally if and when you qualify and/or are promoted.

  This can be tricky as well, but still the traditional route to internal mobility is still engrained in the enterprise. And for the qualified few of you who do have an interest in taking on more responsibility and maybe even an IT supervisory/management role, then follow the bouncing political ball on how to get there. This is where not only your skills and experience play a role, but also your internal networking ability combined with your business insight. Meaning, you can articulate the context of how you can and will impact the business further if promoted. Remember, make that business case.

- **Lattice moves**—the progressive moves that take you to new cross-trained realms within your organization.

  This is the optimal path of course. The one that is embedded in the agile enterprise where the fluidity of today's workforce—full-time, part-time, contract—is understood by management and developing you and the teams you're on as needed are part of the ongoing business growth strategy. Being able to reconfigure on-demand is a competitive imperative, so giving you the stretch assignments that increase fluidity makes for the lattice-driven organization.

Here come more balls, by the way.

smack

■ **Mindful Moment**   In larger organizations, usually there are multiple IT reqs open at any given time unless there's a hiring freeze, which happens. For the most part, opportunity abounds in the form of mobility opportunities, at least for the right person, and the same competitive nature of the beast you've dealt with looking for new work can also be just as brutal for internal opportunities. Remember, practice some of the same "no-smack-talking" tactics I discussed in Chapter 15, no matter how unhappy you are in your current role.

Referrals, Referrals, Referrals

Referrals are still the best way to get in from both the outside and the inside. Whether the statistic is 30 percent of hires are from referrals, 40 percent, 50 percent, or higher, getting the referral is the best way to find your possible next move inside the organization. In smaller companies, that's pretty damn easy because you're likely to hear about the opportunities (especially if you're the unfortunate one being replaced). Larger organizations have internal online job boards, talent community posts, and direct recommendations from your boss (you hope, during the regular one-on-ones you have).

If you've ever been claustrophobic, you know what it feels like to be trapped in a confined space for any length of time. That maddening feeling from the dark recesses within suddenly catches fire in your neocortex, and the only thing you can think about is that you have to get out. Now. Maybe you're ending the year, crying about your claustrophobic career. Maybe you think that your choices are as low as the jobs-to-job seekers ratio out there, even if your employer added other relevant IT opportunities for you and your go-to peers. However, in the midst of your panic attack, maybe you need to realize it's as simple as keeping your internal windows open, letting in the fresh air of possibility. I know, it doesn't seem all that intuitive, but that breeze will bring in that go-to choice and opportunity.

Look for the referrals, referrals, referrals!

The traditional corporate model of stable full-time jobs with benefits continues to disintegrate and/or be reconfigured into contingent work, project-based work, online work, and an infinite number of combinations of these. So be thankful you have that new full-time job. To remain a go-to in the company and be able to uncover future opportunities, it means you'll have to:

- Take ownership of your career development and convince your employer of why you should.

- Take on related (or sometimes not) projects that will stretch you and give you new skills.

Take a deep breath and stay frosty. Know when you should move, take a dive, or when you should stand still and catch what's coming. The opportunities are flying your way, in the form of nation balls.

smack

Mindful Moment It's really simple—be a go-to employee who gets the job done while also getting the inside scoop on future internal opportunities. Own your career development and push your employer to support you in that process. You've got the job—now make a future out of it!

Careers in Cloud Computing and Mobile Technology

The New Religion, Part I

There's no way that company exists in a year.

—Tom Siebel

This well-known statement from the founder of Siebel Systems, made back in 2001, was in response to what Salesforce.com was already becoming—a force to be reckoned with.[1] A Dreamforce to be reckoned with, actually, Dreamforce being the annual one-week Salesforce.com customer appreciation and partner conference that over 85,000 (in 2012) businesspeople attend.[2] If you've ever attended, you know it gets more interactive and extravagant each year, and 2012 was no exception. The conference was held at Moscone Center in San

---

[1] http://money.cnn.com/magazines/fortune/fortune_archive/2001/06/25/305460/index.htm.

[2] http://www.salesforce.com/dreamforce/DF12/.

Francisco. In the grassy space between two of the conference buildings, huge HD screens projected the keynote speech to passersby, as well as to an audience lounging on bean bags, taking a break and checking their smartphones or tablets, or enjoying the free WiFi. Yep, bean bags and free WiFi. Everywhere, in all the Moscone Center buildings and in nearly every nook and cranny in between the buildings. The conference is an amazing business extravaganza— I've never seen so many tieless men in sports coats, and women in pants suits, even in Silicon Valley. There weren't as many men or women wearing jeans as I would've liked, but there were still enough to be true to California casual.

Into the Cloud

Cloud computing is alive and well. Salesforce is a sales and marketing, collaboration, performance management. and employee-recognition cloud-based software platform with a gazillion apps and partners in its AppExchange, as well as being a developer community to create even more apps and SF integrations. Salesforce has been number one on *Forbes* magazine's list of most innovative companies for two years in a row, with $3 billion in annual revenue.[3] That's nowhere near Oracle's annual revenue of $37 billion, but for a company (and technology platform) that was compared to the likes of Pets.com, they're doing just fine, thank you very much. By the way, Oracle founder Larry Ellison once said that his successor should be a software engineer—there's hope for you yet.

Maybe you've never worked for Salesforce, or for any of the companies it has bought lately, like Radian6, Buddy Media, or Rypple, and so maybe you don't care. But if you've been part of any cloud-based company in the past ten years or so, you know that the platform is much bigger and broader than the general public realizes. Software runs the world, and the world now floats atop the cloud that runs the world. The days of installed software, with the costly customizations, the upgrades, the annual licensing and consulting fees, are becoming olden times. No, cloud computing hasn't completely replaced legacy ERP software systems like Oracle or SAP, but there's a reason Oracle and SAP have been buying up the cloud-based companies that have gotten the formula right. It's why Workday, a totally cloud-based human capital management platform, is taking on the big boys by going public as well this year.

---

[3] http://www.forbes.com/sites/victoriabarret/2012/09/05/why-salesforce-com-ranks-1-on-forbes-most-innovative-list/.

The Growth of the Cloud = Jobs

Every analyst firm, from Gartner to IDC to Forrester and many others (I worked at one of the smaller players in 2011 called Ventana Research, covering the HR technology space), have released relative numbers claiming that cloud computing will grow revenues in the gazillions over the next five to ten years, creating millions of direct programmer jobs and many new jobs we don't even know about yet. According to research sponsored by Microsoft, and conducted by IDC in 2012, spending on public and private IT cloud services will generate nearly 14 million jobs worldwide from 2011 to 2015.[4] And according to the 2012 Gartner CIO Agenda Report, the top three priorities for that year were analytics and business intelligence, mobile technologies, and cloud computing.[5]

When I entered the HR and recruiting technology space nearly 13 years ago, the Internet had just started to transform the way companies recruited, hired, and managed their workforce. Regardless of the industry, the technological transformations have been astounding, with all things now social, mobile, and cloud computing, just to name a few tech fields.

And what's been cool to watch is how these technologies have helped to innovate the very talent-acquisition and talent-management software systems that are used to recruit, hire, onboard, and develop tech pros like *you*. These technologies are all about getting to the "short list" of qualified applicants faster and more accurately, as well as managing more accurately, faster, and better all the employee life-cycle data.

This application is really exciting for me. I continue to see some innovative cloud-based talent platforms, like the one I currently work for called BraveNewTalent. Human resources, recruiting, training, and talent-management professionals are responsible for providing the highest quality and most efficient workforce processes to the entire organization. Yes, from my vantage point—and yours as job seeker—there's obviously still a lot of work to be done a decade into the 21st century, but mercy, it's still magical at times.

And Then There's Mobile . . .

Think about it: creating applications for smartphones and tablets that will help promote workforce mobility and interactivity. Utilizing social media for recruiting and evaluating talent for hiring. Deploying integrated talent-management applications and adopting workforce analytics and metrics across

---

[4] http://www.microsoft.com/en-us/news/features/2012/mar12/03-05CloudComputingJobs.aspx

[5] http://imagesrv.gartner.com/cio/pdf/cio_agenda_insights.pdf

cloud platforms. Maybe it sounds a little like marketing jargon, but trust me—this is cool stuff. It's what I call "talent management re-imagined": to acquire, to empower, and to retain—you.

The new business technologies like social networking, mobile applications, and cloud computing (we'll talk social analytics and big data in Chapter 19) are still in the early, mass-adoption phase at most companies. Remember, you've got some companies still recruiting via job boards and email, and then managing the process with spreadsheets. Ack! But for more and more companies, the cloud computing innovation is happening across departments—finance, operations, IT, supply chain, sales and marketing, and every other facet of business today.

Just don't sit there and blink because, in the next five to ten years, you could be reading about how nano-technology and charging your devices in the new and improved inductive cloud are what's hot. Use your imagination.

Most of the coolest innovations are about bringing together people and technology in order to increase productivity and performance for greater competitive advantage. Business today requires us to communicate and collaborate via a variety of tools and services, including email, phone, instant messaging, video chat, the social networks (Facebook, Twitter, and LinkedIn), other online networks, webinars, podcasts, blogs, wikis, the company intranet—and even face-to-face contact from time to time. And to do this, of course, we use landlines, cellphones, smartphones, tablet computers, laptop computers, desktop computers, the Internet, and the magic of cloud computing.

You can't turn around these days without seeing a smartphone or a tablet or netbook in your colleagues' hands; and in the next few years, the market will be flooded with an even wider array of choices. The growth of the global virtual workforce, combined with the diverse "ways we now work," has fuelled mobile development The combination of social media, collaboration, and mobile technologies is increasing the demand for real-time communications and 24-hour data access in the palm of every job seeker's and employee's hands.

The installed-based, on-premise software market continues to get compressed, with more and more companies moving to SaaS and cloud deployment to meet all their software needs. So the term "cloud computing" may be hip and fresh today; but for those of you who've been around the block more than once, you know it goes back to the days of the early Internet. Let's talk about the different cloud technologies that are out there and the skills required to use these platforms.

Get me some of that new, cloud-computing religion!

▨ **Mindful Moment** Cloud computing has dramatically changed how software is developed and deployed, making it more cost-effective for organizations and a more efficient way to manage all kinds of business processes. The good news for you is that billions will be spent on cloud technologies in the next 5-10 years, as well as generating millions of jobs.

Lots of Cloud Computing

Just to be clear, "cloud computing" is the implementation of computing resources—both hardware and software—that are delivered as a service over a network, which usually means the Internet. According to most folks in the tech industry, the name comes from the practice of drawing stylized clouds that represent networks in diagrams of computing and communications systems. It is also what the early Internet was called.

Now, by no means am I cloud computing expert, but I do know that there quite a few flavors representing the cloud. Just try searching for "cloud computing" jobs in California, using a job- search tool like Indeed.com. When I did this, nearly 3,000 jobs came up, from software developers to network administrators.

Because there are many types of public and private cloud computing existing in the marketplace today, let me briefly review and reiterate what is already widely accepted.[6]

Software as a Service (SaaS)

Software as a service (SaaS) is the form I'm most familiar with, as a software product marketer and a consumer. It's also called "on-demand software" or "Web-based software" and it entails delivering software and data that are centrally hosted on the "cloud." SaaS is typically accessed by users via a "thin client," or what's known as a computer dependent on another system like a server, via a Web browser.

Many business applications are delivered via SaaS these days, including human resource management, recruiting, and training, as well as other business activities like accounting, collaboration, customer-relationship management (known as CRM), management information systems, enterprise resource planning (know as ERP), invoicing, content management, and service desk management.

---

[6] http://en.wikipedia.org/wiki/Cloud_computing.

Platform as a Service (PaaS)

Platform as a service (PaaS) includes the same kinds of cloud computing services as SaaS, but provides a specific computing platform for a variety software components and modules. Users can also control the software configuration and deployment. The PaaS provider offers the networks, servers, storage, and related services.

Infrastructure as a Service (IaaS)

Infrastructure as a Service is considered to be the most basic cloud service model, whereby cloud providers offer computers to run usually as virtual machines. The virtual machines can have many operating systems that are also known as "guests." They can run at the same time on a single host computer, creating what's called a "hypervisor," or a virtual machine manager (VMM). These configurations can scale quite nicely to support many virtual machines. IaaS providers include Amazon EC2, Rackspace Cloud, Terremark, and Google Compute Engine.

Desktop as a Service

Desktop as a service, which is usually called "desktop virtualization" and "client virtualization," keeps the personal computer/desktop environment separate from the physical machine using the client-server models—separate computers that use the Internet to access servers of information. In larger organizations, the server information is stored via the virtual desktop, as opposed to remote client local storage. This means that users can access all their applications, programs, processes, and data on a centrally run server, giving them the opportunity to run apps on a smartphone.

Data as a Service (DaaS)

Data as a service (DaaS) is closely related to SaaS. DaaS means that the data, which is the product, can be provided on demand to any user, no matter where it is located in the world. Service-oriented architecture (SOA) has given data the ability to reside almost anywhere.

Storage as a Service (STaaS)

Storage as a service (STaaS) is when that large service providers offer subscriptions for leasing storage space. Because they can scale storage easily, the service providers can give customers a better deal than even their own storage could ever give them, as well as offsite backup alternatives.

Security as a Service (SECaaS)

Security as a service (SECaaS) is when large service providers offer subscriptions for security services. Again, because they can scale these services easily, the service providers can give customers a better deal than their own security infrastructure could ever provide, including services such as antivirus, antispyware, authentication, and more.

Test Environment as a Service (TEaaS)

Test environment as a service (TEaaS), also known as an "on-demand test environment," creates a delivery service for software test environments where the software and data are centrally hosted in the cloud and accessed via a browser over the Internet.

API as a Service (APIaaS)

API as a service (APIaaS) allows for the development and hosting of APIs (application programming interfaces). These APIs can help generate multiple origins for API calls, including REST, XML Web services, and TCP/IP.

IT as a Service (ITaaS)

IT as a service (ITaaS) creates a marketplace for in-house, enterprise IT organizations to purchase any of the above "as a service" services.

The Right Cloud Computing Skills

So now that you're familiar with all the variations of cloud computing, and you want to get that next great position in cloud computing, let's review WANTED Analytics most commonly advertised job titles for IT talent with cloud computing skills.[7] WANTED Analytics is the exclusive data provider for The Conference Board's Help-Wanted OnLine Data Series,[8] the monthly economic indicator of hiring demand in the United States.

These titles may vary as time goes by, but consider:

1. Software engineer
2. Senior software engineer

---

[7] http://www.wantedanalytics.com.

[8] The Conference Board is a global, independent business membership and research association. For more information head to http://www.conference-board.org/.

3. Java developer

4. Systems engineer

5. Senior systems engineer

6. Network engineer

7. Senior Java developer

8. Systems administrator

9. Enterprise architect

10. Websphere cloud computing engineer

Maybe you've held similar positions and have some cloud computing experience. Either way, there are key skills that you need to zero in on when applying for jobs or looking for further internal opportunities if you're gainfully employed.

Here's a list of key skills you'll need in cloud computing:

- Cloud computing
- Java and Javascript
- Linux
- Structured query language (SQL)
- UNIX
- Software as a service (SaaS)
- VMware software
- Salesforce CRM
- Python extensible programming language
- Practical extraction and reporting language (Perl)
- .NET

But besides the technical skills, you also need skills that will "round you out" as a valuable specialized IT business problem solver:

- Business and finance
- Enterprise architecture and business needs analysis
- Project management
- Contract and vendor negotiation

- Security and compliance

- Data integration and analysis (see Chapter 19)

- Mobile app development and management (what's next)

Mindful Moment   Hey, there are lots of "[fill in the blank] as a service" opportunities out there for you if you've got the right IT skills and experience—or you're going to get the right IT skills and experience. Remember everything this book has presented about how to package and present yourself.

Mobile Rules the World

I love my mobile devices. I love my iPhone, iPod, and iPad (sorry to those who don't). I love the fact that all of my devices, including my Macbook Air and Macbook Pro, synch wirelessly and update one another automatically, no matter which one I'm using. I love the delirious number of applications I have to choose from for my mobile devices—from business productivity, to GPS, to banking and finance, to book apps, to educational games, to toddler games, to mindless games. I love the fact that my two- and four-year-old daughters use the iPod and iPad effortlessly, as if they had been playing with them in utero (which they kinda were).

So that means for those of you who are mobile computing and mobile application developers, I love you. In a strictly plutonic, slightly stalkerish way. No need for the restraining order.

According to a 2012 World Bank study, three-fourths of the world's inhabitants now have access to a mobile phone.[9] Also, the number of active mobile phone subscriptions worldwide, both prepaid and postpaid, has grown from fewer than 1 billion in 2000 to over 6 billion now, of which nearly 5 billion are in developing countries. The number may even exceed the total human population at some point in the near future. And lastly, more than 30 billion mobile applications were downloaded in 2011.

There are nearly 700,000 active mobile apps available in the Apple app store,[10] and over 500,000 Android active mobile apps; [11]and there are thousands of

---

[9] http://web.worldbank.org/WBSITE/EXTERNAL/TOPICS/EXTINFORMATIONANDCOMMU NICATIONANDTECHNOLOGIES/0,,contentMDK:23242711~pagePK:210058~piPK:210062 ~theSitePK:282823,00.html.

[10] http://148apps.biz/app-store-metrics/.

[11] http://www.appbrain.com/stats/number-of-android-apps.

new ones being developed every day. Earlier this year, the Apple app store reported receiving about 26,000 submissions every week.[12]

And just as I did for "cloud computing," I searched for "mobile computing" jobs in California, using the job-search tool Indeed.com. Nearly 1,500 jobs came up, from software engineers to mobile security. (Of course, you can search for jobs geographically in any search tool like Indeed.)

The Right Mobile Computing Skills

You want me to love you? Well, then I want you to be the best mobile computing expert you can be, and that means loving:

- Java and JavaScript
- Objective C
- C++
- C#
- .Net
- HTML5

You also need to choose the operating system—the mobile platform—you want to develop for, such as Google's Android or Apple's iOS, or both, then learn the programming languages (above) and software development environment (below) for that mobile platform.

Android and RIM (Blackberry)—Eclipse

Eclipse is a multi-language software development environment, as well as an integrated development environment (IDE), written mostly in Java.[13] It can be used to develop mobile applications in Java and other programming languages, including Ada, C, C++, COBOL, Haskell, Perl, PHP, Python, R, Ruby (including Ruby on Rails framework), Scala, Clojure, Groovy, Android, and Scheme, by also using other plug-ins.

iOS (Apple)—Xcode

Xcode is Apple's development environment for creating iPhone and iPad apps.[14] Xcode includes everything you need to develop—the Instruments

---

[12] http://articles.latimes.com/2012/mar/14/business/la-fi-tn-apple-26000-20120314.

[13] http://www.eclipse.org.

[14] https://developer.apple.com/xcode/.

analysis tool, iOS Simulator, and the latest Mac OS X and iOS software development kits (SDKs). The Xcode interface integrates code editing, UI design with Interface Builder, testing, and debugging in a single window.

Windows Mobile—Visual Studio

Microsoft Visual Studio is an integrated development environment (IDE).[15] It's all about Windows development and is used for console and graphical user interface (GUI) applications and Windows Forms applications, websites, Web applications, and Web services. This includes both native code development and managed code for all platforms supported by Microsoft Windows, Windows Mobile, Windows CE, .NET Framework, .NET Compact Framework, and Microsoft Silverlight.

Symbian

Symbian is a mobile operating system (OS) and computing platform for smartphones and maintained by Accenture.[16] The latest version, called Symbian^3, was released at the end of 2010 and first used in the Nokia N8.

Mindful Moment   Mobile devices are going to exceed the global population at some point in the near future, as well as will most likely usurp laptops and desktops, so you definitely want to get in on this job market. Cloud and mobile computing will generate millions of new jobs in the next 10 years, and in this quick "innovate or die" world of work we live in, that's the new reality of career security.

---

[15] http://www.microsoft.com/visualstudio/eng/whats-new.
[16] http://en.wikipedia.org/wiki/Symbian.

Careers in Big Data and Social Analytics

New Religion, Part II

> Machines don't make the essential and important connections among data and
> they don't create information. Humans do.

> —Jim Stikeleather, Executive Strategist, Innovation for Dell Services

I'm a huge *Freakonomics* fan—the books, the blog, the podcasts. Journalist
Stephen J. Dubner and award-winning economist Steven D. Levitt really do
give their fans and readers "the hidden side of everything."[1]

And a lot of that means analyzing the raw data in a unique and interesting
ways—ways that for the longest time couldn't be done simply because the
computing power and storage capacities just didn't exist until the 1980s and
1990s. In fact, it wasn't until the 1990s, when true business intelligence
systems (BI), arising from what was known as decision support systems in the
1960s and then developed in the mid-1980s, were born. It was in 1989 when
Howard Dresner, a business intelligence and performance management
thought leader and former Gartner Research Fellow, proposed "business
intelligence" as an umbrella term that included "concepts and methods to
improve business decision making by using fact-based support systems."[2] Right
on, Howard. Hence all the software companies at the time—like Oracle, IBM,

---

[1] http://www.freakonomics.com.

[2] http://dssresources.com/history/dsshistory.html.

HP, SAP, SAS, and a slew of others old and new, big and small—jumped into the BI business to help companies manage all their disparate data siloed in various systems and databases. And there were the storage hardware and server companies that created cost-sensitive and cutthroat businesses so organizations could store more data in smaller spaces—spaces interconnected around the globe via a mishmash of outdated and spanking brand-new telecommunications technologies under the sea, underground, from towers atop buildings and mountains, and in space.

Are You Ready to Pass Out?

But then something else technical in nature was born—the Internet. Suddenly everyday people could access "data" fairly easily via their phone lines. And the online data combined with business data worldwide has grown exponentially over the years—to a point that now, according to IBM, human beings create 2.5 quintillion bytes of data. Every day. [3]

Did you get that? That's 2,500,000,000,000,000,000 bytes of data. I'm just excited that my oldest daughter, who's four, can count to 20.

Oh, and by the way, that volume of data is just an average over the past two years. Can you imagine the next two years? For those of you keeping score at home, big data in the IT world is a collection of data sets so large and complex that it becomes difficult to process using smaller database management tools. It takes pretty powerful software, hardware processing power, and multiple servers to process it all, which we have today. In fact, software startups that are crunching somewhat large amounts of data for their customers can quite affordably lease the computer power and server storage needed to do so. Barriers to entry in the big data world are smaller than they've ever been.

Today big data is everywhere: Internet search, finance and business information, HR and recruiting information, biological research, meteorology, physics, environmental research, and much more. It's also being collected from all over the place, everywhere: climate sensors, mobile devices, remote sensing, software logs, social media posts, digital pictures and videos, microphones, radio-frequency identification readers, purchase transaction records, and cell phone GPS signals. Just to name a few.

2,500,000,000,000,000,000 bytes of data. Every day.

According to DOMO, a business intelligence company founded in 2011, the amount of data generated on the Internet every minute by a global Internet population of 2.1 billion people includes:[4]

- 48 hours of video on YouTube
- 684,478 pieces of content shared on Facebook
- 3,600 new photos shared on Instagram
- 27,778 new posts published on Tumblr

I've seen other, similar daunting stats. I mean, how do we make sense of all this? Maybe all this "big data" doesn't rock you to your very core as it does me, but you've got to admit it's a little unsettling. And even a little silly.

Don't you think?

---

[3] http://www-01.ibm.com/software/data/bigdata/.

[4] http://www.domo.com.

Rubber Chickens in Space

Equate the Internet to space; we inject a lot a silly crap into space because we can. We're sending up more and more of it into our atmosphere every day, cluttering the view of the heavens. That's why it's comical that one of those objects sent into space earlier this year was a rubber chicken.

Work with me here. I am going somewhere.

Yes, a group of California students launched a rubber chicken into space, all in the name of science, and they named it Camilla.[5]

And then I dreamt that I received this email:

> *Hi Kevin,*
>
> *Camilla added a pin to Space-Bound Rubber Chicken Infographics.*
>
> *Click here to check it out.*
>
> —Ben and the Pinterest Team

Yes, it was a bad dream, one that I'm never "pinterested" in having again. Because there's enough silly crap in our own atmosphere, closer to home, online. Beyond the big three of social networks—Facebook, LinkedIn, and Twitter—some new social networks on the scene have grown quickly and dramatically. While I'm not an active user of Pinterest, Comscore had reported that Pinterest was the fastest independent site to hit 10 million monthly uniques in the United States. [6,7]

What comes next? Noise and spam. A lot of it. That's what happens when any new social channel gets big enough to bring regular value to early adopters and early mainstreamers—more content shared means more noise means more spam. The spam comes because it gets more difficult these days to differentiate between what's legitimate and what's garbage.

Check out another faux Pinterest email that an old colleague of mine received:

> *Hi!*
>
> *Ivana Tosten mentioned you on a new pin that was added to "My Style":*
>
> *"I never thought losing weight could be so easy, but it turns out that there are products that actually work! See newsrapid2012.com it's AMAZING!"*
>
> *Click here to reply.*

---

[5] http://www.huffingtonpost.com/2012/04/21/rubber-chicken-camilla-sp_n_1442805.html.

[6] http://www.comscore.com.

[7] http://www.fastcompany.com/1834177/content-curators-are-new-superheros-web.

Click here to follow back Ivana

—Ben & the Pinterest Team

Sure, many of you would get the fact that this was contextual spam, but there are those who wouldn't and be pulled into the outer rings of crappy space.

Automated content curation and social analytics are still pretty new, but thank goodness they're here, considering how much help the world needs (that they may not even be aware of) to aggregate, filter, read, and redistribute relevant content from across the realms of junked-up space—including Tweets, blog posts, news articles, Facebook Shares, LinkedIn Shares, Pinterest posts, and tons more.

Put a Lens on It, Baby

Putting a lens on all this data is something that's needed more and more to make sense of it all. More specifically, and to be metaphorically correct for this chapter, you need to put a telescope on it to see past the space junk and focus in on what exactly you want to curate and use (like a social Hubble telescope).

Putting a lens on the same social noise in order to discover and analyze who's talking about what company, person, product, or thing is also quite valuable for organizations, as well as for who's voting for whom in the elections, what news stories are trending, and endless streams of Internet big data trending hotness. That's what it's all about these days.

And if you really want to reach Camilla the rubber chicken in the upper atmosphere, then good for you. Make sure to put a pin in it for me.

Through all of this, what's fascinating to me is how all this relates directly to the quote from Jim Stikeleather at the beginning of this chapter. No matter how much data is out there, no matter how powerful the data analysis algorithms are, it still takes humans to connect the dots between what's really happening and what's not. It takes us to see that "hidden side of everything."

For example, in one recent Freakonomics report, one of the producers went to Fort Benning in Georgia, where a whole bunch of feral pigs were devastating the land and equipment on the base. So, a cash bounty was provided to those hunters who eradicated the pigs, bringing in the pigs' tails and details of how and where they were killed. What ended up happening was that, after three years and over $125,000 in bounty money, the pig population had actually grown dramatically, not declined. It was a head-scratcher, indeed. What they found out after crunching all the data, and then looking at it through the human lens, was that all the bait they had put out to attract the pigs had actually spurred their reproduction—hence, the unintended economic consequences of what was originally conceived.

Amen for the humans. And the jobs big data and social analytics are creating.

Mindful Moment The sheer volume of data in the world today is unfathomable. The number of zeros alone at the end of the bytes of data pumping through our veins daily is enough to make me pass out multiple times. But the good news is that all this data of the democratization of the Internet is creating a whole bunch of big data and social analytics jobs.

The Biggest Data of All Is in the Works

I'm telling you, there are lots of big data jobs out there. But as with all constantly changing tech jobs today, you've got to have the right skills and some contextual experience.

According to management consulting firm McKinsey & Company, the United States could be in a pickle by 2018, with a shortage of up to 190,000 people with "deep analytical talent" and upwards of 1.5 million people capable of analyzing data that would enable business decisions.[8]

Based on the research I did, there are lots of jobs available. But there's just not a definitive "big data" profession; the skill sets required reach across almost every business and industry. Just search for "big data" jobs using Indeed.com. At the time of this writing, nearly 18,000 jobs came up, from architect to engineer to programmer.. And there were nearly 2,700 on Dice. com. (I'm listing both job boards again because Indeed.com aggregates the universe and Dice.com is used predominantly by companies and recruiters sourcing for specialized tech jobs.)

Tech experts agree that math, statistics, data analysis, business analytics, natural language processing, creativity, communications skills, and Hadoop are all critical to creating big data analytics frameworks and applying them to benefit businesses. Hadoop is an open-source software framework that supports tons of data and enables multiple applications and computers to work together. Hadoop can be learned via classes or can be self-taught.

Again, because there's not a "big data profession" per se, here's a list of the most common jobs with the skill sets required based on Computerworld research:[9]

---

[8] http://www.mckinsey.com/insights/mgi/research/technology_and_innovation/big_data_the_next_frontier_for_innovation.

[9] http://www.computerworld.com/s/article/9231445/Big_data_big_jobs_.

Data Scientists: Today, these are the smartest folks in the room with the deepest of analytical insight, who are also assuming leadership positions in businesses. Lots of math and statistics here as well as artificial intelligence, natural language processing, and/or data management.

Data Architects: These are programmers who can put the method to the madness when it comes to that mountain of disconnected data. They usually have statistical backgrounds as well as programming and BI, and have the ability to look at data in new and innovative ways.

Data Visualizers: These are the folks who interpret the data and analytics for everyday business use. They give the data context and understandability for all in business to consume and learn from and to apply to daily operations.

Data Change Agents: These are the quality management and change management folks who use the data analytics to improve operations and processes. They are clear communicators and help to ensure the data analyses stick.

Data Engineer/Operators: These are the folks who take the big data building blocks and create the infrastructure and manage it, ensuring that business needs are met and systems and processes are performing as they should.

Mindful Moment   While there's not a "big data profession" per se, there are more and more jobs available today including data scientists, data architects, data visualizers, data change agents and data engineers/operators that require sophisticated skill sets. Do you have what it takes? If not, get it while the gettin's good.

Social Insights Can Be Pinteresting

No, I'm still not "pinterested" in what you're sharing on Pinterest, but there are billions of dollars at stake for many companies that do. In the past few years alone, companies like Radian6, now part of the Salesforce Marketing Cloud, have been aggregating and analyzing what consumers have been saying, online across social networks and the greater Internet, about specific companies, products, and services—called "sentiment analysis." This has spawned myriad sentiment analysis firms, also known as "social listening" software, trying to make sense of all the online chatter on behalf of their client companies.

While this kind of social listening is important for consumer businesses, business-to-business companies are finding more value in curating and sharing relevant and highly targeted content for their buyers, influencers, and even internal employees and applicants. They are drinking from the firehose and freezing the data "water" into flavored ice cubes so they don't drown. This includes firms like Curata and SocialEars.

As a long-time marketer, I know that all this analyzed information can be valuable as long as it's kept in the context of who you're targeting and why you're targeting them. But the intricate algorithms that go into slicing and dicing all this social data is up to you smart folks. Advanced analytics pros are in very high demand. The fact that traditional enterprise business intelligence reporting and query tools have made it into mainstream cloud computing products today and has given an edge to growing numbers of companies offering predictive analytics, data mining, text analytics, and other analytics techniques—all of which are still pretty new. But like big data architects, advanced analytics professionals need both technical and business skills. It takes time to acquire this combo, but it can be done. Analytics experts also work shoulder to shoulder with marketing experts and statisticians, making formidable allies in the new world of work.

When I searched for "social analytics" jobs, nearly 9,000 came up on Indeed.com and 400 on Dice.com, and they ranged from software engineers to social listening analysts. And according to WANTED Analytics, the occupations that most often demand in-depth analytical skills include:

- Computer Systems Analysts

- Management Analysts

- Market Research Analysts

- Software Engineers (Applications)

- Industrial Engineers

- Operations Research Analysts

Mindful Moment   Analyzing social data and providing the right insights to businesses today has only just begun. Developing the right algorithms via predictive analytics, data mining, text analytics, and other analytics techniques will help harness the wild horses of today's Internet data, creating millions of new jobs for data analysts tomorrow.

Traditional IT Careers Today

Gender, Social, and the Innovation Evolution

And I said, "Well, gosh, can't we—can't we find some—some women that are also qualified"? I went to a number of women's groups and said, "Can you help us find folks?"' and they brought us whole binders full of women.

—Governor Mitt Romney, 2012 Presidential Candidate

Three things: My two little girls, social media, and why we—as the "world of work" consumer (both employee and customer)—are transforming IT innovation. All through the writing of this book, these are the three things that kept seeping into my mind and filtering my perception of the technology world today (and tomorrow).

For those of you who have children, you know as I do that we only want the best for them. We want them to have more opportunities to excel in school and work than we ever did. I see how bright and smart my girls are; and then when I read about the continued disparity between how many women go into science and technology versus how many men do, and how many women who do go into technology get compensated less than their male counterparts, of course I'm compelled to pull for the women. This situation has been slowly changing, and I hope to be a catalyst for changing it further. Guys, I'm not saying you don't deserve to be where you are, but I do want more women—my daughters, included—to deserve to be there as well when they work just as hard as the rest of us to get there.

Then there's social. It has democratized everything. It has given us the content we want in the media we want, when we want it. It has given us the ability to connect and collaborate with anyone, anywhere in the world. It has given you, the job seeker, an insider view into organizations, and it has given organizations the same insider view into you. It has even helped to topple dictatorial regimes, for goodness' sake. Social has given us, the workplace consumers, the power to transform how, where, when, and why we work.

These are the traditional IT careers of today, and at this level of employment democratizion, we are developing some amazing hardware, software, and networking technologies at an exponential pace. Early adopters have to take Dramamine these days to be able to manage all the waves of change.

But, yes, there's still a limit on how far we've come. With all the online tools, social and professional networking sites, and job services available today, we've got political candidates looking for world-of-work gender equity in binders full of women.

It was funny, and it did get a lot of comedic mileage, but the reality is that no U.S. administration has ever really had a significant impact on job growth, career development, and the tech industry. In fact, most economists agree that the right recipe to spur job growth via startups and significant GDP increases wouldn't garner many popular votes. Taxing employee healthcare benefits, for example. Or doing away with the mortgage interest write-off. Or by obliterating any and all federal and state business taxes, so that companies will reinvest their earnings in job growth. Maybe.

Not gonna happen in million years.

But these are all things that are out of our control. When it comes to skilling up, networking inside and out, making yourself more marketable and finding work, these are things that are within your control.

That is why I wrote this book. When I left a great job two years ago for a business endeavor that went awry fast, I didn't realize that the sometimes painful yet amazing journey I was about to embark on—the walkabout through the business wilderness during the height of the deep recession—would teach me to adapt and learn new skills quickly. I bought a domain and then launched a new website to reposition myself and my experience in the HR B2B technology space; but instead of using free blog services, I learned how to use WordPress and I refined my social marketing skills.

So what, you say? You're right; I'm not programming relational databases. But I was reprogramming my career and my life—that's what we have control over. Here's the point: no one's going to manage your career for you. This is the new millennium of specialization, from advancing yourself technically to becoming business and marketing savvy.

We went back to school. We learned new skills. We took the contract work. We got ourselves cross-trained, and we volunteered to stretch ourselves. We were given assessments and we passed background checks. We built a powerful online profile. We researched the employers we wanted to work for. We leveraged our networks and worked with recruiters. We found mentors and joined professional associations. We used all the latest job-seeker tools at our disposal. We made our business case and got the final interview. We were interviewed online. We got the job and fought hard to be onboarded and trained for the long haul. We skilled up on the inside and kept our internal mobility opportunities open. We found opportunities in cloud computing and big data and more.

We did all this. Men and women alike. Nontraditional ownership of our own career development. Amen.

Boys and Girls Can Play Nice

Back to reality and the binders full of women, though. Come to think of it, in the IT world they've all been binders full of men. Unshaven men wearing "Alcatraz" T-shirts and smelling of taco trucks and Mountain Dew, and playing Rock Band or World of Warcraft or Words with Friends.

Okay, that's an unfair exaggeration, and the chapter-opening quote has already filled a season's worth of SNL cold openings. And my apologies to my tech brethren, but it is true that every single technology company I've talked shop with and worked for of late has had mostly men, at least nine out of every ten team members, who are creating system architecture, managing IT infra-structure, setting up databases, working out UI, crunching code, fixing bugs, and dressing up the software. (No, you don't smell of taco trucks.)

Mostly men, with the exception of one recent interaction where there was one woman in a development team of six. Interestingly enough, I've seen more female founders and CEOs in Silicon Valley than practicing technology professionals, so that may make more of a difference at some point.

In fact, most of my career in tech marketing, HR, and recruiting has included more female counterparts than men. Really. Although certainly not equal in opportunity and pay, there were more women in the workforce in the last two years, outpacing the men. And of the 15 job categories projected to grow the most in the next decade in the United States, all but two are occupied primarily by women.[1] However, an IT World article from early 2012 about IT professionals stated:

> While hard numbers related to the number of women who work in high-tech as technical support or managers in the private and public sectors in the U.S.

[1] http://www.bls.gov/ooh/About/Projections-Overview.htm.

*today are hard to come by, some studies estimate women constitute 15% to
25% of the ranks at most, and about 8% of managers. . . . To be sure, women
in the U.S. aren't coming out of undergraduate and graduate programs in
computers sciences in huge numbers. As of 2009, only 18% of graduates in
computer science were women.* [2]

Time to evolve, ladies and gentlemen, for all of you to benefit—and our
children. My two little girls, both of whom take smart device usability to
uncanny levels, may want to be in IT some day, and I'm going to be right there
urging them on through school and into their careers. According to a study
by the Anita Borg Institute, there needs to be a culture shift inside companies
today.[3] They need to recruit from bigger candidate pools and advertise
positions more neutrally, removing stereotypes and culture references that
tell "diverse" candidates to stay away.

If you're in a position to hire, you can make a difference: Make sure that at
least one woman is in the running for every tech job, as well as making women
part of the recruiting and hiring management teams.

We're not talking about rocket science here. I'm sure that most of you reading
this book, regardless of gender, would agree. You want to work with the best
team, doing the best tech work out there, in the best companies around the
world—or at least something pretty damn close.

In fact, finding the right opportunity can easily start online and in person
today, with professional networks, circles, pools, communities, playgrounds
even—whatever you want to call them. You can meet and network with like-
minded IT pros, male and female alike, who are interested in specific yet
gender-neutral careers, skills, hobbies, technologies—you name it. You can
communicate with one another, challenge one another without malice,
commiserate and collaborate about career commonalities. Brothers can
encourage more of their sisters to go into tech, and sisters can encourage
their brothers to stay in tech.

Either way, you'll share binders full of growth opportunities with one another,
just like the big open network playground we work together in today.

And yes, you can still play video games (I've actually heard more women play
video games these days than men. Really.)

---

[2] http://www.itworld.com/networking/256428/least-1-woman-should-be-interviewed-every-it-
job-opening-advocacy-group-says.

[3] http://anitaborg.org/. The Anita Borg Institute is an organization dedicated to increasing the
role of women in technology.

No Matter What You Call It

Listen boys and girls, what's new will soon be old. If you've been in tech for any length of time, especially the past two decades, you know innovation is rapid and never-ending. Every technology I've discussed in this book—cloud computing, mobile, big data, social analytics, and more—will evolve and become something new. But they're all built on the great IT foundation of hardware, software, and network development, production, programming, and project management.

So, in a sense, it's an oxymoron that innovation makes what's old become new again. This is why it's critical that you constantly "skill up" to keep yourself relevant and marketable, not only for a new job but also to progress in the one you have—go back to school, upgrade your skills, cross-train, or basically all the things I've pointed out in this book.

Hey, the U.S. automotive industry is experiencing a renaissance of sorts. At the time of this writing, over 8,000 automotive engineering jobs have come up on Indeed.com nationally and nearly 400 on Dice.com. (I'm listing both job boards again because Indeed.com aggregates the universe and Dice.com is used predominantly by companies and recruiters sourcing for specialized tech jobs.) This includes a variety of other manufacturing industries (over 42,000 manufacturing engineering jobs came up on Indeed.com recently and over 3,700 came up on Dice.com). Engineering—from aerospace (over 9,500 on Indeed.com and over 1,600 on Dice.com), to biomedical (only 60 on both, but still), to nuclear (60 on both), to petroleum (30 on both)—is becoming more and more specialized and can offer lucrative opportunities for you, and you, and you, if you all get the right combination of skills, experience, and business know-how.

And many of the traditional IT skills are just as hot as the new ones. Case in point: according to *Computerworld*'s 2013 Forecast, the following are the top ten skills for 2013.[4] In fact, 33 percent of the 334 IT executives who responded to their forecast survey said that they plan to hire in the next 12 months. That's up for the third year in a row.

1. *Programming and Application Development:* According to the survey results, companies that have delayed application development projects during the downturn are now ready to rock. This includes finding people with experience in Java, J2EE, and .Net.

2. *Project Management:* I highlighted this earlier in the book. Project management skills are more and more critical to development projects, and if you want to

---

[4] http://www.computerworld.com/s/article/9231486/10_hot_IT_skills_for_2013.

open up those lattice growth opportunities out there, you'll master some basic leadership and coordination skills here. Development projects are getting more complex, involving coordination of global teams and getting applications to talk one another correctly.

3. *Help Desk/Technical Support:* With the complexity of business today, and the creation of new systems and electronic records applications, more and more technical support folks are needed to help others use these systems. Help desk technicians are a growing job market.

4. *Security:* Hacking for ill will is something companies grapple with every minute of every day, losing billions in lost data, time, and revenue every year. CIOs and other IT leaders have made security a number one priority, and the complexity of the tech world today hasn't made it any easier. So for you security buffs out there, and for the hackers now turned to the light, look sharp.

5. *Business Intelligence/Analytics:* As I mentioned in Chapter 19, "big data" and analytics are big time right now; they are a top priority for many companies, second only to security. Those who succeed in big data have a math/statistical background, technology background, and sound business skills. Data scientists and data analysts are tough to come by, so get to skilling up and make it happen.

6. *Cloud/SaaS:* As I discussed in Chapter 18, "cloudy" days ahead are where it's all at. Companies are moving from installed-based software to Software as a Service and cloud computing to save on licensing fees, overhead, and maintenance, so they need those of you with the cloud computing skills and experience.

7. *Virtualization:* This is a new one, but could be a growth opportunity for many of you. If you understand storage and virtual server clusters, and have some experience creating them, then this is a space for you.

8. *Networking:* Hey, that's the networked world we live in and we wouldn't want it any other way. Companies need networking pros who've got the experience, still one of the most wanted skill sets in the IT world.

9. *Mobile Applications and Device Management:* Again, in Chapter 18, I described how this is hotter than hot and will continue to be so for the next decade. More people globally are jumping online via their smartphones and tablets to access apps representing everything from entertainment to workplace management and productivity software. App development continues to lead the glamorous life in tech today.

10. *Data Center*: The older core-tech skills are still vitally important to the IT organization. Data center management, server, storage, and data backup skills are all quite high in demand.

■ **Mindful Moment**   When it comes to IT skills, what is old is new again, and what is new will become old—faster than you can shake a stick at, as my Pop used to say. IT is hot—yes, indeed— and even in industries such as automotive, manufacturing, aerospace, and energy, there are lucrative jobs to be found. But again, you've got to have a highly specialized skill set, direct experience, and the contextual business savvy, especially if you want to have a bigger role in the company long term.

The New World of Ongoing Engagement

According to the Gartner 2012 CIO Survey, the world has become exponentially more complex and competitive, and is closing in on CIOs and IT leaders.[5] In fact, 20 percent of them have reduced budgets yet again, and deciding where the IT investment is to be made is getting more difficult, impacting what the heck they do next. But according to the survey, they do agree that the "customer experience is the best opportunity for IT innovation." Of course, this means investing in customer-relationship management, document management, mobile applications, supply-chain management, sales and marketing and services technologies, analytics, and social media.

See a pattern here? Customer interface doesn't just mean your "buying customers." It also means you, the employee or contractor customer, which also means that the IT and technology can now drive innovative business inside and out, as it should. At any given time, we can be employees and then we can be customers. The perpetually transparent (the ability to see inside and out of companies) grows and the ongoing engagement cycle repeats over and over again; social technology has democratized—and many conservative folk would say exacerbated—it all.

Meaning that now more than ever, we are the captains of our own industry. No longer does the evil empire hold us at bay (and in a dark, bleak hole in the applicant-tracking system). We're the ones who brought the smart devices to work when work said you couldn't play on Twitter or Facebook. (Or even LinkedIn, for that matter; I've heard of companies still blocking the professional

---

[5] http://www.gartner.com/technology/cio/cioagenda_findings.jsp.

network site at work.) We're the ones who created the entertaining and collaborative apps for our smart devices that we brought to work. We've become the customer experience that drives IT innovation.

We are IT innovation. We are the nontraditional transforming the traditional.

And that was when my finger refused to post the benign tweet. The simple, straightforward tweet about the recent Recruiting Trends panel discussion on social media, transparency, and competitive advantage in the world of work, recruiting, human resources, and career management.[6]

You see, social media present ourselves as transparent or, rather, as out there in full view, driving the enterprise (crazy) to do the same, and it's making things wilder and to some, scarier than ever. You've read the stories of social media gone bad in the workplace, and you may have colleagues whose poor decisions landed them in the unemployment line or even in court. Or of organizations that, conversely, make the wrong calls on social activities. Consider the following:

My finger rested right above the Return key. And then, before I pressed it, I heard, "Well, at first I posted to my blog anonymously because I didn't want my boss knowing I was writing about my vagina."

Nervous laughter. Pins dropped. Uncomfortable shifting. Even the usually outspoken smarty pants blogging contingent I know all too well hesitated. I know, because I turned to look at them in the back row and they were all frozen in place. Only for a moment, but frozen mouths ajar nonetheless.

The vagina quote came from a refreshingly candid and smart Meredith Soleau, a human resource manager at a mega car dealership in the heartland. Meredith is also a humorist who writes her "Life's Crazy Joke" blog.[7] To be clear, as I was growing up, I was heavily influenced by my mom and my sister. Now I've got the Mama (the affectionate name I call my wife) and two young daughters, and I am quite in touch with all gender-scapes within myself. Really. But based on conversations with all kinds of organizations and professionals during the past few years, this literal and figurative metaphor of the unruly social world is all too real.

It's social gone wild; it's out of control, so organizations are still trying to figure out a way to control it, although we keep driving the IT innovation to "uncontrol" it. Remember that email and the public Internet were first viewed to be business destroyers, not enablers.

---

[6] http://www.recruitingtrends.com.

[7] http://www.lifescrazyjoke.com.

Now, not everyone should be allowed to shoot social from the hip, I get that. You probably work with or have worked with some psychos who've been trying to friend you on Facebook every week for the past year, or who have posted the most political or gender-biased or bigoted blogs you've never wanted to see. Ever.

Personal responsibility and impulse control don't come easily, if ever, to everyone, including organizations themselves. But I'd argue that most of us do know better—the employed and the contracted, or those looking to be employed and contracted—in this ever-transitioning and fluid world of work. We're already out there across a vast network of online and face-time configurations —co-mingling, venting, joking, laughing, offending sometimes still (unfortunately), engaging, sharing, learning, discussing, and developing ourselves and one another.

This is the new world of ongoing, transparent engagement and it's a huge continuous opportunity for IT and technology innovation—and for you because of the jobs it has and will continue to generate. Choosing companies that create continuous learning and development environments and that encourage this kind of ongoing engagement around professionally relevant content—across any and all "customer" populations—is what you have control over, and ironically what the orgs have control over, too.

If you're looking for application development work today and tomorrow, then seek out a company that shares relevant application development content freely, from the corporate site, to social sites, to professional networking sites, to associations, to everything else under the glorious sun. And then do it in a way that you and I can informally "skill up" at the same pace as the organization's recent hires and current employees do (who continue to do more and more on their own, anyway). This will make you more relevant and hireable at some point in the future. That could mean you get a job with that firm, or maybe you show up on the radar of one of their competitors. Either way, it's a win-win-win for you all.

This can all be done via local networking events, conferences, association meetings, Facebook pages, LinkedIn groups, Twitter streams, and other online professional networks, as well as true talent community platforms' the key is being social and, again, acknowledging that "customer experience is the best opportunity for IT innovation."

Don't be afraid to be selective and engage with companies that are willing to engage with you as the universal customer, especially when you and I are already doing it without them.

Godspeed, my friends.

Tweet

Mindful Moment   You are the customer. You really are. And you should be treated as if you're in the market for a large purchase and investment, because that's exactly what it is in this crazy light-speed world of work. Organizations that want the best IT talent—you and you and you—will welcome the transparent, innovative nature that we, as prospects, exhibit today; they can't call all the shots as they did in the old days. Nearly every man, woman, and child is touched by nearly every single piece of hardware, software, and network you help to develop, QA, manage, and maintain, so the power you hold is greater than the sum of what makes you up. Don't you ever forget that, kids. Good luck to you and let me know when you get that great new gig. Contact me at kevin@reach-west.com.

Appendix
We All Need Lists of Stuff

Look at all this stuff. Career management stuff. World of work stuff. Informative IT stuff. Eclectic educational stuff. Business/economy stuff. Happy brain stuff. Hey, at least it's in alphabetical order.

This is my appendix and it includes lots more IT, business, and "life" resources for you that I didn't include in the book. Not everything here is literally about career "development," but it comprises things that could be important for you to keep up to date and rounded out in the world of work. By no means is it an exhaustive list, but it does include sites, shows, resources, and publications I frequent as well as others recommended to me from all my very smart HR, recruiting, career management, and technology friends, all of whom are well above my pay grade.

Good luck and enjoy. And if you've got a resource you dig that I didn't list, please send it my way to kevin@reach-west.com. I'll make sure to include it the next time.

40Tech

http://www.40tech.com

I love this: technology, the internet, hardware, software, gadgets, and video game articles and stuff "written from the perspective of the 40-something average guy." Well, that's me. There's useful information here for any age, but older folks rock. And occasionally still roll. Evan Kline is the founder of 40Tech.

99% Invisible

http://99percentinvisible.org

This podcast/radio show is a favorite of mine. The host and producer, Roman Mars, creates shorts about design and architecture—but not always literally. It's a great way to get those synapses firing in new and creative ways.

Allison Doyle

http://jobsearch.about.com/bio/Alison-Doyle-2335.htm

Allison is a long-time job search and employment expert who's been writing for About.com since 1998. She's got tons of experience in career development, online job search, HR, and the world of work in general. She is a great resource in any market.

All Things D

http://allthingsd.com

This website is a Dow Jones news site devoted to all things technology, the internet, and media. It includes analysis and opinion. A great mix of media and content here.

Amplify Talent

http://amplifytalent.com

Lars Schmidt is a friend of mine and currently the Senior Director of Talent Acquisition & Innovation at NPR (I am a big NPR fan). Lars is all about empowering and developing talent and he provides straight talk on all things HR, recruiting, and career management.

Ars Technica

http://arstechnica.com

Founded in 1998 by founder and editor-in-chief Ken Fisher, Ars Technica is all about the "alpha geeks"—IT and tech pros to the core. The site covers all that's fresh and hip and popular. Quality content makes them a trusted place for tech news, policies, and whatever is latest and greatest in IT.

BetaBeat

http://betabeat.com

According to the editorial team, they're all "about the characters who make this [tech] scene hum: the ambitious young angels, the eccentric hackers and the non-stop networkers. We're here to take you behind closed doors for an inside look at how the deals really get done." Right on. I'd check it out if I were you.

Bloomberg Businessweek

http://www.businessweek.com

Speaking of business sites, this is one of my favorites. A great range of business topics including lots of tech and innovation and solid writers.

Brazen Careerist

http://www.brazencareerist.com

Brazen Careerist is all about virtual recruiting events and solid career advice and education to help folks of all types to "discover their strengths, refine their skills and find a job they love." The keyword being *love*, the thing that often eludes us.

Business Insider Tech

http://www.businessinsider.com

A great business site covering finance, media, technology, and other industry verticals. They bring the best of the web together for your business learning pleasure.

CareerDiva

http://www.careerdiva.net

I'm all about gender balance, and Eve Tahmincioglu is someone you should check out. She's been writing about business, career management, and the world of work for two decades and her stories have been have been published all over the place—including the *The New York Times*, *Time*, Salon.com, and *Businessweek*. She also has a weekly MSNBC.com column called "Your Career."

Career Rocketeer

http://www.careerrocketeer.com

I know Chris Perry, who founded this site, and he's a very smart career development guy. His site is a career search and personal branding blog that's all about owning your career path.

Career Sherpa

http://careersherpa.net

Hannah Morgan is all about helping the "lost" job seekers improve the way they look for work today, giving "no-nonsense" job search advice.

CareerTrend

http://careertrend.net

I've known Jacqui Barrett-Poindexter for a few years, and she's the genuine deal when it comes to helping folks in career transition and those looking for a jump start.

Coursera

https://www.coursera.org

This is one of three online resources I didn't include in Chapters 2 and 3, and they should be duly noted now (these related to the MOOCs I wrote about in Chapter 3—Coursera, Khan Academy and Udacity). The first is Coursera, an online learning portal with courses that include humanities, medicine, biology, social sciences, mathematics, business, computer science, and many others. This site can help you improve your skills and hopefully advance you along your career path—all for free.

Cube Rules

http://cuberules.com

Do you love your cube still? If so, check out this career site from Scot Herrick. Scot will give you advice on how to land your next job and keep it.

Daring Fireball

http://daringfireball.net

Apple evangelist may not be the right word for John Gruber, but from what I've learned in a short time, he's brilliant on all things Apple. John's site is new to me, but this is why I already love it:

"If Daring Fireball looks goofy in your browser, you're likely using a shitty browser that doesn't support web standards. Internet Explorer, I'm looking in your direction. If you complain about this, I will laugh at you, because I do not care. If, however, you are using a modern, standards-compliant browser and have trouble viewing or reading Daring Fireball, please do let me know."

Digital Inspiration

http://www.labnol.org

Amit Agarwal writes a personal technology column for *WSJ India*. He is a published book author and founder of Digital Inspiration, a blog about computer software, consumer gadgets, and web applications. Check it out.

The Economist

http://www.economist.com

Another one of my favorite pubs. *The Economist* has excellent writers who give insight and opinion on international news, politics, business, finance, science, and technology.

Fast Company

http://www.fastcompany.com

You haven't heard of *Fast Company*? C'mon. *Fast Company* is a sweet publication with an editorial focus on tech innovation, ethonomics (ethical economics—love it), leadership, and design. Where smart and hip business and tech meet.

Freakonomics

http://www.freakonomics.com

Love. This. Stuff. I eat it like sugar. This is where New York journalist and author Stephen J. Dubner and award-winning economist Steven D. Levitt write about "the hidden side of everything." Really. Must read and listen.

FreelanceSwitch

http://freelanceswitch.com

Here's another freelance resource for you. FreelanceSwitch is a global freelancer community where you can search for work and talk shop.

Ghacks

http://www.ghacks.net

Ghacks is a technology news blog founded in 2005 by Martin Brinkmann. It's a comprehensive, latest tech news site with five authors and regular contributions from freelance writers as well.

GigaOm

http://gigaom.com

Om Malik launched the GigaOM blog in 2006. It is, today, all about the intersection of business and technology.

HackCollege

http://www.hackcollege.com

HackCollege positions itself for college students, but hey, we're all lifelong learners, right? This site educates all about the when and why of open source software.

JibberJobber

http://www.jibberjobber.com

I know, you need another job search service like you need a hole in the head, but Jason Alba's JibberJobber service is a sound one. It's like having a personal relationship manager that helps you do everything you need to do to manage a job search and improve your networking. For those of you at home keeping score, Jason's background is in IT and business strategy.

Keppie Careers

http://www.keppiecareers.com

Miriam Salpeter is a fantastic career management resource. She's a social media strategist and consultant for job seekers and entrepreneurs. She also considers herself "a new economy job search coach" (love it), a resume writer, speaker, and author.

Khan Academy

http://www.khanacademy.org

The Khan Academy is a not-for-profit that provides free education for "anyone anywhere." They currently offer over 3,500 videos on arithmetic, physics, finance, history, computer science and many more. You can access their video library as well as participate in different interactive challenges and assessments from wherever you can access the internet at your own pace, which is really the only way to learn as far as I'm concerned (and informal learning research).

Lifehacker

http://lifehacker.com

Adam Pash is a self-taught software developer and the chief editor of Lifehacker, a site that includes "tips, tricks, and downloads for getting things done." Right on.

Lost in Technology

http://www.lostintechnology.com

Lost in Technology is all about, well, dealing with technology. So deal with it.

Mashable

http://mashable.com

You may have heard of it, but if not, Mashable is a great mainstream source for news, information, and resources about digital innovation. Mashable has over 20 million monthly unique visitors and 6 million social media followers.

The Next Web

http://thenextweb.com

Founded in 2008, *The Next Web* is an online publication with international news and about internet technology, business, and culture.

NPR Planet Money

http://www.npr.org/blogs/money/

One of my economic and business faves indeed. I love their description:

"Imagine you could call up a friend and say, 'Meet me at the bar and tell me what's going on with the economy.' Now imagine that's actually a fun evening. That's what we're going for at Planet Money."

Personal Branding Blog

http://www.personalbrandingblog.com

Dan Schawbel's personal branding insights are spot on. His blog is about how to create your career and take ownership of it via personal branding. Learn how to make the business case that shines.

ReadWrite Web

http://readwrite.com

ReadWrite web was founded in 2003 by Richard MacManus. It's considered to be smart and sound tech that you should read.

Scobleizer

http://scobleizer.com

Robert Scoble is a very smart guy who is an employee of Rackspace, a cloud computing and hosting company. He calls himself the "chief troublemaker," which means you should read his stuff.

Scripting News

http://scripting.com

I did not know this, but Dave Winer created the internet. No, that's not right. He actually helped create real simple syndication (RSS). The rest is history.

Six Revisions

http://sixrevisions.com

Six Revisions was founded in 2008 by professional web developer/designer Jacob Gube. The site publishes useful articles for designers and web developers.

TechCrunch

http://techcrunch.com

Like Mashable, TechCrunch is a well-trafficked technology site that profiles startups, and it reviews new internet products and other "breaking" tech news. TechCrunch was founded in 2005 and now has 12 million unique visitors per month and more than 37 million page views per month.

Tech Republic Career Management Blblog

http://www.techrepublic.com/blog/career

As many of you may know, *TechRepublic* is an online trade publication and social community for IT professionals; on the same site there's a great resource for career management. Check it out.

Unclutterer

http://unclutterer.com

The Unclutterer is all about getting organized and staying that way. Good God, I need constant refreshers.

Udacity

http://www.udacity.com

Udacity was founded by three roboticists who dig higher education and believe it should be free. There are lots of great courses offered in math, science and IT, so please do check out this site. The internet has now democratized education and Udacity brings together great teachers from all over the world to provide learning content you, the student.

The Unofficial Apple Weblog

http://www.tuaw.com

Founded in 2004, TUAW is a great source for Apple news, information, and analysis. The site is a rich Apple resource for developers, designers, and others as well.

VentureBeat

http://venturebeat.com

VentureBeat is a great business and tech site. It provides news about innovation and a variety of technology trends such as social media, mobile, clean technology, games, and chips.

Wired

http://www.wired.com

Another hip technology publication, *Wired* covers the latest technology trends.

WNYC's Radiolab

http://www.radiolab.org

And speaking of shows that help you rewire your brain, Radiolab is an amazing show and a feast for the auditory senses. The subjects of science, philosophy, and human experience all converge here. Listen to it.

Index

CPSIA information can be obtained at www.ICGtesting.com
Printed in the USA
LVOW12s0243130215

426894LV00001B/97/P